Numerology,
Astrology and Dreams

Numerology, Astrology and Dreams

by Dusty Bunker

1469 Morstein Road
West Chester, Pennsylvania 19380 USA

International Standard Book Number: 0-914918-74-5
Library of Congress Catalog Card Number: 87-62095

Astrological charts by Stephen Erlewine from the Circle Book of Charts.
Copyright © 1972 Circle Bookstore, Inc.
Reprinted with permission.

Published by Whitford Press
Distributed by Schiffer Publishing Ltd.
1469 Morstein Road
West Chester, Pennsylvania 19380

Manufactured in the United States of America

This book may be purchased from the publisher.
Please include $2.00 postage.
Try your bookstore first.
Please send for free catalog to:
Whitford Press
c/o Schiffer Publishing, Ltd.
1469 Morstein Road
West Chester, Pennsylvania 19380

Contents

For Skip, my dream come true

Acknowledgement

I wish to thank Julie Lockhart, my editor, for two reasons: (1) It was through her suggestion that this book became a reality, and (2) her gentle and wise editing made the process of surgery less painful.

Introduction

The danger of the written word is that it freezes ideas in time. In the reader's mind, the writer does not grow beyond that stage, but remains locked in a mind set that does not reflect her growth in the future. But hopefully, the ideas a writer leaves on a page spiral out to nourish others and become enriched expanding entities in the reader's mind.

We all drop seeds as we go through life; some we will see bloom, others we will never know about. And, in turn, we are recipients of the seed thoughts of others—sort of a botanical exchange which keeps the planet green and growing. This book is an attempt to drop seed thoughts. It combines numerology, astrology and dreams which may seem an unlikely union but, for me, it is as natural as the phases of the Moon. Perhaps these subjects are wedded in my mind because I have been lecturing about them for more than ten years and have witnessed first hand the effectiveness of using the knowledge of numerological trends, geometrical symbols and astrological factors to interpret and understand dreams. And conversely, using the messages gleaned from dreams to guide us through current experiences in our lives.

When you are aware of your personal rhythms, you can immediately target a specific area of your life that is being stimulated for change and growth. Your dreams reflect this ongoing process. They are the best source of information, encouragement and guidance available to you because they rise out of the deeper parts of your being.

Small portions of this book contain information from my former work, *Dream Cycles*. I have decided to include these because the information has been unchanging and still applies to this work. However, this edition is entirely restructured and contains ancient esoteric information about geometry and numbers, as well as astrological material — some of which is looked at a bit differently — and new approaches to interpreting dreams through personal number cycles, number philosophy and astrological symbolism.

You will find that I use the terms wo/man and s/he in the generic sense. Since the spelling of each of these words includes female and male, I find this the most equitable way to incorporate both sexes. These words are, in truth, inclusive. And, I use the word Divinity to represent Goddess or God, because I find it is less gender specific.

Also, the comments I have made about religious beliefs concern those who have abused the basic mystical traditions, the early church fathers whose patriarchal view of the world has been, at best, inequitable, and at worst, cruel and inhuman. (One of the people I most respect is Mother Teresa who goes about her holy work non-judgmentally, living her philosophy and giving unconditional love. She is one of many beautiful spiritual souls who perform their missions through their particular belief systems.) In this book, religious history is brought up when it is pertinent to the matter at hand.

Now, in order to co-ordinate numerology, astrology and dreams, we must first lay the foundation for each subject singly. For those readers who have been with me before, I ask your indulgence as we go over the basics in each subject. Keep in mind that we learn through repetition and, since I am a few years older than when I wrote my last book and hopefully a few years wiser, even these basic presentations will reflect my new experiences and will offer you something fresh. For the first time reader of my works, welcome. I hope you will find some measure of pleasure and reward in the reading of this book.

1

Numerology

Numerology is the study of numbers; numbers are the structure upon which the material world is built. The first part of the preceding sentence is clear enough but you may find the second half — numbers are the structure upon which the material world is built — a bit obtuse. I agree, so let's examine this statement and put it in terms we can understand and apply in useful ways.

On a mundane level, it is obvious that we define much of the world around us through measurement. In numerical terms, our calendars and clocks tell us about time, our odometers and yardsticks measure distance, our scales give us weights, our thermometers register temperature, and so on. When we make a dress or construct a skyscraper, we need to know how much material is needed. When we arrange a party or a business meeting, we determine the number of people who will be present and the amount of supplies necessary. When I talked with my editor about this book, she asked how long my manuscript would be and when it would be completed. We plan our schedules around the predictable rising and setting of the Sun or, in some cases, by the cycles of the Moon. In our everyday lives, we are caught up in the "number" of things.

This begins on the conscious level at a very early age. My seven-year-old grandson, Joshua, has been seeing the world through numbers since he began to read and write three years ago. He now carries a clipboard and a pen with him to keep count of everything, from the number of cars that go by his house in an hour to the number of times he wins Hangman. He sees numbers in the loose threads of his pants. One day he looked at his five-year-old brother who was covered with chicken pox, and asked his mother if he could play "connect the dots" on Adam's body (a game which, of course, requires numbers).

Through our senses we constantly measure the stimuli we receive from our environment. Modern research finds that "all our perceptions begin from an innate capacity in the brain/mind to recognize (count) periodic patterns of energy frequency which our nervous system has transformed into neural rhythms."[1] In other words, the distinctions you make in perception, between a flower and a chair for instance, begin from your ability to COUNT the patterns of energy frequency coming from the flower and the chair, and to distinguish them as different from one another and from other patterns in your field of vision. Therefore, *the first act of perception is counting.* This counting of patterns of energy then is transformed into images. "Even smell, touch, taste and hearing elicit an image-formation response, though it is subjective and often amorphous."[2] This may be why the Greeks looked upon the simple act of counting as so important. Plato wrote, "everything is number," and St. Augustine concurred with ". . . numbers are the thoughts of God . . . The Divine Wisdom is reflected in the numbers impressed on all things . . . the construction of the physical and moral world alike is based on eternal numbers."[3]

Austrian philosopher Rudolph Steiner wrote, "Those who deepen themselves in what is called in the Pythagorean sense 'the study of numbers' will learn through this symbolism of numbers to understand life and the world."[4]

This discussion of the process of counting in our everyday lives and the findings of modern science concerning the capacity of the brain/mind to count the vibrational energy patterns of what we perceive begins to lend some credence to my earlier statement: numbers are the structures upon which the material world is built. Now, let's take this statement into the metaphysical realm.

Pythagoras, a Greek philosopher and religious teacher who lived about 580 B.C., is generally known as the father of mathematics and the founder of the Pythagorean Theorem which we all remember from high school math class — right? It states that the square of the hypotenuse (the slanted side) of a right triangle is equal to the sum of the squares of the remaining two sides. This mathematical truth has hidden implications, one of which can be applied to one's name and birth date. Some of that information can be found in an earlier book Faith Javane and I wrote, *Numerology and the Divine Triangle.* But here we are concerned with Pythagoras' teachings that the essential character of the Universe is number, and since all things can be counted, the world as a whole can be interpreted through numbers. Pythagoras said, "When God called the world into existence, He worked as a mathematician."[5] In his school, Pythagoras taught that the numbers one through nine represent universal principles and that life is subject to predictable, orderly and progressive cycles which can be measured by these numbers.

Pythagoras' contention that number is the basic character of the Universe, which of course includes the Earth, was based upon his studies throughout the ancient world in Egypt and Asia, where he was initiated into the highest mysteries. The ultimate truth taught to initiates was the formula behind the creation of the world, a truth that was clothed in words for the general public but was a mathematical formula for the learned. The system employed was *gematria* where each character stood for a letter as well as a number. In other words, a name had a numerical counterpart that was hidden from public view, and this numerical counterpart contained occult significance. The sacred formula of 10-5-6-5 was known to the initiated in secret schools throughout the ancient world — in India, China, Tibet and Egypt — but since we are discussing our Judeo-Christian heritage, we shall use the Hebrew translation of this secret formula. The name that came to signify this formula was Jod-Heh-Vau-Heh or JHVH, and the value of those letters in the Hebrew alphabet is 10-5-6-5. ("Jod" can be transliterated as I, J or Y, so you may see this name as IHVH, JHVH or YHVH.)

It is important to remember that the earliest known religions adored the Mother-Goddess; followers of the Goddess can be traced back to Neolithic communities ca. 7000 B.C., and some claim the Upper Paleolithic Mother-worshipping cultures lived as long ago as 25,000 B.C. By comparison, Abraham lived in Canaan (Palestine) somewhere between 1800 and 1550 B.C., according to most Bible scholars.

The authors of the Judeo-Christian Bible seemed to have "purposely glossed over the sexual identity of the female deity who was held sacred by the neighbors of the Hebrews in Canaan, Babylon and Egypt. The Old Testament does not even have a word for "Goddess." In the Bible the Goddess is referred to as Elohim, in the masculine gender, to be translated as god. Biblical scholars interpreted "elohim" as god although it is a plural form meaning "goddesses and gods." The Koran of the Mohammedans, however, was quite clear. In it we read, 'Allah will not tolerate idolatry . . . the pagans pray to females.'" The pagans were all who would not convert to Father-God worship.[6]

Interesting, but what does it mean? 10-5-6-5 is the code to the sacred trapezoid, a geometrical figure of specific proportions which embodies terrestrial and celestial measurements. (See Figure 1.1.) The Earth is tipped at a 23-½ degree angle to the path it travels around the Sun (the ecliptic). Since every right triangle has 180 degrees, this creates right triangle A, with angles of 90, 66-½ and 23-½ degrees. So, right triangles A and D reflect the Earth's relationship to the Sun and its polar star, or the Earth's place in the Universe. The numerical value of the sides of this trapezoid is 10-5-6-5. Through gematria, the letter counterpart of 10-5-6-5 is JHVH or Jehovah, symbolizing in the patriarchal Cabala the Great Architect who constructed our Universe. (In pre-patriarchal societies, of course, it was the Great Mother who was worshipped as the Creatress of the Universe.)

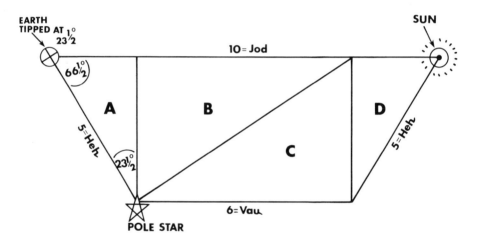

Figure 1.1   The Sacred Trapezoid

If we divide each of the digits of the sacred trapezoid, 10-5-6-5, into 30 (the number of degrees in a zodiacal sign, each of which reflects one month) we arrive at 365.6, the exact number of days in the solar year.

Also, the four right triangles in the sacred trapezoid are based on Pythagoras' right triangle theorem which states that there is an equal relationship between the hypotenuse (the slanted side of the triangle) and the sum of the other two sides or, stated mathematically, the square of the hypotenuse is equal to the sum of the squares of the remaining two sides.

This mathematical truth was personified in the Egyptian trinity of Osiris, Isis and Horus or the Father, Mother and Child. Embodied in this Egyptian trinity is the same truth that is contained in all religious trinities: that the wedding of male (spirit) and female (matter) energies creates life.

When Spirit (represented by the vertical line of the right triangle) descends into Matter (represented by the horizontal line of the right triangle) Life or Nature is created (represented by the slanted line of the right triangle). As Pythagoras said, the joining of the two sides (Spirit and Matter) produces the third side (Nature). This right triangle was called the Eye of Horus, or the All-Seeing-Eye; it is depicted on the back of the American one dollar bill — the eye within the triangle capstoning the pyramid.

There is more information hidden in this simple yet elegantly profound trapezoid constructed of only seven straight lines.

We can see that, in the ancient world, religion clothed science. Religion and science were the same. One spoke to the emotions, to the general public who needed personal contact through familiar embodiments like human personalities; the other spoke to the mind, to the initiate who could relate to the purity of mathematics as an expression of Divinity. But both messages were identical. The tragedy is that we have come to hate, fight and kill each other over semantics, over the different methods we use to describe our faith.

The exact dimensions of the sacred trapezoid can be found throughout the world in the construction of furniture, temples and churches, on the floors and walls of these buildings, and inscribed on coins and amulets. Many ancient keystones were carved in the shape of the sacred trapezoid. The Masonic apron and the shoulders and arms of the Egyptian sun god Ra embody these dimensions. These sacred dimensions are represented in various ancient cultures, and have been carried down the centuries through the arts so faithfully that we have to believe there was an innate understanding of "the proportion, order and harmony" of the Universe created by the Great Architect. This is why the Masons, the Builders and the Carpenters were sacred professions.

This discussion serves to reinforce the idea that numbers reflect the underlying construction of the Universe. By reflecting and meditating on the sacred trapezoid, perhaps we all can discover more truths that will amaze and enlighten us.

The universal principles of numbers are reflected in metaphysical literature around the world. The seven days of creation spoken of in the Old Testament Bible are not seven "days" as we know them, but rather seven stages of creation carried out in a preplanned sequence. The numbers One through Seven symbolize these seven days prior to the manifestation of the material world. In other words, in order for the material world to exist, the first seven principles must be enacted. They are the forerunners of all manifestation which then occurs under the eighth principle. The number Nine rules the dispersement of matter.

These nine universal principles are orderly steps in the process of a "thing," whether that thing is an idea, an action, a business, a country or a human being. These principles apply not only to the cycle of creation but also to the recycling of things. As we shall see, the nine stages of recycling also occur in our personal lives.

First, let's imagine that these nine principles or steps are the original blueprint of all life and that all life is born in the Awareness of Divinity. The ancients said that Divinity is a circle whose center is everywhere and whose circumference is nowhere. So, using the circle or the Zero as the symbol of Divinity and the nine numbers as the steps in the blueprint of creation, we shall examine the meaning of the Zero and the natural numbers One through Nine.

Zero: Divinity

Zero is derived from the Arabic "sifr" meaning "something empty." The dictionary describes Zero as "the origin of any kind of measurement, naught; nothing, a root."[7] If we perceive our material reality through a perception of numbers or counting as research shows, and if the nine numbers are the original blueprint which created that reality, then the Zero, which is the "origin of any kind of measurement," has to symbolize Divinity, the source from which all reality emanates.

The Encyclopedia Americana states that "although 0 has no reference in isolation, a temptation remains to treat words like 'zero,' 'no,' 'nothing,' and 'nobody' as standing for extraordinary entities having a shadowy kind of existence." Divinity also has "no reference in isolation" because it has no form and exists in the void, in "nothingness." And, certainly in our feeble attempt to describe the Source of the Universe, we might call it an extraordinary entity having a shadowy kind of existence in this material world.

The Encyclopedia goes on to say that the Zero "seems to have odd and mysterious properties that set it apart from the natural numbers" (the natural numbers are One through Nine) and that "the mathematician ignores the problem of a logical definition of Zero and is content to treat 0 as a symbol." We have trouble defining the Zero because it represents a concept, a force that cannot be confined or described in a material mode. Words are fences that enclose ideas, therefore words cannot describe that which cannot be enclosed, the indescribable, such as Divinity.

An ancient sect called Neminians worshipped a "being" called Nemo (Nobody), the same Nemo referred to in Biblical writings. Divinity has no body (Nobody), no form, because it is greater than and not of the material world. Rather the material world exists in it. The Zero or ellipse is Divinity, Cosmic Awareness, Superconsciousness. It has absolute freedom from any kind of limitation. It is the Zero "in which we live and move and have our being." We might think of the Zero as the Universe in which we live, the Cosmic Egg laid by Mother Goose.

In ancient Egypt, Mother Goose was Mother Hathor who lived in the Nile goose. Her Golden Egg was the Sun, embodied in the Sun god Ra. She was called the Creatress of the world because "she produced the whole universe in a primordial World Egg."[8] The story of Jack climbing the beanstalk in search of the goose who laid the golden egg actually describes the ancient shamans who climbed the Heavenly Vine to reach the realm of the solar deity. This brings to mind the umbilical cord that connects the child to the mother. In this case, the cord, the Heavenly Vine, connects the Earth to its Creatress, the Great Mother. We can learn a great deal by examining fairy tales and nursery rhymes!

According to the Lakota Indians of Wyoming, tradition teaches that "the female principle precedes the male. It is first, what must happen before anything else can. The female principle is the number before all numbers start. It is the womb, the starry night sky; it is the great void, the source of all possibility."[9]

In terms of the recycling of matter, in mathematics, Zero is used as a place holder, representing the transition point from one series of nine numbers to the next series of nine numbers. When we count from Nine to Ten, we end the first cycle of nine numbers and begin again with the second cycle of nine. To identify this transition, we use the 0 with the 1 in the form of the number 10. In this sense, the 0 allows repetition, a recycling of the nine natural numbers. Metaphysically, this repetition is the promise of eternal life, of reincarnation, the continuum of life's energy. We have a constant reminder of this promise always before us in our hands with their ten fingers. And since it is logical to assume that early people used their fingers as the first tool with which to convey the idea of numbers, most counting systems are based on units of ten. We can learn about the structure of the Universe by studying our own bodies. The ancient axiom, "As it is above, so it is below," is again revealed.

The Zero, therefore, is Divinity, which laid the cosmic egg in which all life exists and recycles without end.

One: Action

Here, the essence of life, the seed, the primordial impulse, awakens to the desire to move out from its center to explore life and, in so doing, to discover its individuality apart from the Whole, the Oneness, the Zero, which is Divinity. One is the outbreathing of Spirit, the Ego, the self-consciousness of Self and the awareness of that Self's need to express.

Two: Attraction

Science states that for every action, there is an equal and opposite reaction. Occult science teaches that when any force begins to work in the Universe, another force opposed to it arises at the same moment. When the One moved out, it caused the opposite reaction, a moving in or the law of attraction. At this moment, duality was born, the polarity of opposites that underlies all manifestation: day and night, up and down, good and evil. Two is the mirror of illumination where the Self sees and knows itself through reflection of its opposite. There would be no "short" unless there were a "long" against which to measure it. There would be no cold unless there were a hot. Two collects and assimilates. It is the gestation period.

Three: Expansion

In the Three, the pairs of opposites are united and harmonized. The principles of One and Two are now in the process of unfoldment, working outward, looking forward to manifestation. In this number we find multiplication and growth. In mathematics, the triangle with its three sides is called the first perfect shape because it is the first form that can be constructed with straight lines. The triangle is a symbol of the three fold nature of Divinity in most cultures: Christianity teaches Father, Holy Ghost (which was originally the Mother) and Son; the Egyptians had Osiris, Isis and Horus; in Scandinavia, it was Odin, Frey and Thor; and in the Hindu religion, Shiva, Vishnu and Brahma. The trinity or the Three is the number behind manifestation, reminding us of the expression, "Things happen in threes."

The downward-pointing triangle is called the Yoni Yantra, and it was adored by worshippers of the Great Mother just as the cross is revered by Christians. It represented her genital area, the source of all life. In time, She conceived a spark in Her Yantra which grew into an upward-pointing triangle (the male) and thus the hexagram or six-pointed star was born, symbolizing the union of Goddess and God. Worship of the downward-pointing triangle, the Yantra, was meant to induce oneness with the Mother of the Universe.

Four: Formation

The result of the expanding Three is Four, or the square, the second perfect shape in mathematics. In Four, the Ego clothes itself in matter. Four
is the number of the Earth: the four elements, the four seasons, the four
phases of the Moon, the four winds and the four corners of the Earth (the
latter seems a strange expression because the Earth has no corners, although this might be disputed by members of the Flat Earth Society.) The
point is that, corners or not, we still relate the number Four to the Earth.
Four brings order, measurement and classification. Memory is also a function of Four because it is in the body that time becomes linear with a yesterday, today and tomorrow. The physical body with its memory is the cross
(four extremities) we must bear. I imagine that our higher Self finds the
body a dense vehicle in which to reside. Perhaps that's why some babies
are so fussy. Their Selves are having a hard time adjusting to these heavy
bodies that won't do what they want them to do.

Five: Change

The life essence, now in the body, discovers that it must learn to be versa-
tile so that it can adapt to the conditions of the physical world. Five is
an active number in which the decisions that are made become vital in
the future evolution of the Self. Freedom and independence come through
the ability to make correct choices. Five is a critical number; it is here
that experiences will provide the information to enable us to choose between good and evil.

   Five is said to play a critical part in the development of illness and
the healing process. "The fifth week and the fifth day, or the fifth hour
of the day, are known to be important not only in illness but for things
in general that are wrong or can be amended, for example, 'The fifth
Trumpet in the Apocalypse of St. John is the summons to a decisive crisis'
(Steiner)."[10]

   Also, this number rules the five senses which take in experience and
influence the decision-making process. Five is the development of conscious thought. With the five-pointed pentagram as its symbol, the Five
represents evolving humanity striving toward its destiny. Halfway between One and Nine, Five is the pivotal point in the blueprint of creation.

   It is interesting to note that up until the late nineteenth century, the
Catholic Church's Doctrine of Passive Conception declared that the soul
entered the fetus during the fifth month of pregnancy. It was called "the
quickening." Prior to that time, the fetus had no soul, therefore abortion
before the fifth month was not a crime.

Six: Balance

After Five has stirred up things through its contact with its environment and the subsequent results of its decision making process, Six sets out to bring balance and harmony to these situations. Six takes on the social responsibilities brought about by the decisions made in Five.

This number rules the balance of opposites, the co-operation of male and female. Its symbol is the Philosopher's Stone, the six-pointed star comprised of two triangles, one pointing up and the other down. These two perfectly balanced triangles represent the harmonious joining of Fiery Will (the upper triangle) and Watery Feeling (the lower triangle.)

Six seeks peace in the environment through love, compassion, beauty, truth and justice. According to the Christian Bible, the world was created in six days therefore, to the ancients, Six represented completed perfection of the planning stages of the blueprint.

Seven: Rest

Divinity rested on the seventh day, but this use of semantics is deceiving for, although Seven brings temporary cessation of externals, the mind now sets to work. We are created in the "image" or "imagination" of Divinity. So, it is in the mind or thought of Divinity that we are born.

Seven is "a bridge for the Superconscious to perceive the material world."[11] Thought precedes reality. You, your family, your home, your job and your city were thoughts before they became realities, and that is why Seven precedes Eight. Seven is the promise of things to come represented by the rainbow with its seven colors. Seven is a complete cycle in the sense that it symbolizes the cosmic blueprint that precedes physical manifestation.

Eight: Manifestation

Physical reality is the result of the first six steps in the cosmic blueprint energized by thought in the seventh step, so Eight, manifestation, is the result of energized thought. We've certainly seen enough books on the market about the power of positive thinking to lend some credence to this idea. Although Four represents Form, it is the IDEA of form in the blueprint; it has yet to become a reality. In Eight the idea of form takes form in the physical world. Eight gathers all the ideas generated through the cosmic blueprint and gives birth to them in the material. The seven days of creation are the pattern leading to the physical plane of the Eight. The blueprint is now a working reality. In the Eight we begin to understand that all pairs of opposites (opposite forms of expression) are effects of a single cause from the One. Eight is the physical embodiment of the previous principles of the cosmic blueprint One through Seven.

Physical embodiment or the Eight is symbolized by the cube. Salt crystallizes in cubes, and we are called the "salt of the earth." Salt was considered the most material of the minerals by the alchemists. Here on Earth, in the physical body which is the cube, the stone the Masons work on and the temple not built by human hands, the Ego has taken on the most material of all cloaks.

All matter eventually dissolves, therefore death belongs only to the material world, the Eight. However, the Eight represents an unending cycle suggested by its glyph 8, the only number that can be drawn over and over without lifting pen from paper. (Technically, the Zero is not a number.) The point of crossing between the two equal circles in the 8 is the point of transition from earthly life to the spiritual and back to the earthly, and so on ad infinitum. The eighth day, or the first day of the week, emphasizes the repetitive theme. Medieval writers said that Eight represents immortality. The glyph for Eight, 8, placed on its side, ∞, is the mathematical symbol for infinity.

The first seven "days" in the creation story are the separate pieces of the whole pattern. In the Eighth day, the pieces are assembled. The material world is born and reborn and reborn. . . .

Nine: Dispersement

Nine is the number of completion, fulfillment and attainment in the physical. It encompasses all, contains all and continually returns. For example, any number times 9 returns to 9: $4 \times 9 = 36$; $36 = 3 + 6 = 9$. Any number added to 9 returns to itself: $4 + 9 = 13$; $13 = 1 + 3 = 4$. Because Nine contains all, it embodies wisdom. The cat, symbol of practical wisdom, is reputed to have nine lives. Key 9 in the Tarot is the Hermit who turns to shed the light of wisdom for those who follow. When we want it all, we say, I want the "whole nine yards."

The wisdom of Nine knows that the material world is illusionary and transitory, that it exists for a period of time then must be dissolved and used as fertilizer for the next cycle of experience. The Nine therefore gives back to the Universe what it has learned so that the Universe will be richer. Knowing it will return, the Nine gives freely. Nine is letting go of the material.

Ten: Rebirth

Ten is One starting again. Ten is reflected in the Ten Commandments, the Ten Hierarchies, the Ten steps on the Cabalistic Tree of Life, and Aristotle's Ten Categories which reveal the secrets of the material and spiritual worlds. Goethe in *Faust* speaks of the "significant totality represented in the first ten numbers." And the French mystic Louis Claude de Saint-Martin, referring to the tenth page in the "Book of Man," wrote: "It is without doubt the most significant, and actually the page without which all the preceding ones could not have been known. It is the closest relationship to the first page, from which everything proceeds."[12]

Time for a breather. All this metaphysical stuff may sound wonderful and spiritual and logical but, the big question is, how does it apply to your personal life? I respond to life's experiences much as a baby does — if it satisfies my needs, then it's useful. Metaphysical theory has to have some practical value. So let's examine the taste and pleasure factor in number philosophy — or how it works in your life — by first examining the cycles in nature around you and then discussing the cycles that affect you personally.

Cycles in the Universe

Recycling is part of the order of the Universe, inherent in the cosmic plan. Order in our world has always been obvious, even if misunderstood. From the beginning of human awareness, we saw that the Sun appeared in the morning and disappeared at night. This led to our awareness of a day. Eventually, we saw the Moon wax and wane in rhythmic patterns encompassing approximately twenty-eight days, and saw that this lunar cycle was divided into seven-day segments of quarter moons.

As time progressed we discovered that the Sun did not revolve around our Earth; rather, the Earth revolved around the Sun. As new planets were discovered, we saw that they, too, revolved around the Sun in an ordered amount of time. In those parts of the world where the seasons' changes are obvious, we were cognizant of the four seasons of the year and the months that made up that year. Here was further proof of the phenomenon of cycles.

Today, the cyclic nature of life is becoming more obvious as science delves ever deeper into the mysteries of the human body and its responses. Body timing is affected by three main rhythmic cycles: the Earth's daily revolution, the Moon's monthly orbit around the Earth and the Earth's yearly journey around the Sun. Blood pressure, pulse, body temperature, breathing and hormonal activity rise and fall in tune with the spinning of the Earth. Our circadian (about a day) rhythms even seem to be tied to our abilities, temperaments and resistance to disease. A disruption of the circadian rhythm is experienced when we travel at high speeds from one time zone to another, resulting in what we call "jet lag."

Laboratory tests have shown that mice injected with pneumonia germs at 4:00 AM survive at higher rates than mice injected at any other time during the day. This implies that there is a rhythmic response to either the contraction or the rejection of disease. This is something that deserves close attention considering the frequent administration of vaccines to so many children and adults today.

Statistics show that birth and death rates seem to be cyclical. Between midnight and 6:00 AM more babies are born and more heart attacks occur than at any other time of the day. And more babies are born in May and June than in November and December.

Japanese professor Maki Takata discovered a direct relationship between the activity of the Sun and the response of the human bloodstream. A few minutes before sunrise each day the blood undergoes a sudden change as if anticipating the break of day.[13] (We might also wonder if the blood is anticipating the close of night.)

We can see in nature and the Universe, and in our bodies' responses to nature that there is a cyclical process in life that repeats in an orderly fashion and at predictable intervals.

Now, where do you fit in? As a creature in the natural world and part of the Universe, you also respond to this cyclical process. Numerology is one method for determining and understanding the recycling pattern of your life. You'll find that this pattern repeats every nine years in keeping with the cosmic blueprint. This does not mean that the same events happen over and over every nine years. That would not be logical or useful. You are in the physical plane to learn and to grow. You learn through repetition and you grow through awareness of that repetition but, in this case, the numerical cycles in your life do not bring a repeat of identical events. Rather, there is a *recycling of your same attitudes or mental patterns every nine years.* This is an important distinction. For example, let's say that nine years ago you were in what is known as a 3 cycle and you took a trip to England. This year you may be taking acting lessons. You are repeating the same cycle of nine years ago but the event is different. The need for expansion in your life, however, remains the same. Both the trip to England and the acting lessons will aid you in expanding your ideas about yourself and your understanding of the world around you and your place in it.

Your life's lessons are learned through examining the events that are drawn into your life because of the attitudes you have. Once you can see the physical results of your mental attitudes, you can eliminate the negative ones and concentrate on the positive, which in turn will create a new and better world for you. This is the law of the cosmic blueprint. Mind (Seven) creates matter (Eight).

Personal Year Cycles

Let's find out what cycle you are in right now because the needs of this cycle will influence your dreams. And if you examine the meaning of your dreams, you will find ways to better use the cycle you are presently in.

Numerology involves simple addition. To determine your present cycle, add the numbers that make up the full date of your last birthday. Be sure to use the full year, i.e., 1987, and not an abbreviated form, '87, because the shortened version will give an incorrect total.

Example 1: July 9. As of this writing, October 1986, the last birthday would have been July 9, 1986. July is the seventh month.

July 9, 1986

$7+9+1+9+8+6 = 40$

Reduce the number 40 by adding again.

$4+0 = 4$

The individual in our example is in a personal cycle 4 from July 9, 1986 to July 9, 1987.

Example 2: November 22. As of this writing, October 1986, the last birthday was November 22, 1985. November is the eleventh month.

November 22, 1985

$11+22+1985$

$1+1+2+2+1+9+8+5 = 29$

To reduce the 29, add the two digits.

$29 = 2+9 = 11$

To reduce the 11, add again.

$11 = 1+1 = 2$

This individual is in a personal cycle 2 from November 22, 1985 to November 22, 1986.

Your cycles change with each birthday so if you are in a personal cycle 7 now, on your next birthday you will be in an 8, the following year you will be in a 9, the following year a 1, then a 2 and so on. The nine cycles repeat throughout your life. This holds true for any "thing" that has a birthday so you could examine the cycles of your family, pets, friends, famous personalities, your town, a business, a country or an idea.

Your first year of life does not necessarily start with a one cycle. To find the number you were born under, add your original birthday: e.g., November 10, 1939 or $1+1+1+0+1+ 9+3+9 = 25$. $25 = 2+5 = 7$. This person was born under a 7 cycle, so during the first twelve months of the person's life, the 7 cycle was in operation. At age one, the individual went into an 8 cycle; at age two, into a 9 cycle; at age 3, into a 1 cycle; and so on. I point this out because some people think that because they are 34 years old, for instance, they are in a 7 cycle ($34 = 3+4 = 7$).

Another point I wish to make here is that there is some discussion on whether your personal cycle starts on your birthday or on January 1st, the beginning of the current calendar year. My contention has always been that the personal year is just that, your personal year. It starts on the day you were born.

If you were born in December, for example, you were not even in the womb on January 1st of that year. According to the January 1st theory, if you were born at 1:00 AM on December 31st, your entire first personal year of life consists of twenty-three hours. This doesn't make sense to me, and it doesn't seem fair. We should each have the benefit of the full twelve months' experience in each of our personal year cycles.

I believe that the January 1st system connects us to the year we are born through a social consciousness. For example, you were part of the graduating class of '61. Or you might look back in your life and say, "I remember 1942. I was in grade school and we used to take our dimes in every Friday to buy stamps for our Savings Bond Books to help the war effort." We tend to think in yearly periods when referring to larger social events in which we participated.

But, as I say to my classes and in all my writings, try it for yourself. It has to taste good and please you.

Following are basic descriptions of the nine cycles. I am going to describe the types of events that can occur under each personal cycle. However, it is important to remember that these cycles are more than external events. On a deeper level they indicate the attitudes you are experiencing. Each personal cycle shows where your MIND is focused for that period of time. I like to say that each birthday brings a new mental homework assignment for that year. The personal year cycle represents an INNER EVENT that usually manifests in your outer world because mind creates physical reality.

Of course, every set of possible circumstances that could occur in your life cannot be described here, but you should get the general idea. As you read these definitions and apply them to your own life, you might keep in mind our discussion of the cosmic blueprint so that you can see how everyday events and your overall personal year tie in with the meanings of the basic nine numbers.

Personal Year Cycle One: Action

This is the beginning of a brand new cycle in your life. You might say that you are born again during this time. You have the urge to reach out and try new experiences.

You are not so willing to take the advice of others and this is as it should be. You need to make your own decisions now. You may feel a sense of isolation, of being alone, even if you are surrounded by people. This should not worry you because you need to feel somewhat removed so that you will not be unduly influenced by others.

You must think of your own needs before the needs of others during this cycle. This may go against what you have been taught, and it does not mean you should disregard others altogether. But during your One cycle, *you* must come first. You have to fill your own well before others can drink from it.

The decisions you make now will influence your life for many years to come so it is necessary that they are made to fit your lifestyle and your present requirements. Your independence may cause some concern to those around you so explain that this year is "your time."

Dare to do those things that you might not have attempted before. You have the pioneering instinct now and are mentally preparing for accomplishment in every phase of your life: relationships, business, on the home front, creatively, financially. The reins are in your hands and you must decide which road to take.

During this cycle, one new person who will be a great influence in the coming years may enter your life.

Personal Year Cycle Two: Attraction

This year requires you to accept a calm, receptive, waiting attitude. The events you set into motion last year are now gathering energy. This is an incubation period during which those seeds you have sown are being nourished behind the scenes. If you have seen the smock worn nowadays by pregnant women with the message "under construction" and an arrow pointing down, you know what this cycle is all about. This is your "under construction" period. Many hidden events are taking place.

You need to be quiet, patient and cooperative. You may have upset the status quo last year with your energetic drive. Now is the time to set things straight, to be the mediator and to balance anything that is disturbing in your environment. You are now receptive to the feelings of others and find that companionship is important. You may be more sensitive during this cycle so try not to take things too personally. Instead, use this sensitivity to draw upon your creative source which is being stimulated now. Recognition from unexpected quarters is possible.

You want peace but don't pursue it at any price. Balance is the key.

Sudden events can occur during this personal year so be prepared for all eventualities. If you have to make quick decisions, examine the fine print before you agree to anything.

Do not push affairs now. Instead, watch and wait, accumulate and assimilate. All sorts of partnerships are possible under a Two cycle.

Personal Year Cycle Three: Expansion

This is your year of activity, expansion, travel and luck. You need room to move and express yourself freely. All the experiences you encounter now have one purpose — to help you grow and expand your horizons. If a long trip to another part of this land or another country will do the job, then the opportunity will present itself. You will meet people who enlarge your idea of the world and your role in it. Positive feedback will encourage you to speak out and express yourself as never before.

Since this cycle is very social, you may be invited to parties and various public functions where you suddenly become the center of attention. You are very noticeable when in a Three cycle. Because of this new exposure, you take stock of your appearance and indulge yourself with a new wardrobe. This is important because your appearance makes a difference with those you are contacting now. You are blossoming. Take acting or elocution lessons, or become involved in other activities that will help you express yourself more fluently.

This could be a very lucky period. Enter every free contest and buy those one dollar tickets from your local organizations. Play the sweepstakes or lottery. Because you feel lucky, you transmit positive energies which draw positive results back to you — the law of cause and effect. During this cycle, if you operate wisely, more money is available. But beware of the one pitfall of this cycle. DO NOT OVERINDULGE. It only takes one ticket to win. Too much expansion can bring on bankruptcy.

Expansion is the key word — there is growth and fertility in all areas of your life. The creative life force is active.

Personal Year Cycle Four: Formation

The emphasis this year is on work, order, budgeting, foundations and close physical relationships. You have such an urge to organize your life that you clean the attic, the cellar, the closets, desks and drawers, the garage and shed, and the office. No corner is safe from your organizational energy. Your need is to build a strong, secure and orderly foundation in your life. Your subconscious takes suggestions from what you feed it every day so if you live in an organized environment, your life will run more smoothly. You understand this truth and realize its importance in your life at this particular stage of your growth.

Material things become important. You want money and possessions because they add to your sense of security and satisfy your heightened physical desires and needs. You may purchase goods or services that require setting up a budget and making payments. Land and property, building and remodeling come under this cycle. Be economical and practical now, organizing your funds wisely. Take care of your money and it will take care of you.

Your body is your physical home and, after last year's expansive mood, you may find that your body expanded along with your attitude. So out come the jogging pants, the diet book and the bathroom scale. Since Four highlights the physical, health is an issue; eat well, rest and have a check-up.

Money that comes to you now is in direct proportion to the amount of work you do. Work well and you will be paid well.

Since all things physical reign in the Four cycle, your sexual relationships can be very rewarding and physically stimulating now. You are aware of sensations that are often muted under other cycles.

This cycle asks that you look at the physical plane — your body, money, possessions, earthly ties — with respect and understanding, realizing you are only a steward of these things. Own them, use them wisely and with honor, but do not let them own you.

Personal Year Cycle Five: Change

Communication, change, experience, decisions and sexual magnetism are key issues for you this year. You are so busy and totally involved in the activity of life — meetings, errands, answering mail and the telephone, making arrangements, attending parties — that you might want to consider installing a revolving door in your home. Suddenly everyone needs you. This whirlwind of activity is a result of the changing cycle of Five. These many experiences are necessary so that you will have enough information available to make the decisions that eventually must be made during this period. Experience is your most important lesson and change will be the end result. You are at a turning point in your life when you can look back over the past four years and decide if you like the direction in which you are headed. If you are dissatisfied, this is the time to make the change.

You feel a restless energy that keeps you on the move, propelling you into the mainstream of life. You don't want to miss anything because your curiosity is at its peak. Because learning is part of the curiosity you feel now, you should consider taking courses in some area that you find stimulating as well as practical for the future. Absorbing information is easier now because your mind is as active as your body.

During a Five cycle, the opposite sex suddenly discovers you. Your date book fills as you become the life of the party, surrounded by admirers. This attention is part of the cosmic plan that becomes more obvious under the Six.

Your nervous system is highly activated so avoid alcohol and drugs, drive with care and resist temptations that would undermine your effectiveness. With that in mind, it's time for fun, excitement, sexual relationships, experience and learning. Make the necessary changes and flow with them.

Personal Year Six: Balance

Love, home and family, justice, beauty and social responsibility are accented now. The emphasis is usually on the home and family members, and there probably will be changes on the domestic scene. Family members may enter or leave the home. Children go off to school or get married. Babies are born. Relatives need financial assistance or may move in with you temporarily for some reason. Responsibility on the home front increases. After your Five cycle of sexual encounters, you see how the home situation can change.

This is a time for seeking balance at the very roots of your being, which manifests in your home, your relationships and yourself. You may express this need for balance by remodeling or redecorating your home to bring beauty into your environment.

Your sense of artistic proportion is sensitized, therefore you can create things that express great beauty and deep feeling. Your heightened sense of proportion may manifest in your need to get involved in community projects that beautify your town or city, or in legalities that bring justice and unity to the political scene.

You also may feel impelled to donate your time and services to local organizations like Big Sister/Big Brother, Paratours, or other social groups where you can become intimately involved with people who need the wise counseling and healing energy you emit during this cycle.

Your sense of fairness is so keen now that others seek your advice in settling their differences. You become Mother/Father Confessor; buy a thick towel for your shoulder because everyone will be crying on it. Any pending court decisions could be settled here also, because Six seeks to restore balance and harmony. If balance is not attained, disruptions occur. Six expresses the peace or war syndrome.

However, this can be a warm and loving year. Express your love and compassion for others and enjoy the wonderfully nurturing and fulfilling feelings this cycle can bestow on you.

Personal Year Cycle Seven: Rest

Rest, perfection, health and analysis are the key issues for you this year. You need this period of retreat because you are more tired than usual and don't want to socialize. You need to be alone, to think, meditate, reflect and retreat within yourself. It is a good time for vacations, weekends at the mountains or by the sea, or just being by yourself in your home. You would rather be alone now, or at least with people of a more contemplative nature who complement your own mood. Divinity rested on the seventh day; this is your time to rest.

Outside activity and interests will slow while your attention is transferred to your inner world. You will do a lot of necessary thinking now, synthesizing the experiences you have gained. This is a pause in the life cycle during which you need to become partially conscious of your spiritual side, your inner world. You have done enough outside work — now let nature take her course.

This introspective period is the best time to perfect skills you already have. You may want to take a course to polish your existing talents, or begin philosophical or metaphysical studies such as history of religions, yoga, mind awareness courses, astrology, numerology or dream interpretation.

Set material worries aside. The things you have been worrying about will mysteriously take care of themselves. You should not push or be aggressive in your attempts to accomplish worldly goals. If you persist in these attempts, you may become ill. The cosmic blueprint says stop, look and listen to your inner world. If you do not heed this message, you may be placed where you have time to listen — in bed. Slow your pace and take care of your health.

Your intuitions are strong now. Dreams, visions and telepathic experiences are all possible as you delve into the mystical side of life.

Personal Year Cycle Eight: Manifestation

Karma, responsibility, business, finance, sex and power become your personal issues this year. If you have ever been in doubt about how effective you are in the material world, now you will find out. Karma reigns; the law of cause and effect is complete and you will get exactly what you deserve. You could receive a raise, a promotion, public recognition, or some other honor or award. There's even a possibility of legacies. Or, there can be material loss, financial hardship, unemployment and sometimes bankruptcy. The difficult side of this cycle does not mean you are a "bad" person, but it does indicate that you have not handled your past cycles wisely.

This is your power year. If you have an idea, take it to the top. People in high places are more willing to listen to you now. Eight is the cycle of material domination. Business and government are ruled by this number. (Note that the 800 wats line connects you to the business world.) You may feel more pressure on the job, whether your job is inside or out of the home. Additional responsibilities, however, can bring you more income.

Intense sexual relationships are needed, but pure physical enjoyment must be balanced with the spiritual. There must be a meeting of mind and body, heaven and earth so that both partners unite on an equal and sharing basis. Eight requires a union of equality.

Examine this cycle carefully because it points out in the clearest ways how effectively you have grown through your past seven cycles. Here you will find limitation or freedom.

Personal Year Cycle Nine: Dispersement

Endings, transition, charity, friendships and wisdom are key issues in this cycle. Cycle Nine says you must let go of those things that are no longer necessary in your life. You may not know what you need, so if you cannot or do not want to let go of certain "things," then the Nine will do it for you. People may leave your life. You might change jobs or relocate, and things that you have grown attached to may have to be relinquished. Nine is the clearing house in which you make room for the new.

This can be an emotionally trying time if change and transition are difficult for you, and you may need time to sort it all out. Do some serious house-cleaning: physically, mentally, emotionally and spiritually. Remember, when endings occur, there is something new just around the bend.

You have gathered many experiences during the past eight years. Now it's time to give back to the Universe some part of what you have gained. This is tithing time. Your giving is a demonstration of your faith in the unending flow from the cornucopia of life. Work with others for the common good.

Be sympathetic, compassionate and understanding toward all whom you encounter. Old friendships become especially meaningful now. Gifts and favors may be yours. Observe this cycle closely; many of your goals will have been accomplished and you should finish any that are still uncompleted. Much wisdom can be gained here through observation.

Be open to change. This can be an uplifting and promising year with the freshness one feels after a cool shower on a hot summer's day. This cleansing renews and invigorates, preparing you for the exciting new cycle ahead which will begin with your next birthday. Allow the winds of change to sweep out the old and make room for the new.

Well, there you have it — the nine basic cycles that relate to the cosmic blueprint.

Many people find that constructing a chart large enough to cover the cycles throughout a lifetime is very revealing as a learning tool. This life cycle chart also can help you spot trends that may arise in the future.

To do this, you need to determine the number under which you were born. I discussed this process earlier on in this chapter. Add the numbers of your birthdate, for example, November 4, 1937.

$$11 + 4 + 1937$$

$$1 + 1 + 4 + 1 + 9 + 3 + 7 = 26$$

$$26 = 2 + 6 = 8$$

This individual was born under an eight cycle.

Next, take a sheet of poster paper or three pieces of standard 8-1/2 by 11 paper scotch taped together side by side and draw nine, evenly-spaced horizontal lines. (See Figure 1.2.) Mark off a narrow margin at the left and write the numbers One through Nine in it. These numbers represent your personal year cycles. Divide the remaining space vertically into eleven columns.

Now, refer back to the number under which you were born and write "age 0" next to the appropriate personal year number on your chart. Remember, you are not one year old until twelve months have passed therefore, when you are born, you are 0 years old. The person in our example was born under the 8, and would write age 0 in the column next to the number 8. (See Figure 1.2.)

At age 1, this person enters a Nine cycle so place age 1 next to cycle 9. The following year at age 2, the person enters a 1 cycle. She would go to the top of the next column and write age 2 next to the cycle 1, and so on. Fill in your entire chart up to the age at which you wish to stop.

Next, fill in the blocks with the events that have happened in your life. It is very unlikely that you will remember every event right off the top of your head so write down the ones that you remember at the moment. As time goes by, you will recall others. You can talk with relatives and check old photograph albums or newspapers, too, and eventually more memories will come back to you.

As new things happen to you that you feel are important, enter these on the chart as well. Don't neglect to write down your moods if they persist for extended periods of time for they also reflect the cycle you are experiencing.

By tracing your cycles horizontally across your chart, you will see certain patterns forming. For instance, in every Six year, you may discover that there were changes in your home, even when you were a child. Examine these changes and see how they affected your life. By discovering these patterns you will have more power over your future. Plan to work *with* your cycles rather than responding to them unaware.

1		AGE **2**:	AGE **11**:	AGE **20**:
2		AGE**3**:	AGE**12**:	AGE**21**:
3		AGE **4**:	AGE **13**:	AGE **22**:
4		AGE**5**:	AGE **14**:	AGE **23**:
5		AGE**6**:	AGE **15**:	AGE **24**:
6		AGE **7**:	AGE **16**:	AGE **25**:
7		AGE**8**:	AGE **17**:	AGE **26**:
8	AGE **O**:	AGE**9**:	AGE **18**:	AGE **27**:
9	AGE **1**:	AGE **10**:	AGE **19**:	AGE **28**:

Figure 1.2   Life Cycle Chart

Notes

1. Lawlor, Robert, *Pythagorean Number as Form, Color and Light,* Lindisfarne Letter, 14 (Stockbridge, MA: The Lindisfarne Assoc., 1982), p. 32.

2. Ibid., p. 32.

3. Bond, Frederick Bligh and Lea, Thomas Simcox, *Gematria* (London: Research Into Lost Knowledge Organization, 1977), Epigraph.

4. Stebbing, Lionel, *The Secrets of Numbers* (London: New Knowledge Books, 1963), title page.

5. Ibid.

6. Stone, Merlin *When God Was a Woman,* (NY: Harcourt, Brace, Jovanovich, Publishers, 1976), p. xviii, introduction.

7. *The Random House Dictionary of the English Language,* Jess Stein, editor in chief (NY: Random House, 1969).

8. Walker, Barbara, *The Women's Encyclopedia of Myths and Secrets* (San Francisco: Harper & Row, Publishers, 1983), p.349.

9. Ann Kreilkamp, "Saturn/Uranus in Sagittarius: Conceptual Repatterning," *Welcome to Planet Earth, Aries 1987,* Vol. 6, No. 10, p. 32.

10. Stebbing, p. 32.

11. Schmalz, John Barnes, *Nuggets from King Solomon's Mines* (Ferndale, Mich: Trismegistus Press, 1980).

12. Stebbing, p. 65.

13. *Reader's Digest Strange Stories, Amazing Facts* (Pleasantville, NY: The Reader's Digest Assoc., Inc., 1976), p. 52.

2

Astrology

Once upon a time, long ago, wo/man looked to the heavens and began
to wonder. In a time when s/he had little or no control over the environment, s/he looked for signs from above to reduce the anxiety s/he felt
and to suggest a dependable presence and order in life.

The cycles of the Moon and the Sun were the most obvious to early
people. And it appears that the Moon was observed and honored first,
suggested by many findings including 10,000- to 25,000-year-old notched
reindeer bones and mammoth's tusks, presumably marked in accordance
with the phases of the Moon.

Humankind has always known intuitively that we were connected
to the cosmos by invisible energies. Despite the reasoning of the Age of
Science, which denied any but a mechanical connection of the human organism to the environment and the cosmos, the inner knowing persisted.
Ancient teachings passed down through the millenniums have remained
the same. As above, so below. We are microcosms of the macrocosm; what
we find in ourselves, we find in the Universe. And we are intimately linked
to the subtle yet pervasive influences of terrestrial and celestial energies
and cycles that we cannot see and, until recently, were not able to measure. We are not controlled but influenced by these energies and cycles.

Through the continuing "discoveries" of science, ancient teachings
are being substantiated. In the 1940s, "the Russian Tchijevsky demon-
strated how human behavior and metabolism were affected by ions, elec-

trically charged particles floating in the atmosphere. This was proof of a very fine sensitivity on the part of the human system."[1]

More recently, two German scientists, Konig and Reiter, "found that the human organism is incredibly sensitive to waves of extremely low frequencies and correspondingly weak energy. It was theoretically unthinkable that man could register energy changes of such infinitesimal magnitude . . . "[2]

Although clothed in modern technological language, these findings corroborate the teachings of ancient wisdom. Astrology is based upon identical information, although it was a "knowing" that we are "incredibly sensitive to waves of extremely low frequencies and correspondingly weak energy." Astrologers understand that distant planets like Pluto can affect our own planet's energy field and each of us here on Earth.

Until recently science believed that space was a vacuum, void of any living substance. Yet all cultures have passed down traditional spiritual teachings about a space teeming with living energies, known as the ether. The kahunas of Hawaii believe that space is filled with *aha* threads, and that you are connected by this thread to every person you have contacted in your lifetime. The more contact you have with a particular person — either physically or psychically — the stronger the aha thread between you becomes, so that eventually you "know" when something is happening to that other person because the aha thread begins to vibrate. It's rather like a cosmic telephone.

Science now has validated the ancient teaching that space is neither static nor empty. "The artificial satellites have shown clearly that space is filled with an infinity of corpuscles and waves buffeting our earth, affecting everything that lives on its surface."[3]

Scientists call it "corpuscles" and "waves buffeting our earth," the kahunas talk about "aha threads," philosophers and alchemists refer to it as "the ethers." Science looks down its nose at this "primitive" wisdom. They play mental gymnastics, leaping superficially over a body of wisdom that has survived for thousands of years in many different cultures, then couch the same information in technical terms and declare it has been "discovered."

A professor of biology wrote that science's truths are "uncertain 'shifting sands.' The 'truths' of one generation may become absurdities of a succeeding one. Our treatises in science demand steady revisions, not simply to add the new 'truths' but almost equally to shed that which has meanwhile ceased to be 'true.' "[4]

Despite the "uncertain shifting sands" of scientific truth, scientists continue to attack astrological teachings as superstitious nonsense although the "truths" of astrology have persisted for five thousand years — unlike most scientific "truths."

A European scientist once said that if statistics prove astrology, he would throw out statistics. Because of personal prejudice, he denies himself a holistic view from his personal center by mindlessly rejecting astrological knowledge that has permeated cultures from the beginning of recorded history. Healthy skepticism is a good thing, but I feel some scientists miss out on a body of truth by refusing to examine some of the old teachings.

Western astrology, as we know it today, had it beginnings 5,000 to 6,000 years ago in Mesopotamia, a land that lies between the Tigris and Euphrates Rivers, roughly in the area where modern Iraq now exists. The Sumerians, who lived in the southern part of Mesopotamia, observed the skies with care for they were aware of the lunar and solar cycles that affected the seasons and the growth of their crops. This knowledge, essential for their survival, became an integral part of their lives.

They were an advanced culture; the world's oldest written documents were found in Sumer. Goddesses were honored by this civilization. "Females were worshipped and adored all through Sumerian history . .

but the goddess who outweighed, overshadowed, and outlasted them all was a deity known to the Sumerians by the name of Inanna, 'Queen of Heaven,' and to the Semites who lived in Sumer by the name of Ishtar. Inanna played a greater role in myth, epic, and hymn than any other deity, male or female."[5]

The story of Inanna, as seen by Diane Wolkstein, is "the archetypal Moon Goddess: the young woman who is courted; the ripe woman who enjoys her feminine powers and generously offers her bounty; and the mature woman who meets death in the underworld."[6]

This lends more credence to the theory that the earliest cultures were matriarchal and worshipped the Moon, paying tribute to the Great Mother whose essence often was embodied in the Moon.

The Sumerians were conquered by the Babylonians whose greatest period was from 2,800 to 1,750 B.C. Both Babylonian and Chaldean priests (the Chaldeans were a dominant people who originally occupied the southerly part of Babylonia) studied the movement of the heavens from watchtower observatories high above the cities. These towers, which were about 270 feet high, were called *ziggurats* which means "cosmic mountains." The Christian Bible speaks of the ziggurat as the Tower of Babel (Genesis 11:1-9).

The ziggurats or towers were seven-tiered, each layer representing one of the seven known planets (Uranus, Neptune and Pluto were not discovered until 1781, 1846 and 1930 respectively). The base of the ziggurat was *Sheb,* Saturn, and was colored black; the second level was *Marduk,* Jupiter, orange; the third was *Nergal,* Mars, red; the fourth and middle level and exact center was *Shamash,* the Sun, which was covered with plates of gold; the fifth was *Istar,* Venus, pale yellow; the sixth was *Nebo,* Mercury, blue; and the top platform was *Sin,* the Moon, silver. This layer was left unfinished or open in order to be used as an observatory.[7]

The Moon was especially sacred to ancient peoples. One reason was that it was linked to fertility. The Moon's cycles corresponded with the menstrual cycle of the fertile woman who, as the producer of life, was considered closest to Divinity, the Great Mother. Also, planting was done according to the phases of the Moon. Without food, these people could not live. Their existence was intimately connected with the Moon, the Great Mother, who operated through the females in their environment and through Mother Earth, who produced new life and nourishment without which they would die.

Although in more temperate climates, we tend to look to the Sun for our pleasure, in those areas around the equator, the Sun can be harsh and unforgiving, drying the earth and depriving the people of their precious water supply and destroying food crops. After a burning day, the presence of the Moon was a sweet relief and a respite in the arms of the Great Mother.

The Mesopotamian trinity embodies these early people's attitudes toward the Moon. "The great triad in that country was Sin the moon-god, who was masculine and the most powerful, Shamash the sun-god, feminine, and Ishtar, the goddess of love."[8]

Modern translations of these ancient carvings and teachings have to be taken in the light of patriarchal thought. Traditionally male scholars, or those trained in the patriarchal institutions of the last few thousand years, have attempted to interpret the intentions of the ancient people who, in many cases, were matriarchal. " . . . we must reevaluate all female images that have been despised by previous generations of male scholars."[9]

It is typical of this mode of thought to call Sin, the moon-god, "masculine and the most powerful." The description of this god is as follows: "Sin was pictured as a strong man with a beard of lapis lazuli who travelled across the sky in his boat, the lunar crescent."[10]

First of all, the word "powerful" is often associated with males because men have traditionally lived out the domination syndrome. A recent television special on cats noted that most women prefer cats, but men almost universally choose dogs because they can dominate dogs. So, in the modern patriarchal mind, if the god is the most important, he must be masculine and powerful.

Also, has it been overlooked that this god travelled in the "lunar crescent," symbol of the Moon, the Mother Goddess' representative, who protectively circles the earth in predictable cycles. It appears that Sin was born out of the Cosmic Womb, the crescent Moon, and that his authority was dependent upon Her support and nourishment.

Today's patriarchal interpretations have forgotten or do not know that "male spiritual authority was dependent on marriage . . . between the ruler or a land and his goddess, or the mandatory husbandship of priests who were not allowed to contact deities unless they had wives."[11] In Asia, wives embodied their husbands' power, and certain ceremonies could not be performed if the priest had no wife. The word marriage comes from the Latin *maritare,* or union under the Goddess Aphrodite-Mari.

Because the Goddess presided over all aspects of marriage, the early Christian fathers passionately opposed marriage. St. Jerome said that "the primary purpose of a man of God was to 'cut down with an ax of Virginity the wood of marriage.'" St. Ambrose claimed marriage a sin against God. St. Augustine "flatly stated that marriage is a sin."[12] St. Paul said that to marry was only better than to burn. And so on.

To support this contention that the Moon, emissary of the Great Mother in matriarchal societies, was the most powerful deaty (feminine form of the masculine "deity"), the early people measured time by the Moon. Calendars were lunar, consisting of twelve lunar months of 29½ days each. To adjust to the seasons, a thirteenth month was inserted every few years. The sun calendar was introduced around 800 B.C. In our own country, in this century, the Native Americans spoke of time in terms of "many Moons ago."

With the conquest of Chaldea by Alexander the Great in 331 B.C., the Greeks turned from their mythological pantheon and adopted Chaldean astrology from the priests, building it into the system which is very close to the one practiced today. By the time Babylon, the old capital of Babylonia, was destroyed by fire in 125 B.C., astrology had become an integral part of Greek culture.

Pythagoras, the Greek philosopher and father of mathematics, was born around 580 B.C. (We mentioned him in the first chapter on numerology.) He travelled throughout Greece, Egypt and Asia in search of ancient wisdom. Well aware of Chaldean astrology, he taught this celestial science along with mathematics at his school. He believed that the essential character of the Universe is number and that everything could be interpreted through number. "All things can be counted therefore number was a fundamental part of the world's framework."[13]

Among many other ideas, the Pythagoreans taught the following:

The Pythagorean theorem, supposedly discovered by Pythagoras, on which, it is speculated, most of Euclid's first book in *Elements* about geometry is based;

The spherical nature of the Earth — the Pythagoreans may have been the first to teach this;

A central fire around which the planets and fixed stars revolved. This preceded Copernicus' heliocentric view of the solar system in 1543 by a thousand years.

A few hundred years after Alexander had conquered the known world, Greece was defeated by the Romans who then took up astrology. "From the fourth century onward, everyone in Rome believed in astrology," and every emperor had his personal astrologer.[14] In fact, the astronomers who have come down to us through history, were astrologer/astronomers. The two systems were inextricably bound until the seventeenth century.

The names of the seven original "planets" we use today — the Moon and the Sun (which are not planets but are grouped with the planets for convenience), Mercury, Venus, Mars, Jupiter and Saturn — evolved from the Babylonian to the Greek into Latin and finally into the English translations of today.

The Horoscope

Your horoscope is a picture snapped at the precise moment you took your first breath. It is a geocentric (Earth-centered) view of the solar system with you in the exact center of the wheel, surrounded by the planets as they were positioned on the day of your birth. That moment in time is filled with the specific energies you inhaled as a new life form on Earth, taking in the "prana" or life force of the Universe. Those energies permeated every cell in your physical body with their specific creative pattern. You became that moment, joined in a cosmic marriage in time. As Carl G. Jung, the well-known Swiss psychologist, wrote: "We are born at a given moment, in a given place, and, like vintage years of wine, we have the qualities of the year and of the season in which we are born. Astrology does not lay claim to anything more."[15]

In Ruth Montgomery's biography *Born To Heal,* Mr. A. is quoted as saying, "At birth, the first breath of life is our direct supply, our lifeline with the Universal Power . . . So long as this energy is established and flows without obstruction, we are in tune with the Universal supply of energy."[16]

The horoscope depicts your relationship to the world, how you see your environment and how you perceive the events that occur around and to you. At the precise moment of your birth the energies of the Sun, Moon and the planets struck the place where you were born at specific angles, and formed unique angular relationships to each other and to you. These planetary positions and angular relationships tell the astrologer how you are likely to express yourself in your environment and how easily or difficult this is for you.

Three of the major angular relationships that can form between the planets are known as the square (a 90-degree separation between two planets), the opposition (a 180-degree separation) and the conjunction (technically 0 degrees of separation). For years, astrologers have spoken of the problems alloyed with these particular planetary configurations. The scientific community has rejected such interpretation as, at best, superstitious nonsense, and, at worst, an attempt to defraud the public. RCA communication analyst, John H. Nelson, however, understood in 1951 that "the quality of radio reception depends on sunspot activity" but that "a conspicuous variance remained unaccounted for."[17] Nelson knew that some other force was at work. According to him, "certain specific planetary configurations cause disturbances in radio reception: those in which, in relation to the sun, the planets find themselves either at right angles to each other, or in conjunction, or in opposition."[18]

Scientists find this phenomenon "difficult to explain," yet astrologers have been using these same angles for many thousands of years. The correlation between Nelson's "discovery" and ancient astrological knowledge seems obvious.

The Signs of the Zodiac

The present order of the signs of the zodiac is as follows: Aries, Taurus, Gemini, Cancer, Leo, Virgo, Libra, Scorpio, Sagittarius, Capricorn, Aquarius and Pisces. (See Figure 2.1.)

In Tropical astrology (that which is practiced most widely in the West), these signs do not correlate with the constellations that go by the same names. Rather, they represent a pattern for the exchange of energy between celestial forces and the human organism (or country, business, relationship — whatever you are examining through astrology; you can cast a horoscope for just about anything).

These twelve signs are the formative principles through which we guide our collective lives. They represent the underlying principles that affect each of us regardless of our nationality, our philosophical/religious

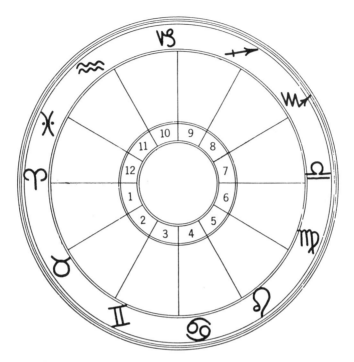

Figure 2.1   The Natural Chart

beliefs or cultural training. The basic numerological formula for the creation of the Universe is Four but, once the umbilical cord to the mother
is severed, we as individuals resonate to the Twelve, the instinctual patterns governing life on this planet and represented by the twelve zodiacal
signs.

The first six signs — Aries, Taurus, Gemini, Cancer, Leo and Virgo
— represent your personal development, action and response to your immediate environment.

In Aries, you recognize that you are, that you exist.

In Taurus, you realize you need. There are certain specific possessions that are necessary to ensure your survival, substances such as food
and water.

In Gemini, you become aware that you can act upon your circumstances in some manner. Communication and people become factors.

In Cancer, you discover that one special person creates a womb of
nurturing protection in an uncertain world. This nurturing is essential for
your survival.

In Leo, you begin to play, to express your ego, your individuality within your family unit, to show your love in your own way.

In Virgo, your play develops into skills that individualize you apart from others. These skills will serve you when you step over the line into the remaining six signs of the zodiac.

The remaining six signs are Libra, Scorpio, Sagittarius, Capricorn, Aquarius and Pisces. In these, you reach out beyond yourself into the world and learn to interact with others on all levels.

In Libra, you reach out to one other person to form some kind of a union.

In Scorpio, you and that other person join resources to ensure that the life you have created will survive. That "life" could be another human being, a friendship, a business or any joining that requires the cooperation of two people.

In Sagittarius, your understanding expands. You realize that it is necessary to protect the resources that will ensure the continuity of life. Your social conscience develops.

In Capricorn, you build an enduring framework in which society as a whole can exist in harmony and to the mutual benefit of all members.

In Aquarius, you go beyond the established laws and structures that will support society. You look outside your immediate environment and see that others may need assistance. Your humanitarian feelings develop and you reach out to others indiscriminately, with unconditional love.

And in Pisces, the boundaries dissolve between me and you, mine and yours, my ideas and your ideas, my base and your base, my love and your love. Recognition of the Oneness of all life permeates your consciousness.

This is the law of Twelve, the underlying principles which guide our collective lives.

We know that there are cycles within cycles within cycles, just from observing something as fundamental as time: a second within a minute within an hour within a day within a week within a month within a year within a decade within a century, and so on. More than one principle is in operation at any given time. If we refer back to the laws of both Four and Twelve which govern us, we can see this expressed as the four elements that contain the twelve signs of the zodiac.

The Four Elements

The earliest cultures revered the Four, geometrically expressed as the sacred trapezoid discussed in chapter 1, because it was the formula for the creation of life. In a mundane sense, it was expressed as the four corners of the Earth (the points on the compass), the four seasons, the four winds, and the four phases of the Moon. Early astrological charts were drawn as squares.

The four elements are fire, water, air and earth. They are not only an integral part of astrology but also have been represented in a variety of esoteric and symbolic ways in most cultures throughout history. All the presentations originate from the same formula of Four found in the Sacred Trapezoid, the secret formula for the construction of the Universe by the Great Architect.

The ancient concept of the four elements was not meant to convey the same information as the present day periodic table of chemistry. We know there are more than four chemical elements. The elements of which the ancients spoke and which are represented to this day in a variety of symbolic ways are not identical to those identified by science. They are the basic laws of this solar system, and indeed, may be the basic laws of the Universe. The four elements are the unseen builders of the material world and all that resides in it. They are the four basic energies that are contained within the Primary Energy, Divinity.

The elements are an integral part of astrology, as well as of time, nature, language, psychology, religion, architecture and games around the world. They are hidden from the casual observer's eye in awesome structures such as the Sphinx, and in the most common of pastimes, the ordinary deck of playing cards. The four elements are at the foundation of metaphysical science.

In Tibetan cosmology, the elements were considered to be "the fundamental energies of the cosmos." In Tibetan Buddhism, the *Stupa* is a symbolic structure of creation. It is constructed of five levels, representing fire, water, air and earth, as well as ether. Ether is the Source or container of the four elements and, as such, represents the All or Divinity from which all life is born and in which all life dies. Ether permeates space and all living matter. A similar idea is held in the holy scriptures of India.

The Ancient Greeks based their philosophy on the four elements, equating them with wo/man's four faculties: "moral (fire), aesthetic and soul (water), intellectual (air), and physical (earth)."[19]

The Greeks also postulated the "Four Ages of Man." The first was the Golden Age when humans lived like gods. The second was the Silver Age when "a race of feeble and inept men . . . obeyed their mothers all their lives (i.e. it was a matriarchal age)." The Bronze Age, in which men "delighted in oaths and warlike exploits. 'Their pitiless hearts were as hard as steel . . . '" was the third. The discovery of metals and attempts at civilization occurred during this period. The fourth was known as the Hero-

ic Age, the Iron Age, "a period of misery and crime . . . Thus they explained the progressive degeneration of mankind."[20]

These four worlds are not only a blatant example of a punishing patriarchal view of creation, they also depict the four elements: *fire,* the Golden
Age of the Sun, where men were in the exalted position they deemed they
merited; *water,* the Silver Age of the Moon, when matriarchy ruled over
"feeble and inept men;" *air,* the Bronze Age of oaths and pitiless hearts,
of discovery, where the mind ruled; and *earth,* the Age of Iron, an element
of great hardness and density, symbolic of entrapment in "a period of misery and crime."

These four ages are in direct descending order of the creation of the
Universe as taught by all adepts. The "progressive degeneration of man"
refers to the life force entering into the physical body and having to deal
with the temptations and pains of the physical world. These Greeks tended
to overlook the joys of the physical world, but of course, such things pertain
to a matriarchal view of creation.

Medieval Europe spoke of four "humours," which applied to four
specific human temperaments. This information was applied liberally in
medical diagnosis. Hippocrates, the father of medicine, enumerated four
humours: blood, phlegm, yellow bile (choler) and black bile. He considered
these four to be the root of disease. Literary people of that day wrote
of four temperaments in human beings: sanguine, phlegmatic, choleric and
melancholic.

Carl Jung spoke of the four human Functions: intuition (fire), feeling
(water), thinking (air), and sensation (earth).

Tradition has it that the four elements are also represented by the
four fixed signs of the zodiac: Taurus, the bull (earth), Leo, the lion (fire),
Scorpio, the eagle (water), and Aquarius, the wo/man (air). We find these
four symbols reproduced in the Sphinx in Egypt which stands as guardian
before the Great Pyramid. This composite creature is made up of "the
head of a Woman, the body of a Bull, the paws of a Lion, and the wings
of an Eagle."[21] In *Isis and Osiris,* Plutarch wrote, "The Sphinx symbolizes
the secret of all occult wisdom." The Sphinx, representing the four Elements through the symbolic bull, lion, eagle and woman, is an architectural
representation of the one true formula of creation embodied in the sacred
trapezoid.

Hathor, Queen of Heaven, and mother of all goddesses and gods,
was said to have incarnated in the Sphinx. Her name, Hathor, became
part of all royal names to insure the matrilineal succession.[22]

The four Elements represented by the woman, the bull, the lion and
the eagle, are also found in bas relief over a doorway into the Chartres

Cathedral in France. The Church says that these four symbolic figures represent the four apostles, Matthew, Mark, Luke and John. (Some researchers believe that the twelve apostles symbolize the twelve signs of the zodiac. In light of the Christian attitude toward astrology even today, it is interesting to note that Christians still revere twelve apostles, which correspond to the twelve zodiacal signs and represent the underlying principles in our collective lives.)

An ancient axiom — to know, to do, to dare and to be silent — verbally transmitted the symbolic message of the four elements through the woman (to know, using human intelligence to set goals and understand the process of arriving there), the bull (to do, the patience to carry out our daily duties methodically), the lion (to dare, courageously asserting our individuality and making a place for ourselves in this world), and the eagle (to be silent, to energize our plans by keeping them silent until the moment comes to act, knowing that excessive talk dissipates energy). In this axiom, we find the four elements describing the proper way to live our lives.

Our modern deck of playing cards, which some claim dates back to A.D. 1120, in China, contains the four elements in the form of the four suits: clubs (fire), hearts (water), spades (air), and diamonds (earth). The fifty-two cards symbolize the fifty-two weeks in the year; the suits of twelve cards plus the ace represent the twelve solar months and the thirteen lunar months in each year. An in depth discussion of the playing cards can be found in *Nuggets From King Solomon's Mine,* by John Barnes Schmalz, (Trismegistus Press, 23136 North Woodward, Ferndale, Michigan 48220, 1980).

The Tarot, a deck of picture cards which may have been the predecessor of our modern playing cards, also contains esoteric information about the four elements. In the Minor Arcana, a division of the Tarot deck, are four suits: wands (fire), cups (water), swords (air), and pentacles (earth). This was not an arbitrary division but one based upon the occult knowledge of the four vital forces that create life, the four elements.

Some historians believe the Tarot was invented around A.D. 1200 and used in Morocco as a communication tool for the many adepts from all over the world who met in Fez. Since language was a problem, they embodied the ancient wisdom in a book of pictures "whose combinations should depend on the occult harmonies of the numbers." The bones of this invention was a "simple system of numbers and letters afforded by the Qabalah . . . "[23] Others believe that gypsies, migrating from their ancient home in Hindustan, brought the Tarot to Europe. This suggests an even earlier origin.

As the Chinese, Japanese and Koreans know, pictures provide an effective method for conveying information. These people speak more than seven different languages yet, if they know how to read and write, they can communicate easily because the Chinese language is made of pictures. Perhaps this accounts for the Chinese proverb, "A picture is worth ten thousand words."

Interpreting the message of the four elements into mighty structures and common playing cards ensured that this wisdom would always be there for those who wished to see.

Everything we have talked about in this section relating to the four elements can be found in the sacred trapezoid. Its four sides whose numerical value is 10-5-6-5, or Jod-Heh-Vau-Heh, symbolize the four worlds of creation contained within the Primary Energy, Divinity.

As we discussed earlier, Joh-Heh-Vau-Heh is a geometrical and numerical formula. It is a noun form from the Hebrew verb HVH meaning "being, woman, life." "Correctly translated, it means 'That which was, that which is, That which shall be.' THAT, not HE."[24]

JHVH (representing the four elements of fire, water, air and earth) are therefore verbal symbols for the four basic energies that bring all things into existence. It was called the Divided Name, "considered to contain all the Forces of Nature." (See Table 2.1, which shows how the secret formula of the creation of the Universe is expressed in many ways.)

It must be remembered that this formula was sacred because it represented the perfect order of the Universe as conceived in the mind and heart of Divinity. Without this order, no life would be possible. Wo/man's survival depended upon an awareness of the cycles of the seasons, determined by the Sun, and the proper planting of the crops, determined by the cycles of the Moon. Adoration of the planets in their dependable orbits was humankind's way of recognizing and giving thanks to the Universe which sustained it.

In an astrological chart, the four elements indicate the characteristic manner in which a person thinks, behaves and reacts. They describe disposition and temperament — just like the Greeks' four faculties, the medieval four humours and Jung's four functions.

If you have an emphasis on one of these four elements you express that particular disposition more often. An "emphasis" means that more than just your Sun is positioned in one of the elements, although you can begin to understand your temperament by looking at your Sun sign. For instance, you may have an Aries Sun, which is fire, but four planets in Taurus, an earth sign. Therefore, the earth element would be predominant. For those of you who are unfamiliar with the planetary placements at your birth, you can obtain a copy of your natal horoscope by mail from

THE FOUR ELEMENTS
The Building Blocks of Life

THEIR EXPRESSION IN THE PHYSICAL WORLD

Elements	Fire	Water	Air	Earth
Seasons	Spring	Summer	Fall	Winter
Tarot suits	Wands	Cups	Swords	Pentacles
Playing card suits	Clubs	Hearts	Spades	Diamonds
Tetragrammaton	Jod	Heh	Vau	Heh
Sacred trapezoid	10	5	6	5
Serpent signs	Leo	Scorpio	Aquarius	Taurus
Astrological types	ardent	emotional	intellectual	practical
Apostles	Mark	John	Matthew	Luke
World myth figures (i.e., Sphinx)	lion	eagle	woman	bull
Nature spirits (Paracelsus)	salamander	undines	sylphs	gnomes
Greek philosophical qualities	morality	aesthetics	intellectuality	physicality
Human	spirit	soul	mind	body
Human functions (Jung)	intuition	feeling	thinking	sensation
Human bodies	vital/ etheric	emotional/ astral	mental/ causal	physical

Table 2.1   The Four Elements: The Building Blocks of Life

a number of outlets. (See Appendix for the addresses of some astrological services.) Your chart will indicate the elemental emphasis in your horoscope.

If you have an emphasis on the element earth (Taurus, Virgo and Capricorn) in your chart, you tend to be practical, patient, persevering, conservative and well-organized, with a well-developed sense of values. You have a sensual connection to the Earth and want physical contact with life. You process your experiences and react to the circumstances around you by filtering them through this particular frame of reference. If you are too attached to earth, you become excessively materialistic and overly concerned with the body and its needs, placing too much importance on money and sensual pursuits.

If your chart is dominated by air signs (Gemini, Libra and Aquarius), your characteristic behavior is social and intellectual. Communication is a key factor in your life. Your initial reaction is to gather and dispense information, which you can use to make decisions and judge fairly. This leads to understanding the larger principles that will benefit humanity. You are more attuned to the abstract than those people whose charts have an earth emphasis. An imbalance weighted toward the air element can cause aloofness and detachment from your own and others' feelings. People with too much air are impractical and live in ivory towers.

If water (Cancer, Scorpio and Pisces) is the predominant element in your chart, you are sensitive to moods and to your environment. You have deep feelings that are influenced strongly by unseen energies. You perceive and process your world in a nurturing and responsive way. An excess of water brings on self-pity, self-indulgence and overly emotional responses that are the result of an overworked imagination.

When fire (Aries, Leo, Sagittarius) is your dominant element, you are outgoing and direct in your behavior and reactions. You are enthusiastic and ardent about your experiences in life, and caught up in the joy of living. You are adventurous and sometimes impulsive. Too much fire can create a bossy, forceful and boisterous personality. Usually you are unaware that your behavior irritates others, but even if you do realize this you don't care.

Next time someone says. "You're in your element," you'll know what s/he is talking about. You are doing what you do best, what really fits your personality, or, in other words, expressing the qualities of the emphasized element in your natal chart.

In the above descriptions of the elements, I mentioned what the behavioral effect is of an abundance of each element in your chart. I would like to emphasize that no element or sign or number is "good" or "bad."

The energies simply are; what you do with them is entirely up to you. An overabundance of one number in your name or one element in your astrological chart does not mean that you have to express that energy negatively. Rather, you need to control it and watch how you are externalizing it because it can run away with you if you are not aware.

Knowing which element dominates your chart (if, indeed, one does) will help you understand the types of dreams you experience. This knowledge should be kept in the context of your current personal year cycle as well as the circumstances surrounding the time of that dream - all of which will be covered in more detail later.

Birth Charts and Worldviews

Later in this book we will be discussing Sigmund Freud, Alfred Adler and Carl Jung, three individuals who deeply influenced psychology in this century. For now, let's look at their astrological charts in light of what we've talked about so far. We can see how their particular theories fit in with their personal views of the world — in accordance with their natal horoscopes.

It is not within the scope of this book to go into depth about these men's theories. Our purpose here is to show how much of what each man "saw" in his world was the result of his basic character as revealed by his astrological chart. The law of attraction draws to us those things that are on the same frequency as our own emissions, much like a radio station only picks up what is on its own frequency. So, it becomes a self-fulfilling prophecy when we examine the world — which is really "our" world — and find that it fits into our expectations and "proves" our theories. We build our philosophies and theories based on our individual worldviews. Our philosophies and theories can contain part of the truth but not the whole truth because we cannot see the whole truth while in the physical body. We are limited by the extent to which our senses and our minds process and comprehend information.

Freud

Sigmund Freud (1856-1939) was an Austrian psychoanalyst who pioneered many theories. His major work, *The Interpretation of Dreams*, appeared in 1900. In it he surmised that dreams were associated with our conscious thoughts and problems, and did not occur as a matter of chance. He felt dreams contained some sort of meaning, but often were so heavily

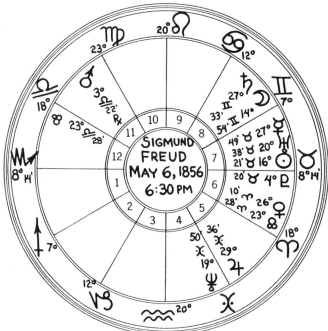

Figure 2.2   Freud's Chart
(*See note on page 59)

veiled that the messages were almost undecipherable. Freud is credited with theories of disguised wish fulfillment; the Oedipus complex in which sexual desire for the parent of the opposite sex creates rivalry with the parent of the same sex; penis envy or the female's envy of the male symbol of power, the penis, and her repression of the desire to own one; castration anxiety; and a tripartite division of consciousness into the id, ego and superego.

Let's first examine the elemental distribution in Freud's chart. (See Figure 2.2.) We find that he had four planets in earth signs (Sun, Mercury, Uranus and Pluto in Taurus) and three in air signs (Moon and Saturn in Gemini, Mars in Libra). (I don't always give the outer planets — Uranus, Neptune and Pluto — the same emphasis as the inner seven because the outer planets describe generational influences. However, in Freud's case, they are closely connected to his personal planets.)

His earth signs gave him the determination and perseverance to spend countless hours organizing his material and to continue his work even though it evoked severe criticisms from his colleagues throughout his life. He stuck to his guns with typical Taurean stubbornness.

The earth element also showed in his love of things from the Earth. He had three rooms of his own which were full — "one might almost say cluttered" — with artifacts from all over the world, particularly Greece and Egypt. He loved archaeology and followed the excavations of his time with great interest.

The air in his chart shows his intellectual and social interests. He was thirsty for knowledge and was fascinated with how the minds of other people worked. After collecting ideas in order to enhance his own understanding of the world, he then dispensed this information to others through his books and lectures. The air element helped him maintain a more abstract point of view than earth alone would have allowed. However, without the earth element, he might never have placed the seat of his pants on the seat of his chair and actually written what he had collected.

I find his chart extremely interesting in light of the theories he presented, many of which were sexual in content. The Oedipus complex described how the child's desire for the parent of the opposite sex created a jealous rivalry with the parent of the same sex. Freud also believed that females suppressed the desire to own a penis (penis envy), a symbol of male power. And he elucidated on castration anxiety. In 1905, he wrote *Three Essays on the Theory of Sexuality,* in which he described infantile sexuality and adult sexual perversions as stemming from it. Freud was thought a crank when his "startling conclusion that various psychoneuroses were caused by unconscious sexual conflict" reached the ears of the public. With four planets in Taurus and Scorpio rising (on the eastern angle, the sunrise position on the wheel) and his Moon in Scorpio's natural house (the eighth), he was immersed in sensuality and sexuality. (When the subject of Taurus-Scorpio arises, I always think of Bob Pelletier's comment that Scorpio has the reputation but Taurus has all the fun.)

Freud's Scorpio ascendant gave him the intense need to investigate the mysteries of sexuality, to know about birth, death and transformation. He was a natural detective. This intense desire to know has given Scorpio its sexual reputation, however, it is the Taurus part of Freud's chart that led him to experience the sensual part of life, to feel, to smell, to taste, to own. He was very aware of his body and its needs, and he transferred those needs to everyone else.

Mars in Libra inconjunct Pluto in Taurus shows his desire to investigate and sort out the feelings he had regarding his own sexuality. And the Moon in the fourth house (which represents the home and mother) squaring Neptune (90 degrees apart) caused confusion in his own mind about the sexuality of women and perhaps his relationship to his own mother.

When his sexual theories first reached the public, a storm of protest arose. Freud never replied to these criticisms, but continued to publish his new findings. This is a behavior we might expect from someone with Scorpio rising — a person who keeps his counsel, choosing to remain silent but steadfast in his beliefs.

There is much to admire about Sigmund Freud and his theories. As with all ideas, however, we must examine them in the light of the personality who presented them, and in keeping with our own feelings and makeup. Some of what he said may fit your personal philosophy; some might not.

Ashley Montagu, author of *The Natural Superiority of Women,* might disagree with Freud's penis envy theory. He would say that vagina envy is closer to the truth. "Ludicrous as it may appear to some, the fact is that men have been jealous of women's ability to give birth to children, and they have even envied their ability to menstruate; but men have not been content with turning these capacities into disabilities, for they have surrounded the one with handicapping rituals and the other with taboos that in most cases amount to punishments. They have even gone so far as to assert that pregnancy occurs in the male first . . . ".[25]

Today, some contend that vagina envy is the basis of men's disapproval of women entering the workplace. (I find this a curious use of the word "work" since a woman has traditionally worked very hard in the home as well as outside it. I wince when a woman is asked if she works, and she says, "No, I'm a housewife.") Since the "workplace" historically has belonged to the male, it was the only place he could be creative, like the woman. Listen to his language when he discusses his business. He births an idea, then nurses that idea. It's his baby. It's the world he has created.

Now, women are invading his world, proving that not only can they create and nurture with their bodies, they can also usurp his position in the business world and do his job as well as he can. What does he have left? It may not be right but it is understandable that his reaction is to put the "working" woman down and pay her less for her services than he gets for his.

Adler

Alfred Adler, the founder of individual psychology, was born in Vienna on February 7, 1870. He began his career as an ophthalmologist but later changed to psychiatry. Appointed chairperson of the psychoanalytical group, originated by Freud as the Wednesday Psychological Group which later became the Vienna Psycho-analytical Society, he broke away in 1911 to form the Society for Free Psychoanalysis, which displeased Freud considerably.

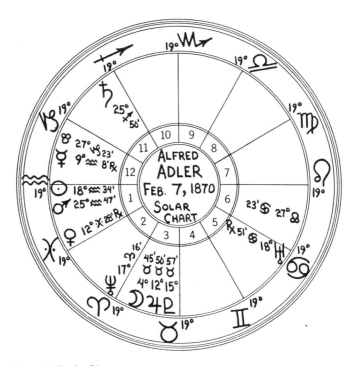

Figure 2.3   Adler's Chart

Adler's ideas attracted a great deal of attention. He theorized that feelings of inferiority develop when a person feels lacking in qualities when compared with others. And "he postulated a basic striving for superiority or self-assertion which leads a person with an attitude of inferiority to seek to compensate."

Adler has two planets in fire signs (one is an outer planet), two planets in water (one an outer planet), two planets in earth (one an outer planet) and three planets in air. (See Figure 2.3.) The Moon changed signs on the day of his birth and since I don't have his exact birthtime, I don't know whether his Moon was in Aries, (fire) or Taurus (earth). However, what is clear is that three personal planets — Sun, Mercury and Mars — were in air.

With the element air, and specifically Aquarius, so noticeable in his chart, Adler understandably was attuned to the abstract and to intellectual reasoning. He was concerned with the individual's place within the world family, and his periodic intellectual aloofness may have left him feeling separated from the crowd. This was only one factor in his entire makeup, however, it is interesting to look at the man in light of it. The founder of "individual" psychology has three personal planets in Aquarius, the most individualistic of all the signs.

Aquarius, as well as its opposite sign Leo, is constantly measuring the individual's expression against the collective expression. The essence of these two signs is love. Leo expresses individual love for its immediate family and requires the homage due a reigning monarch. For Leo, there is one monarch, who constantly measures her/himself against others because of a need to feel superior. S/he needs audience approval and, when it is not forthcoming, s/he can feel inferior.

Aquarius, on the other hand, expresses universal love for the world family. In Aquarius, we are all monarchs. The purpose of this sign is to recognize the superiority of all individuals as unique human beings who deserve a chance to attain their goals.

Goal is a key word in Aquarius; this sign rules the house of goals, hopes and wishes come true. Adler uses the word goal frequently. For example, " . . . let me direct your attention to the fundamental and at the same time, the determining factor in the psychic life of both healthy and nervous people — *the feeling of inferiority.* Similar in nature must be reckoned the *urge toward the positing of a goal,* toward the heightening of ego consciousness, . . . "[26]. And "if anyone doubts the correctness of *the goal of superiority . . .* "[27]

Adler's inferiority/superiority theory is a result of the emphasis on love found in the Leo-Aquarius polarity. A child's feelings of inferiority/superiority are directly measured by the amount of love s/he receives. So, it would be natural for someone with an emphasis on the Leo-Aquarius polarity, like Adler, to evaluate the "goal" of the individual in terms of inferior/superior functioning.

Adler's Sun in Aquarius square Pluto shows that he was very willful at times; he almost seemed to go looking for adversaries. He needed power (Pluto) struggles (square) in his life in order to find his own identity (Sun). His goal was to recognize himself as a worthwhile (superior) individual within the world family.

In addition, his Mars in Aquarius, gave him "the desire for independence to pursue unusual or unorthodox courses of action." He "demanded the freedom to do things (his) own way."[28] I deliberately quoted the definition of Mars in Aquarius from a book on astrological analysis to show that Adler's Mars in Aquarius was part of his personality that drove him to postulate his theory on "individual" psychology. He needed to stand apart from the "norm," to go against tradition, in order to formulate goals that would benefit the larger family. His theories helped him work out his personal goals.

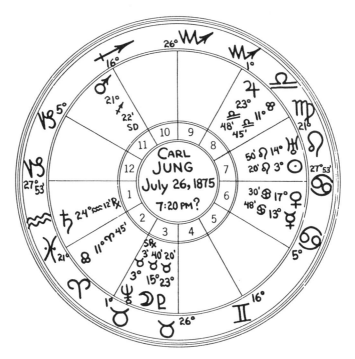

Figure 2.4   Jung's Chart

Jung

Swiss psychologist Carl G. Jung (1875-1961) was strongly influenced by Sigmund Freud, whose methods and conclusions he embraced in 1906. Jung formed the first International Psycho-Analytical Congress, held in Salzburg in April 1908. Two years later, the International Psycho-Analytical Association was born. By 1914, Jung had broken with Freud because of personal and scientific differences.

Jung knew astrology and used it in his work. "The original research of Carl Jung in this area cannot be stressed enough for it was he who first suggested that an astrological chart might provide psychologists with insights not readily available elsewhere."[29]

Jung's chart shows a fairly even distribution of elements. (See Figure 2.4.) He had three planets in fire signs (one an outer planet, Uranus), two in water, two in air, and three in earth (two outer planets, Neptune and Pluto). If his birthtime is correct, his rising sign (on the eastern angle) was Capricorn, an earth sign. From this we can conjecture that his characteristic mode of thought and behavior was balanced, with no particular emphasis on one element. Therefore, Jung was temperamentally disposed to think about the world in as complete and holistic a manner as his past conditioning would allow. He looked for wholeness in the individual, a melding of all facets of the psyche. Actually, what he was expressing was the even distribution of elements in his own natal chart. And he saw dreams as guides toward this wholeness.

Jung coined the word "archetype," a term that endures and is used widely today. "One of the most interesting contributions by Jung is the concept of the *collective unconscious,* made up of racial memories called *archetypes.*"[30] As Jung wrote: "A more or less superficial layer of the unconscious is undoubtedly personal . . . But this personal unconscious rests upon a deeper layer, which does not derive from personal experience and is not a personal acquisition but is inborn. This deeper layer I call the *collective unconscious.* I have chosen the term 'collective' because this part of the unconscious is not individual but universal; in contrast to the personal psyche, it has contents and modes of behavior that are more or less the same everywhere and in all individuals."[31]

The archetype which resides in the collective unconscious is a symbolic model, a pattern of behavior, that is common to all people. It often is found in fairy tales and myths. Images such as the mother, the hero, the beast and the witch are archetypes.

In Jung's chart, Saturn is placed in Aquarius. Saturn rules structures and the past; it represents the past upon which the structures of the present are constructed. When they have outlived their usefulness, they will be torn down by new ideas which, in their turn, will age and become the old structures upon which the future will be built.

Those patterns of behavior that come from the past and with which Jung was so involved are associated with Saturn. Jung's Saturn in Aquarius suggests that he would take an unusual look (Aquarius) at this structure (Saturn) and try to understand the root patterns (Saturn) of the group (Aquarius) and the goals towards which these patterns direct the evolving person.

His Saturn square Pluto indicates a struggle (square) with the traditional ways (Saturn) of understanding the psychology of the individual as well as a need to tear down, regenerate and rebuild (Pluto) these structures in ways that would be liberating (Aquarius) for the collective wo/man (Aquarius).

Jung was able to do this through his Saturn trine Jupiter. This configuration allowed him a creative avenue (trine) through which he could formulate (Saturn) a broader view (Jupiter), a philosophy that would expand and enrich (Jupiter) the thought patterns of society. Jung's "broad view of human oneness" and "the direction in which man's consciousness is slowly striving," his need to find "meaningful expression for the urges" and "his sense of commitment to and participation in group life must be real," were all related to his Saturn in Aquarius.[32] The preceding, a definition of Saturn in Aquarius, seems to sum up Jung's reason for arriving at a theory such as archetypes.

Jung also coined the terms extrovert and introvert. This man had his Sun in Leo, the sign opposite Aquarius where his Saturn was positioned. His Sun appears to have been in the seventh house, the house of relationships. Leo is a positive, fiery, sunny, extroverted sign. Jung's Sun — his sunny extroverted ego — is opposed (in terms of sign polarities) to Saturn, a planet that exerts a restricting, containing, inward-directed influence. We might look at his concept of extroverts (Sun in Leo) and introverts (Saturn) in terms of this planetary opposition in his birth chart.

Notes

1. Gauquelin, Michel *The Cosmic Clocks,* (San Diego: Astro Computing Services, 1982), p. 107.

2. Ibid., p. 108.

3. Ibid., p. ix.

4. Ibid., p. ii.

5. Kramer, Samuel Noah *From the Poetry of Sumer,* (Berkeley, CA: University of Berkeley Press, 1979), p. 71.

6. Wolkstein, Diane and Kramer, Samuel Noah *Inanna, Queen of Heaven and Earth,* (NY: Harper & Row, Publishers, 1983), p. xvi.

7. Higgins, Frank C., *Ancient Freemasonry,* (NY: Pyramid Book Co., 1923), p. 30.

8. Gauquelin, p. 11.

9. Goldenberg, Naomi *Changing of the Gods,* (Boston: Beacon Press, 1979), p. 74.

10. Gauquelin, p. 11.

11. Walker, Barbara *The Woman's Encyclopedia of Myths and Secrets,* (San Francisco: Harper & Row, Publishers, 1983), p. 587.

12. Ibid.

13. *Encyclopedia Americana, Vol. 23,* (NY: Americana Corporation, 1966), p. 50.

14. Gauquelin, p. 23.

15. Jung, Carl *Astrology questions and answers,* (Manchester, NH: Time Data Research, 1980), p. 4.

16. Arroyo, Stephen *Astrology, Psychology, and the Four Elements,* (Reno, NV: CRCS Publications, 1975). p. 91.

17. Gauquelin, p. 71.

18. Ibid., p. 72.

19. Arroyo, p. 89.

20. *New Larousse Encyclopedia of Mythology,* introduction by Robert Graves, (Prometheus Press), p. 93.

21. Papon, Donald *The Lure of the Heavens, A History of Astrology,* (NY: Samuel Weiser, Inc., 1972), p. 21.

22. Walker, p. 365.

23. Case, Paul Foster, *The Tarot,* (Richmond, VA: Macoy Publishing Co., 1947), p. 3.

24. Ibid.

25. Montagu, Ashley *The Natural Superiority of Women,* (NY: Collier Books/Macmillan Publishing Co., Inc., 1952), p. 18.

26. Adler, Alfred *Individual Psychology,* (Totowa, NJ: Littlefield, Adams & Co., 1969), p. 100.

27. Ibid., p. 202.

28. Sakoian, Frances and Acker, Louis S. *The Astrologer's Handbook,* (NY: Harper & Row, Publishers, 1973), p. 152.

29. Papon, foreword.

30. *Encyclopedia Americana, Vol. 1,* (NY: Americana Corp., 1966), p. 622.

31. Jung, C. G. *Four Archetypes,* (Princeton, NJ: Princeton University Press, 1959), pp. 3-4.

32. Greene, Liz *Saturn,* (York Beach, ME: Samuel Weiser, Inc., 1976), pp. 69-70.

* Although today ♂ is widely used as the symbol for Mars, the original symbol was ♁ — Venus inverted.

3

Dreams

One morning I walked into my kitchen and found 100 caterpillar eggs on the floor. I scooped them up and placed them outside on the porch. A short time later, they were back on the kitchen floor so, once again, I put them outside.

I had this dream in the spring of 1976. On the surface it didn't seem particularly awe inspiring, but I awoke with a feeling that the dream was special in some way. The mood one experiences upon awakening is very important, therefore I examined the dream more closely and found a message that foretold a major transformation. Indeed, this dream was so significant that, after all these years, it still stands out in my mind as one of the more important.

There I was in my kitchen, my fortress, a place of safety and comfort, my symbol of my place in life. Not because I'm such a great cook — I hate to cook. Rather, the kitchen is the place where I raised my four children, made school lunches every weekday morning for twenty-one years, conducted cub scout and brownie meetings, taught 4-H sewing classes, made posters for the PTA bake sales and created the school newspaper. It is also the place where I am now sitting at my desk, looking out at a large maple in our front yard. For me, the kitchen is a symbol of the things that make up my life: my family and my writing. The kitchen represents my lifestyle.

The caterpillar eggs in the dream represented imminent change. A caterpillar is a symbol of profound transformation because it changes from a creature creeping on the ground, bound to the earth, into a butterfly, free to waft upon the breath of the wind. And eggs are a symbol of the stage preceding the birth of something.

I felt that 100 eggs had a time implication, therefore I counted 100 days from the morning of my dream. (If you go to bed between 10:00 and 11:00 at night, most of your dreams occur in the morning hours.) I circled that date, a Monday, on my calendar.

The number 100 also symbolizes major change. I mentioned in chapter 1 that the Zero represents the cosmic egg in which all things originate; it is the creative source. When Zero is the last digit in a number (e.g., 20, 30, 40), it repeats the series of numbers One through Nine, ushering in a new cycle of experience.

In my dream, the two Zeros in the number 100 emphasized the change that was to occur. This dream could have come to me four days earlier presenting 104 caterpillar eggs and I would have counted 104 days from the morning of the dream. But the impact of the transformative message would have been diminished. Instead, the dream was given to me 100 days prior to the event that was to change my life. The number symbology was as important as the time element.

I did not know why the eggs had to be placed outside the kitchen twice, but that was to be made clear at a later date.

At the time of this dream, we had no intention of selling our antique colonial home, however, the huge house, barn and three acres of land became too much for us to maintain. It was beginning to own us. Therefore, we put the beautiful old place up for sale. As we left the real estate office, I told my husband that my caterpillar dream must have something to do with the house, and the date I had circled on the calendar might be the day the house would sell. He smiled down at me kindly.

During the following weeks the house was shown to a number of couples. On the Friday before the Monday that I had circled on my calendar, the real estate agent called to tell us that a couple had decided to buy it and would be in on Monday to sign papers. I could hardly wait to tell my husband that my caterpillar dream was right on target! The fact that I put the eggs out twice, though, still had me puzzled.

I bounced out of bed Monday morning full of enthusiasm and anticipation. We had decided not to look for another home until we had an agreement on the one we were in, so I was eager to begin house-hunting that afternoon. At ten o'clock the phone rang. It was the real estate agent calling to tell me that the man who had wanted to buy our home had lost his job over the weekend and, therefore, the sale was off. Although I couldn't believe it I knew the situation wasn't over. This had to be what putting the caterpillar eggs outside twice meant.

One hour later, the real estate agent telephoned again. "This is the strangest thing," he said, "but Mr. and Mrs. Smith have just given me a deposit on your house." I smiled knowingly; the dream suddenly made sense.

Three months later we moved into a small cape built in 1950. All of the doors and windows open and shut easily, and the walls meet the floor squarely. Anyone who has lived in an old house knows what I mean.

This move marked a major shift in consciousness for me. I became more involved in the metaphysical world. Once the responsibilities of the big house had been lifted I had time for the studies that had been hovering on the edge of my consciousness. I began my serious work in this house and since moving here I have written five books. I feel at home. Oddly enough, the number of this house is 36 — my birth number.

Conscious, Subconscious and Superconscious

Before continuing, I want to define the terms conscious, subconscious and superconscious in the way that I use them.

The conscious mind is the part of which we are all aware. It governs your everyday living, your thoughts and the actions you perform each day in order to function in the physical world. It is like an envelope or an egg that encloses you. Unfortunately, this mind often becomes so fixed and hard that it blocks information from other worlds of consciousness that are just as important. And when it becomes too rigid, it does not allow information and guidance from these other levels to come through.

The collective consciousness represents what each individual in a society collectively accepts as truth and uses as the structure of her/his life. The collective consciousness of a country may contain certain religious, social and economic beliefs that each person accepts as a standard by which to live.

The personal subconscious mind is much like an iceberg lying beneath the surface of the ocean: it becomes denser and more massive as it goes deeper. The personal subconscious contains every thought, feeling, emotion and impression that you have ever experienced. Some of the experiences lie near the surface, others exist at much deeper levels. Some people believe that the memories of all your past lives are stored here in what is known as the *akashic records*. Your total experience is registered in the personal subconscious mind. It is like a computer with a limitless memory bank and if you know the code, any information from your personal past is available.

The collective subconscious is that body of information, images and myths that are the common bond between all people, regardless of culture and personal beliefs. Each culture may clothe and name these images differently, but the roots remain the same. It is our human heritage.

The superconscious is all encompassing, like the 0. It contains the personal and collective conscious, and the personal and collective subconscious, encompassing you and me and every other person and thing in the Universe. In this respect, it is the oneness of which we are all a part, and the basis of the mystical experience that All is One. The superconscious is like a great sea in which we live and move and have our being. Here our minds link with one another in a pool from which we all draw inspiration, guidance and truth, and to which we all contribute our experiences.

Now, what is this thing called a dream?

My dictionary describes the word dream as: "a succession of images, thoughts or emotions passing through the mind during sleep."

Images, in this case, are the pictures we see in our dreams. We might wonder why the subconscious sends messages in the form of pictures rather than stating the situation or problem in words. It would certainly make things much simpler and books like this would be unnecessary! But the subconscious is wise and knows many reasons why pictures are more effective than words when it comes to conveying messages.

First, words are loaded with meanings that are not always clear and are subject to misinterpretation. Have you ever misconstrued what someone else has said? I have. I recall one incident in which I believed a man I had hired was overcharging me for his services. When I questioned his fee, he agreed to adjust it with a comment about "not spreading it around." I took this to mean he thought I was not willing to spread my money around. Actually he did not want me to tell anyone that he had made this concession. Obviously I was feeling uncomfortable about bringing up the point or I would not have taken his comment in the way I did. We all interpret words according to our past conditioning. Therefore, language, as the main method of communication in a dream, would be a poor vehicle.

Secondly, in most cases words are not as effective as images, unless you are listening to a particularly eloquent speaker. The expression "a picture is word ten thousand words" is true.

Here's an example. A woman had been told by many professional people that her sculptures were very good and that if she worked at it she would be recognized in her field one day. Regardless of their encouragement, she doubted her abilities and, because of her attitude, her work lacked that special something. One night she had a dream. She was in the center of her town on a day when many people were moving about conducting their daily business. Suddenly, to the east above a body of water, she saw a row of huge mountains rising up out of the flat horizon. A second row, then a third row rose behind them. She was overwhelmed by the majesty and power of the mountains, but at the same time she was frightened by the spectacle. Was the earth beneath her sinking while the mountains rose? Would the mountains encircle her in a prison? Would the town and everyone in it be destroyed?

I asked her to become the mountains and speak to me. She said: "I am the mountains. I am rising out of the sea to show the world my power. I am visible and will last for many centuries. I will give pleasure to those who look upon me."

I didn't have to say much more. From the look on her face, it was obvious that she understood the meaning of her dream. The east, where the Sun rises each morning, signifies the beginning of a new day — her rebirth. The sea was her link to the creative depths of her subconscious. These symbols represented the light of awareness that was about to shine on her consciousness, bringing with it an understanding of her abilities.

Mountains are not something one can easily pass by without noticing, therefore, in this image there is the promise of recognition. And since mountains endure, so her work would endure for many years giving pleasure to those who looked upon it.

Her fear of the earth sinking and the mountains encircling her was her fear of taking on the responsibility that fame could place upon her. She would not be as free as she had been. Her current lifestyle, her foundation, the earth beneath her feet, would undergo change. She feared the weight of these golden chains.

However, this dream gave her the encouragement that many people could not offer verbally. Viewing a picture is often more dramatic than hearing a voice. A picture is indeed worth ten thousand words. It condenses large amounts of information into a small and concise package. Dream pictures are the shorthand of the subconscious.

Also, pictures contain messages that transcend the language barrier; that is, pictures or images can be universal in scope, understood by everyone regardless of language or culture. Many of you are familiar with the Tarot deck. According to tradition, this deck of colorful pictures was once a holy book containing metaphysical truths, revered and used in the initiation of advanced wo/men. As time progressed, and in order to protect this holy information from destruction by ignorant forces, these pictures were incorporated into a deck of playing cards and presented to the public as a game. The ancients were playing a clever game themselves — placing valuable information in the most obvious place in order to protect it, hiding it in plain sight — and it worked. The cards are still in existence today.

The symbolism of these cards is universal; people from different countries and backgrounds can understand the messages contained within them. The Tarot deck is also said to have been used as a communication vehicle by the old-world intellectuals from many countries who gathered at the sacred city of Fez in Morocco. Because they came from different lands and spoke various languages, the Tarot was used effectively to transmit ideas.

According to Paul Christian, in *The History and Practice of Magic*, large-scale drawings of the first twenty- two keys (cards) of the Tarot are hidden inside the great Pyramid where "Thales, Pythagoras, Plato and Eudoxus were the most famous Greeks to pass successfully through all the phases of initiation." [1] If this story is true, we can see the importance learned people in the past placed on pictures as a method of communication.

And then there is the possibility that dreams come to us in pictures because we really do not want to look at some of our problems. If the messages came through from the subconscious verbally, we could shut them off immediately and, like Charlie Brown, say that even our brains are against us. We could turn a deaf ear. Pictures, however, slip through nicely without offending us. So when you begin to tell someone about your dream, thinking that it applies to that mixed-up person down the street, it suddenly dawns on you what the dream means, and whoops — it's too late to escape the truth that what you dislike about that person down the street is really something in yourself. The subconscious is very clever.

Finally, there may be a bit of Sherlock Holmes in each of us, and dreams titillate the imagination. We like to discuss our dreams because they are so unusual or comical or beautiful. Our interest is stimulated and we begin to think. And that is the beginning of discovery.

My dictionary also defines a dream as a series of thoughts. A thought is an idea or a notion arrived at through the process of thinking. Graham Wallas, in *The Art of Thought*, describes four stages of creative thinking: (1) preparation in which the problem is worked on intensely, (2) incubation during which the problem is set aside while other activities are carried out, (3) illumination or insight when the solution is suddenly apparent, and (4) verification or revision, when the details of the solution are worked out. Wallas states that "sleep continues the incubation phase because dream activities also contain material that may provide either a component needed for a solution or an analogy for solving the problem."[2]

We can readily see that sleep is an incubation period during which many problems can be solved. When we need to make an important decision we might say, "Let me sleep on it." Benjamin Franklin, while serving as ambassador to France, waited until he had a good night's sleep before making any important decisions. Harry Truman and Thomas Edison were in the habit of napping when faced with problems for which they had no immediate answers. Even if they were in the middle of a meeting, they left to take a nap. When they returned, they invariably had their answers.[3]

How many times have you gone to bed with a problem on your mind and found, in the morning, that you had suddenly solved it? Or, if you did not wake up with the solution, somehow during the day you worked the problem out nicely, almost instinctively. That instinctive reaction probably occurred because the solution had been arrived at during your sleep.

It seems apparent from laboratory testing that the mind itself never sleeps but continues some kind of activity throughout the sleeping hours. Often, when sleepers are awakened at times other than during a dreaming stage they report that they were thinking. This thinking process resembles that which you typically experience when awake.[4] There seems to be no difference between thinking during the sleeping state and thinking during the waking state.

Thinking during sleeping hours may be the first step in Graham Wallas' description of the creative thought process — the preparation in which the problem is worked on. Perhaps thinking during sleep is the way we lay out the problem clearly, without emotional inferences, so that the subconscious can weave these threads of thought into images — images that reveal much more than words.

If we apply Wallas' four steps of creative thinking to the dream process, the first step — preparation — is the thinking that goes on during sleep, the preliminary process by which the subconscious receives unbiased information about the problem to be solved. In other words, thinking during sleep is like saying: Here is the problem. Create a dream with images that reflect this problem.

Step two — incubation — can occur when you awaken and do not remember a dream, or recall a dream but set it aside because you don't understand it. In both cases, you go about your daily activities focusing on other issues while the incubation process is going on at hidden levels.

Step three — illumination — is that stage, sometime in the future, when a flash goes off in your head and you understand what the dream means. Or, you might go back and review the dream at a later period and suddenly experience insight into its meaning.

Step four — verification or revision — is that time when you refine and make practical use of what you have learned from the dream.

The dictionary also defines a dream as a series of emotions. This does not need much verification when you consider the variety and intensity of feeling that dreams encompass. Even when we wake, we often think we are still dreaming because the emotional content of the dream carries over into our waking consciousness. A dream with high emotional content is easy to recall and makes a lasting impression upon us.

Dreams have been looked upon with reverence from the beginning of recorded history. Ancient societies believed that the dream was a link between the everyday world and the invisible Universe that surrounded them. Indeed, the dream world was as real as their external world. After awakening from a dream in which he was a butterfly, Chuang Tzu (469-386 B.C.) wrote: "Did Chuang Tzu dream he was a butterfly, or did the butterfly dream he was Chuang Tzu?"[5] Many ancient cultures had such faith in their dreams that the spiritual elders were assigned the duty of interpreting the dreams of their people. They believed that dreams had meaning and needed to be examined and listened to for guidance.

From ancient times all major civilizations have regarded the dream as a source of inspiration, revelation and guidance. A 3800-year-old papyrus scroll in the British Museum describes in great detail the secrets of dream interpretation. In ancient Egypt, there were professional dream interpreters, called the Learned Men of the Magic Library, who practiced out of specially constructed temples. The dream of Prince Thutmose IV was inscribed on a stone tablet erected before the great Sphinx of Gizeh in Egypt, around 1450 B.C. During a midday nap "in the shade of the great god," the prince had a dream in which the Sphinx spoke to him. In exchange for clearing the drifting sands away from its body (only the head was visible then), the Sphinx promised Prince Thutmose that he would be Pharaoh and reign over the length and breadth of the earth, enjoying plenty, riches and long years. The best of everything would be his. When Thutmose became Pharaoh, he remembered his dream and ordered the sands removed from the feet of the Sphinx. As promised, his reign was long and fruitful.[6]

In the Islamic faith it is taught that the Koran was given to Mohammed in a dream. Buddha received enlightenment while in a meditative state similar to a dream while sitting under the Bo tree.

Christians are aware of the important role dreams played in the Bible. Joseph's correct interpretation of the Pharaoh's dream about seven fat cows and seven lean cows directed the Pharaoh, with Joseph as overseer, to store food during the seven years of plenty so that when the seven years of famine struck Egypt, the people did not starve. Although seven in the Pharaoh's dream indicated a period of time it also suggested that plans should be made because Seven is the thinking and planning stage prior to taking action in the Eight. Joseph listened and made the necessary preparations. Dreams were also significant in the story of the birth and life of Jesus, the Christ.

The Greeks subscribed to the point of view that dreams were links between the outside world and the invisible Universe around them. Aristotle felt that dreams arose from psychological factors within the individual or from pressures in the environment. Cicero believed that dreams were prophetic, and Plato said that dreams were a means of communication between the soul of an individual and physical reality.[7]

In ancient Greece, temples dedicated to the god of healing, Aesclepius, were built on the outskirts of towns on sites that were known to be especially healthy. When a sick person went to the local temple, after purification, baths, fasting and sacrifice, s/he was allowed to spend the night on a couch near the statue of Aesclepius. The patient then heard from the god in a dream during the night. In the morning, the temple priests would explain the healing procedure that Aesclepius had revealed through the dream. These cures were then inscribed upon the temple walls.[8] Hippocrates, the father of medicine, obtained much of his medical knowledge from the walls of his local temple.

Primitive societies today carry on this ancient belief in the dream as the intermediary between the everyday world and the invisible Universe. The Senoi, for example, are a primitive tribe of 12,000 people living in the jungles of Malaysia. Although we are more sophisticated than the Senoi, they have achieved something we cannot seem to. They are a peaceful people, extraordinarily well-adjusted, and violence is extremely rare in their lives even though there are warlike tribes living near them. In fact, the other tribes are afraid of the "magic power" of the Senoi. These peaceful people spend many hours of each day examining and discussing their dreams. When Senoi children begin to relate their dreams, they are like the dreams of many children, full of monsters and fearful figures that threaten them. By the time they become adolescents, however, through careful and loving counsel by their elders about their dreams, the nightmares are gone and they begin to produce consistently creative messages from their dream world.[9]

Dreams were held in high regard from the beginning of recorded history until the eighteenth and nineteenth centuries, when the Industrial

Revolution and the resurgence of the natural sciences occurred. This period, called the Age of Reason, ushered in a materialistic viewpoint that
affected all aspects of life. Society began to ascribe all phenomena to physical causes, excluding intuition, the soul and the spirit. It became popular
to believe that humans entered this life much like a blank piece of paper,
the *tabla rasa,* upon which would be written the body's experience during
its lifetime. Dreams were thought to be the "grumblings of the body" and
the "twitchings of the brain" and therefore unimportant.

Today, we are paying more attention to the dream. We have come
from the ancient belief that the dream was an actual experience occurring
in another dimension of reality to the modern belief that the dream is closely connected to the inner life of the individual.

When we look at dream research we must consider the source, for
at least two reasons. First, each of us has our own point of view which
differs from others'. No two people will view an experience identically
because no two people are exactly alike. Therefore, to take another individual's experience of truth as *the* truth and base your own beliefs on it
can be misleading and dangerous unless you feel completely comfortable
with that person's postulations.

I am referring, of course, to the theories of Sigmund Freud, Alfred
Adler and Carl Jung that have been used, studied and quoted so widely
during this century. Each theory comes from the personal point of view
of the individual who expounds it. Even the most learned individuals express theories that are part of their own essence, as we found when we
examined the astrological charts of these men in chapter 2. Each of us
expresses viewpoints that are the essence of our experience of our world,
and that experience is necessarily limited by the extent of our sensory
awareness and intuitive functioning. The perfect analogy to this is the story
of the three blind people examining different parts of an elephant.

Secondly, the dream has been viewed through male eyes for thousands of years. Freud, Adler and Jung were bound to examine the dream
from a patriarchal position. As a result, there are few female images of
great power in dream interpretation, and therefore, women have been
denied their mythological roots. Even in dreams, women are placed in an
inferior position. As Naomi Goldenberg states in *Changing of the Gods,*
"behind every witch, dragoness and temptress lies a vision of female power . . . we must reevaluate all female images that have been despised by
generations of male scholars."[10]

Other individuals in this century have added to the body of information on dreams. Edgar Cayce said that dreams are a means of self-preservation. Dr. Ann Faraday, author of *Dream Power,* states that dreams con-

tain "helpful significant clues that help you deal with the realities of every day living."[11] Dr. Rosalind Cartwright, dream researcher at the University of Illinois Circle Campus in Chicago, compares dreaming to digestion: dreams help you whether or not you pay attention to them. Author and lecturer Dr. Frank Caprio says that most of us go through life only knowing one-half of ourselves; dreams help us understand our other half.

Many researchers feel that dreams are a primitive picture language, attempts by the brain to solve the problems we encounter during the day, and that dreams help integrate the information the conscious mind collects during waking hours. This information is then processed during sleep for future reference. Current processed information may be used within the following few days.

There is research suggesting that dreams are important for our physical well-being. The ancient Greeks believed this, which is why they built temples to their god of healing, Aesclepius.

I feel that each of the individuals mentioned above has described some of the truth, like the three blind people feeling different portions of the elephant. Freud's belief that dreams reflect conscious thoughts and problems and can be the result of wish fulfillment makes sense. I would say that wish fulfillment dreams come to encourage you to fulfill the potential you already possess. However, I disagree with some of his other theories, including his penis envy theory because there is substantial evidence to the contrary.

Adler's theory that an inferiority complex results in superior and aggressive behavior is obvious when observing some individuals. I think we each exhibit this in our own lives at times when we feel particularly inadequate.

Jung's collective unconscious as a pool of universal symbols reminded us that we are part of each other. His theory reconnected our umbilical cords to the Oneness "in which we live and move and have our being."[12]

Cayce's suggestion that dreams are a means of self-preservation also makes good sense. Through our dreams, we sort out and integrate disturbing factors from our everyday lives and, in some cases, use them to our advantage. And, as Ann Faraday says, dreams offer helpful clues to help us deal with reality.

As a metaphysician, I understand that we view reality through our own eyes, our own personal numbers and planets if you will, and that we see the "facts" that prove the reality we understand. Each of us has portions of the truth, but not the whole truth. Renowned and intelligent individuals like Freud, Jung and Adler are no different in this respect. I would like to see women writers and researchers become widely quoted authorities in these fields, too, because we are sorely lacking the female point of view.

Dream Terminology

Before I close this chapter, I want to explain a few terms that you are likely to come across in studying dream research and interpretation.

The imagery you experience as you drift off to sleep is called a *hypnagogic vision* or *hypnagogic experience*. Hypnagogic visions take the form of strange conversations and bodily sensations, and unusual phenomena such as faces drifting past your closed eyes. They are not technically dreams but rather images and scenes that you are aware of in a semi-conscious state.

You may have had the experience of waking with a start at the onset of sleep. This startled reaction, perhaps accompanied by a feeling of falling is termed *myoclonic spasm* or *myoclonic jerk*.

A "dream of knowledge" or a *lucid dream* is one that deserves some attention. When you are in a dream state but have full conscious knowledge that you are dreaming — feeling that you are in possession of your waking consciousness while knowing that you are asleep dreaming — you are experiencing a lucid dream. These dreams are exciting and useful but difficult to achieve. They seldom occur to individuals who are not aware that this is possible. During a lucid dream, you must maintain an awareness that you are dreaming, but not become so excited over your power to do what you want in that dream that you wake yourself. By becoming aware during a dream that it is a dream, you can learn to alter frightening dreams to your benefit.

Patricia Garfield writes in *Creative Dreaming* that you can develop lucid dreams by experiencing more flying dreams. This may be possible if what some people say is true — that flying dreams are really astral projection in which we are out of our bodies during sleep and are therefore more alert.

In a lucid dream you are in a favorable position to draw the best from your interactions with the dream and its symbols. Some yogis enter the dream state fully conscious. Their purpose is to never let go of consciousness. Perhaps this accounts for some of their remarkable feats. As Ann Faraday says in *Dream Power,* a lucid dream may be "a way into 'a fourth state of existence' beyond sleep, in which the individual can build up a 'psychic body' capable of transcending ordinary life."[13]

Dream research continues today in laboratories around the world as we search for answers to the age-old mystery surrounding this activity that goes on beneath waking consciousness. All our EEGs and EOGs, tapes and wires, experiments and tests, suppositions and conjectures still leave us with sketchy information about this mysterious world.

We don't know scientifically where dreams come from because "even today the dream and the process by which it is produced are not fully understood."[14] We do know that dreaming is a creative process by which we gather, integrate, digest and store the countless stimuli we encounter each day. Dreams advise, instruct, warn and aid us in solving problems. Dreams care for our physical health. These reasons seem a logical and practical use of the dream function and fit in nicely with today's scientific approach to many things.

But, as Jung said, "we have forgotten the age-old fact that God speaks chiefly through dreams and visions."[15] We can't ignore the psychic or metaphysical aspects of our dreams. There is too much evidence suggesting that dreams encourage, create and inspire. They are precognitive, clairvoyant and retrocognitive. Some people believe that certain dreams reflect astral travel or out-of-body experience; others say that specific dreams put them in touch with past lives. There is probably no way to prove, in the scientific sense, that we have OBEs or past-life dream recall. However, countless people have dreamt of events before they happen, and about events that are happening at distances too great for the dreamer to witness. Others dream about events that happened in the past even though there is no logical explanation for their knowledge.

We have paid homage to our dreams from the "beginning" of time because we realize there are countless things beyond our conscious range of understanding. There is a limit to our conscious perception; there is an edge beyond which we cannot comprehend. Our dreams take us beyond this edge into other dimensions of reality, into a world that seems unintelligible to our conscious mind with its fixed idea of reality. But it is psychic links, such as dreams, that connect us to a greater purpose, a larger whole, a more fulfilling and complete feeling. We intuitively know that dreams are our lifeline to wholeness. Our personal information also registers in the collective subconscious to which everyone has access, so that we contribute to the greater pool of knowledge. Conversely, we draw from this cosmic pool to which everyone else also contributes. It is a nice working arrangement.

Dreams persist night after night (or anytime we sleep) because there is constant stimuli in our environment that needs to be processed and we are creatures that require continual guidance in the form of warnings, scoldings and suggestions. We also need a daily link to those things that inspire and motivate us to be creative individuals and remind us that we are a part of the whole, that what happens to each of us, happens to all of us.

I read once that you cannot pick a flower but you disturb a star. We are reminded through our dreams that, although this beautiful planet Earth is our temporary home, we are the flowers from the stars. Strangely enough, this is a statement of fact. Our bodies and the Earth are composed of the fragments of stars that exploded billions of years ago. We are literally star children.

When all is said and done, perhaps we are not able or meant to understand through our five senses, through our objective, waking consciousness, what goes on at those deeper levels of mind. Perhaps we need another sense or two to see, feel or, even better, to "know" the truth that occurs here. And is it not the search after all that really matters?

Notes

1. Christian, Paul *The History and Practice of Magic,* (NY: The Citadel Press, 1969), p. 88.

2. Bunker, Dusty *Dream Cycles,* (Rockport, MA: Para Research, Inc., 1981).

3. Ibid.

4. Faraday, Ann *Dream Power,* (NY: Coward, McCann & Geoghegan, Inc., 1972), p. 26.

5. Blakemore, Colin *Mechanics of the Mind,* (Cambridge, England: Cambridge University Press, 1977), p. 47.

6. Sechrist, Elsie *Dreams, Your Magic Mirror,* (NY: Cowles Education Corp.), p. 29.

7. Hall, Manly P. *Studies in Dream Symbolism,* (LA: The Theosophical Research Society, Inc., 1965), p. 1.

8. Jung, C. G. *Man and His Symbols,* (Garden City, NY: Doubleday & Co., Inc., 1964), p. 76.

9. Garfield, Patricia *Creative Dreaming,* (NY; Ballantine Books, 1974), p. 84.

10. Goldenberg, Naomi *Changing of the Gods,* (Boston: Beacon Press, 1979), p. 74.

11. Faraday, p. 311.

12. Jung.

13. Faraday.

14. Jung, p. 51.

15. Ibid.

4

The Brain
and Laboratory Research

The human brain is the most complex machine in the world. This maze of wrinkled gray matter weighs approximately three and one-half pounds and within its folds originate every thought, feeling and action we experience. Although, in our everyday speech, we often give credit to other parts of the body — such as clever hands and a courageous heart, it is in the brain that all this cleverness and courage originate. Out of its landscape arose the gift of langauge, the Moonlight Sonata and the wheel. "Incredibly sensitive to internal and external events, it is itself totally insensitive; the brain feels no pain directly, and surgeons are therefore able to work on it without using any anesthesia other than a local painkiller to deaden skin areas of the skull for incisions."[1]

This paradoxical clump of matter is divided into two hemispheres, each with its own special function. The right side has been designated "feminine," ruling the emotional, creative, holistic approach to one's world, while the left hemisphere is called "masculine," controlling analytical, logical, linear thinking. The hemispheres of the brain cross-control the body, i.e., the left, masculine hemisphere controls the right side of the body while the right, feminine hemisphere controls the left side of the body. The ancient concept of the duality of the material world — Yin and Yang, Moon and Sun, night and day — seems embodied in the "two divine revolutions" within the head, the human brain.

I was stimulated into searching for two simple yet comprehensive words to describe the functions of each side of the human brain by a recent television advertising campaign for an automobile. The ad suggests that the vehicle appeals to the "emotional right" side because of certain qualities as well as to the "logical left" side because of other qualities. The implication is that the car satisfies the whole individual, on all possible levels, the emotional and the logical.

I thought about the two words selected by the advertising agency — emotional and logical — and realized what the word "emotional" has come to mean in our society. It is associated with unstable, irrational, and sometimes hysterical people, typically women, who have gone beyond the point of thinking logically and are therefore to be dismissed as unreasonable people. In our patriarchal society, feelings and emotions are viewed as unhealthy and valueless in terms of operating in the everyday world.

Be that as it may, while pondering this heady thought I formulated an association of words to describe the two hemispheres of the brain that I think is perfect. The two I's: Intuition and Intellect.

The "I" is the essence of who you are. When Divinity was asked, who are you, it replied, "I am that I am." Your essence is the "I" within. This "I within" utilizes two methods of perceiving the material world, what I have chosen to label the Intuition (female, right brain) and the Intellect (male, left brain).

The word "intuition" comes from the Latin, *intuit(us),* meaning to gaze at, contemplate. The dictionary defines intuition as "direct perception of truth, fact, etc., independent of any reasoning process . . . an immediate cognition of an object not inferred or determined by a previous cognition of the same object . . . pure, untaught, non- inferential knowledge." I emphasize the word *knowledge.* Intuition is knowledge that is independent of any reasoning process.

Intellect comes from the Latin, *intelligent,* to understand. Its definition is "the power or faculty of the mind by which one knows or understands, as distinguished from that by which one feels and that by which one wills; the understanding; the faculty of thinking and acquiring knowledge . . . Syn. reason, sense, common sense, brains."

Therefore, intuition is knowledge independent of any reasoning process whereas intellect is knowledge that is dependent upon the reasoning process or acquired through thought. Both intuition and intellect function as a source of knowledge; both the right and left hemispheres of the brain supply information that is valid. The traditionally yin "feminine" intuition and yang "masculine" intellect, as methods of obtaining information, are inherently valuable and possessed by every individual in varying degrees.

"Herein lies a great importance of Yin-Yang philosophy: it is a revolution of the thinking world; in it, intellectuality is treated as a part of life, not as the overlord."[2]

The author of this phrase underlined the word "part," an important distinction because, for thousands of years, the idea that the Intellect is superior has reigned. Plato postulated that "the divinest part of us" resides in our head. He believed that mathematics was the purist form of thought and that the sphere was the perfect geometrical shape. Even the Earth, the Moon, the Sun and all the heavenly globes hung in a Universe created by an *Intelligence* that obviously *thought* round.

Divinity is frequently referred to as Cosmic Intelligence. But I wonder if Divinity also imagines, feels and intuits. Actually, I read somewhere that the real meaning of the word in the phrase about "man being created in the *image* of God," actually meant we were created in the *imagination* of Divinity, which makes more sense to me. The former implies that "God" is a big "man" and we are carbon copies or "little men." Certainly this is the height of egotism. The latter, however, suggests we are born in the imagination, in the creative fluid of Divinity. This corresponds to our physical conception and development in the fluids of the womb, and supports the metaphysical axiom: as above, so below. This seems to me to be the battle between Intellect and Intuition, whether we are born in the mind of Divinity or in the imagination of Divinity, whether we are discussing Cosmic Mind or Cosmic Heart. If we keep referring to our Source as Cosmic Mind, we stress the analytical left-brain approach to creation, forgetting that Cosmic Heart, the emotion and feelings of right-brain functioning had an equal part.

Today, we highly prize the intellect, the "male" analytical approach, and often disregard the intuitive, the feminine creative, holistic viewpoint. Our educational systems and intelligence tests traditionally have been left-brain analytical exercises, thus excluding and sometimes demeaning the abilities of those who are more disposed to holistic, creative thinking. At the University of Georgia, B. A. Bracken and his associates have found the those inclined to right-brain creative thinking had more difficulty with linear, analytical, multiple choice-type tests. The solution was to include essay and oral recitation.[3] Perhaps our I.Q. tests suggest that many knowledgeable individuals are designated as less intelligent because they are not able to function as well in the intellectual, analytical, left-brain dominated world. It is my opinion that until we allow both sides of our brains to function freely, and accept the value of their findings in the material world, we are working under a handicap. Granted, some of us will be more right-brained, and others predominantly left-brained, however, both sides function during our lives. Both these functions should be accepted as worthy and productive in society.

The point is that we should value both processes of the human brain — the Intuition and the Intellect — in order to be able to function in an integrated manner with our environment. Once this integration is complete, the "I" within is functioning holistically, combining Intuition and Intellect in a holy marriage.

The Mechanics of Dreaming

Dreams arise from the right hemisphere during sleep while the left hemisphere is more or less suppressed. Not much was known about the process of dreaming until 1953 when probably one of the most important discoveries concerning dreams in this century occurred at the University of Chicago. It revolutionized the course of dream research and the subsequent understanding of dreams.

Under the direction of world famous sleep expert, Professor Nathaniel Klietman, experiments were being conducted on the sleep patterns of infants. The student in charge on that historic occasion, Eugene Aserinsky, happened to notice that the babies' eyes moved synchronously and rapidly under their lids at certain intervals during the night. These rapid eye movements are now known as REMs. To their joy and amazement, the researchers subsequently discovered that REMs occurred only when the sleeper was experiencing vivid dreams. They now knew the times during sleep when dreams occurred.

Before this revolutionary breakthrough, researchers had no way of knowing when a person was dreaming, therefore attempts to awaken the sleeper at the precise moment of a dream were often futile and frustrating. Very little had been learned about dreams and the sleep process in general. Now, with the discovery of REMs, researchers know that whenever a sleeper's eyes move rapidly or jerkily under her/his lids, that person is experiencing a REM dream.

In order to record REM activity, Aserinsky and Klietman decided that, rather than stand over sleepers for hours recording eye movements, they would attach small metal discs or electrodes from an electroencephalograph (EEG) to the scalps of volunteers in order to monitor the electrical activity of their brains while they slept. At the same time, the researchers placed electrodes around the eyes of the sleepers to measure and record their eye movements, a process producing an electro-oculogram. These combined recordings, the EEG and the EOG, supplied them with new information about sleep and dreaming processes which startled the world, and erased long-held myths about what occurs during sleep.

One of the myths concerned the frequency with which we dream. Some people reported dreams every night while others claimed they seldom, if ever, dreamed. Subsequent dream research determined that everyone dreams every night they sleep, and that during an average night's sleep, we experience three to five dreams — approximately one thousand dreams a year. From this fact alone it is easy to understand the excitement aroused by the discovery of REMs.

Before 1953, it was thought that when we fall asleep, we enter one long sleep cycle. As new light was shed on the sleep process, researchers discovered that, rather than one long sleep cycle, the sleep period contains four to six sleep cycles each night. Within each of these cycles are four distinct brainwave patterns, which were subsequently labeled Stage 1, 2, 3 and 4 EEG. (See Figure 4.1.)

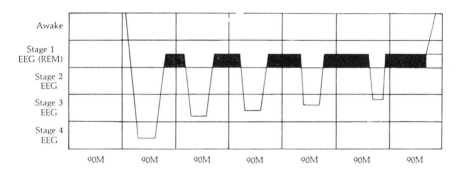

Figure 4.1   Stages of Sleep

When we fall asleep, we quickly descend through Stages 1, 2 and 3 to Stage 4, the deepest sleep, where we may spend half an hour or more before ascending to complete our first nightly sleep cycle. During the second descending cycle, we may or may not reach Stage 4; at any rate, less time is spent at this deeper level during the second cycle. As morning approaches, more time is spent in Stages 1 and 2, and less time in Stages 3 and 4.

Your first dream of the night is about ten minutes long, and the length of each dream increases as the night goes on. In the morning, most of your time is centered in Stages 1 and 2, and REM dreams are the longest just before waking, about forty-five minutes each.

Rapid eye movements occur in the ascending Stage 1 in each cycle rather than the descending stages, and they are directly correlated to the experience of vivid dreams. During REMs, the eyeballs move in a synchronous motion; that is, they move together as they do in normal waking hours. It would seem that the dreamer is watching the action much as he or she would if awake and observing a tennis match or a play. The dreams experienced here in the ascending Stage 1 are vivid and, some say, always in color. Tests have shown that when volunteers are awakened while having REMs, they almost always remember the dream in color. And the colors match those seen during waking hours — the grass is green and the sky is blue. Normally we do not recall our dreams immediately, therefore, elements of the dream, like color, fade from our memory quickly.

When awakened from Stages 2, 3 and sometimes 4, the sleeper may be experiencing a "dreamlet" or more usually a series of thoughts rather than a dream. It is as if the person were thinking at these levels just as s/he would think if awake. Since the dreamlets or thoughts encountered at these levels are not as vivid or emotional (or, as some people feel, not as meaningful) as those which occur at Stage 1, REM dream time, these dreamlets are not considered dreams, but rather fleeting thoughts, sometimes accompanied by pictures. Also at Stages 2, 3 and 4 of sleep, the eyeballs do not move synchronously as they do in REM sleep, but independently. And the movement is not jerky or rapid as it is during REM sleep. These eye movements are labeled nonrapid eye movements, or NREMs. The NREM label is applied to Stages 2, 3 and 4 EEG, periods when the individual is, in some sense, not dreaming.

While researching this chapter I came across something that caused me to leap upright in bed where I lay reading. The author mentioned that the descending and ascending cycles shown in the above graph occur approximately every ninety minutes during the night (or whenever you happen to be sleeping). She went on to say: "the cyclic nature of sleep . . . seems to be an in-built mechanism dependent on some biological rhythm within the body."

"Of course!" I exclaimed out loud, pounding the rumpled covers with a closed fist. Unfortunately my husband was under that part of the blanket sound asleep . . . probably dreaming.

My excitement over this information stemmed from the sudden awareness of the ninety-minute rhythmic sleep cycles and how they *had* to relate to the nine cycles discussed in chapter 1. It seems logical that the cyclic nature of sleep responds to the universal rhythm, the cosmic signature of Nine. Our lives revolve in nine-year cycles and the fetus develops in nine-month stages. English, which is becoming the universal language, has nine parts of speech and our numerical system has nine digits. Both language and digits are products of our collective subconscious response to universal patterns.

Now research suggests a ninety-minute cyclic sleep pattern. The International Encyclopedia of the Social Sciences states ". . . other physiological measures also suggest a ninety-minute period as a unit of sleep time." In tune with this ninety-minute cycle, it continues, ". . . skin conductivity, heart rate, breathing rhythm, eye movements, dreaming occur cyclically." It seems that our biological body rhythms during sleep resonate to this cosmic Nine rhythm.

To synopsize, during a normal night's sleep, we descend and ascend through about five cycles which last approximately ninety minutes each. During each of these cycles, four distinct electrical brainwave patterns, designated as Stages 1, 2, 3 and 4 EEG, can be registered on the electroencephalograph. The most vivid dreams occur in the emerging Stage 1, accompanied by synchronous jerky rapid eye movements, or REMs. This period of sleep, Stage 1 EEG, is called REM sleep. Dreamlets and thoughts occur in Stages 2, 3 and sometimes 4, but here the eyes move independently and more slowly, hence the designation nonrapid eye movements or NREMs. Stages 2, 3 and 4 EEG are referred to as NREM sleep.

During sleep, nerve cell activity in the brain is different from what normally takes place while we are awake. The nerve cells, however, are just as active in sleep, especially during REM sleep. And while the body appears to be very relaxed physically during REM sleep, tremendous activity is taking place in many other ways. The autonomic nervous system registers great variations in respiration, pulse and blood pressure. The brain consumes more oxygen.

Although Stage 1, REM sleep, is similar to light sleep, individuals are not so easily aroused by a touch or a sound as they are from Stages 2 and 3. It may be that they are so involved in the action of the dream that they need a strong stimulus to awaken them. Because of these seemingly conflicting states, REM dream time is called "paradoxical" sleep. NREM sleep, Stages 2, 3 and 4 EEG, is often referred to as "orthodox" sleep because activity here conforms to established sleep behavior and response.

There is evidence that different chemicals are released into the blood stream during each of the Stages 1, 2, 3 and 4 EEG, and each of the four stages of sleep seems to have its own special function.

It appears that Stage 1 EEG acts as a processing station where dreams sort out and integrate each day's information. Perhaps this refining process occurs in the earlier hours of sleep so that by morning we are able to weave all the previous day's stimuli in with memories of our total accumulated past to produce a meaningful dream just before awakening.

Brainwave Frequencies

I think it is important to include here a discussion of Beta, Alpha, Theta and Delta brainwave frequencies in relation to the levels of the mind. The correspondences in the accompanying chart should not be taken too literally because so little is really known about what happens at levels beneath conscious awareness, or Beta. (See Table 4.1.) Keep in mind that normally we change frequencies spontaneously and sometimes rapidly, slipping in and out of levels without conscious awareness. I have designated the "awake" level of consciousness Stage 0. And here I wish to thank my friend, Dottie Limont, for her assistance.

Adult Human Stages	Awareness	Related Name	Cycles Per Second of Brain Frequency
0	awake	Beta	14-40
1	drowsy light sleep	Alpha (light)	7-14
2	light sleep	Alpha (deeper)	
3	deeper sleep	Theta	4-7
4	deepest sleep	Delta	0-4

Table 4.1.   Brainwave Frequencies

Beta: In Beta, Stage 0, our brainwave frequency measures a rapid fourteen cycles per second on up. We are now wide awake, our attention is focused in the "real" world. Information is processed in linear, logical, organized fashion by our five senses — taste, touch, sound, sight and smell. Beta is the only frequency some people use with any awareness and it is the only frequency totally focused in the objective world. Our physical senses operate exclusively here, and since our senses, besides being preconditioned by our unique pasts, often deceive us, this is sometimes called the world of Maya or illusion. This is the world of time and space, where a continuous flow of sensory experiences gives us the illusion of time, and the apparent separation of objects gives us the illusion of space. This is not the best frequency for learning or retention, but it is superior for "super-activity" such as running a foot race and generally being alert to the objective world. Beta is typically left-brain, logical functioning.

Alpha: Alpha, Stages 1 and 2, theoretically can be experienced while you are awake but in a "dreamy" frame of mind. Seven to fourteen cycles per second of brainwave frequency register here. Below fourteen cycles we begin to focus our attention inward where we are psychic, intuitive and creative. Daydreaming, ESP, meditation and hypnosis fall into the Alpha category. The dreams we remember most easily and vividly are alpha or REM dreams.

Research shows that the brain is just as active, and we learn more rapidly and retain information longer, in Alpha than in Beta. We can learn to use the Alpha dimension with awareness and control through biofeedback, meditation and certain other techniques. Most people, however, do not remember Alpha functions unless they have been trained to do so, or unless they are naturally artistic or dreamy. This is the level used for psychic functioning and creative visualization, as well as for lowering anxieties and blood pressure. Alpha is used by such programs as Silva Mind Control and Transcendental Meditation. The American "sleeping prophet," Edgar Cayce, had to relax in order to do his "readings," but unless someone talked to him while he was in Alpha he would slip into deeper Alpha or Theta and fall asleep, unable to "read." Many people think that in the future science will focus on the use of Alpha with controlled awareness. Alpha is typically right-brain, creative functioning.

According to Jose Silva, founder and developer of Silva Mind Control, 10.5 cycles per second is the healing frequency and if that rhythmic beat were played in recovery rooms and hospitals with synchronized music, healing would take place more rapidly.

Theta: At the Theta level, the brain frequencies slow to between four and seven cycles per second. Theta is a slow frequency and ordinarily adults are asleep when emitting these waves. However, babies and children up to about age six or seven use Theta often.

Theta is the emotional frequency; that is, our emotional development is pretty much programmed by the time we are seven years of age and our emotional beliefs come from this period in our lives, unless we examine and change them consciously. Theta is also the level for natural anesthesia and survival. We trigger a natural survival skill or Theta energy when seriously threatened. We can run like a deer, or lift a car, or walk through fire and not feel pain because we are at the Theta frequency. So this level represents our emotional storehouse, our spontaneous survival mechanism and natural anesthesia. We can learn to function at this level with awareness and control, but it is difficult because ordinarily this level is associated with sound sleep.

Delta: Delta, the deepest sleep, measures zero to four cycles per second of brainwave frequency. Newborn babies who sleep up to sixteen hours a day spend most of their time in Delta. Our physiological systems slow down measurably at this level. As observed in sleep laboratories, the body is almost motionless. Delta can be used with conscious awareness or control by highly trained individuals such as yogis, who are able, for instance, to take one breath every six minutes and inhale enough nutrients from the air to sustain their lives.

Because it is so difficult to arouse someone from Delta, some people feel that the moving principle (the soul) is elsewhere. Conjecture has it that we leave our bodies every night in Delta and travel . . . to a deeper source, to our very roots, our true beings or souls. Delta may be more relative to the non-physical or spiritual world than to the planet Earth. Some feel we relate to the spiritual dimension regularly but do not consciously remember doing so. Actually, little is known about Delta except from the feats of extraordinary yogis. Travel at this level is not be confused with astral travel or out-of-body experience.

What happens when we are not allowed to dream? In 1960, Dr. William Dement conducted "dream deprivation" experiments at Mount Sinai Hospital in New York. Volunteers were awakened on consecutive nights during the ascending Stage 1 EEG, so that they were deprived of about 90 percent of their REM dreams. These people automatically each night increased their REM periods, racing through the other stages to get to REMs so that, as the experiment went into the fifth day, they had to be awakened twenty to thirty times to prevent their dreaming. In ten days, the experiments had to be discontinued because the volunteers immediately fell into REM dreams when they were allowed to sleep again. Because of the persistence with which they assert themselves, it would seem that REM dreams are essential to our well-being.

Along with deprivation of REM sleep comes an interruption of dreamlets and thoughts experienced in NREM stages. If we are deprived or REM dreams, we are denied all our dreams. And if dream deprivation is prolonged, the individual experiences "microsleeps" which take the form of hallucinations or delusions. Denied the dream in the normal sleep period, the individual is actually living out the dream experience.

When Dr. Dement's volunteers were allowed to sleep normally following dream deprivation experiments, their REM time increased in some cases up to 40 percent of the total night's sleep, a 15 percent increase over normal adult REM time. The evidence suggests that we have to make up for lost dreams. A late Saturday night escapade tells the story. On Sunday — all things being equal — we feel fine but, when the Monday morning alarm rings, we have to drag ourselves out from between those warm covers. We are hit with a double dose of dream activity on Sunday night. This seems to be the result of Sunday night's attempt to make up for Saturday's lost dreams.

REM deprivation also tends to produce acute discomfort, tenseness, anxiety, inability to concentrate and slight loss of memory even if we get up to six hours of non-REM sleep; therefore the crucial factor is not loss of sleep as much as loss of REM dream time.

However, when adult volunteers, who were not allowed ANY sleep over a period of days, began their recovery period, they immediately raced to Stage 4, the deepest sleep, rather than Stage 1, REM sleep. Research has shown that in Stage 4 body tissue is restored — built and repaired. The glands secrete growth hormones into the bloodstream, especially during Stages 3 and 4, so if this sleep time is denied, repair and renewal of body cells is denied. Heavy exercise in the late afternoon also causes more Stage 3 and 4, sleep than usual that night. Nature wisely decrees that the physical body be taken care of first. Extreme sleep deprivation in children impairs the growth process. Once the body is secured, lost dreams are made up for by an increase in REM sleep.

Most medication, tranquilizers, sleeping pills, barbiturates, even alcohol, suppress REM sleep. Although some may bring on sleep more quickly, they disrupt the dream period, causing heavy drug users a variety of disorders from tenseness and acute anxiety to hallucinations. Use of these products impairs the brain's ability to synthesize protein which helps memory retain the day's events. This, coupled with loss of REM sleep, makes problem-solving difficult for these people.

Dream research continues in laboratories and small groups and by individuals around the world as humanity searches for answers to the age-old mystery surrounding the activity that takes place at levels beneath waking consciousness. All our EEGs and EOGs, tapes and wires, experiments and tests, suppositions and conjectures, still leave us with sketchy information about this mysterious world. Perhaps we are not meant to understand through linear, analytical processes what goes on at these deeper levels of mind. How could Tartini explain the exquisiteness of the dream sonata he barely captured in *The Devil's Sonata*? And was he meant to? Was his longing the passion he imbued into future works? Shouldn't our 'reach exceed our grasp, or what's a heaven for?' Let's leave that to the right brain, and just enjoy it.

Notes

1. Bailey, Ronald H., and the editors of Time-Life Books *Human Behavior, The Role of the Brain,* (NY: Time-Life Books, 1975), p. 8.

2. "The Summer Seminars of Michio Kushi," *Order of the Universe, Vol. IV,* (Boston: Order of the Universe Publishers, 1972), p. 4.

3. "Multiple Choice Tests Favor Left Brain," (Virginia Beach, VA: Perspective on Consciousness & Psi Research), p. 4.

havior, The Role of the Brain, (NY: Time-Life Books, 1975), p. 8.

2. "The Summer Seminars of Michio Kushi," *Order of the Universe, Vol. IV,* (Boston: Order of the Universe Publishers, 1972), p. 4.

3. "Multiple Choice Tests Favor Left Brain," (Virginia Beach, VA: Perspective on Consciousness & Psi Research), p. 4.

5

Symbols

In dream interpretation, the term "symbol" is used frequently. A symbol implies something more than what it appears to be. We use symbols to represent things we cannot totally understand, things that are beyond our ability to grasp fully. Religions use symbolic images to communicate concepts that cannot be described through language. Divinity is usually symbolized by the circle that has no beginning and no end and, as the ancients said, whose center is everywhere and circumference is nowhere. Symbols emerge from the superconscious; they just happen, from out of the void as it were. According to Jung, we "produce symbols unconsciously and spontaneously in the form of dreams" and dreams are "the main source of all our knowledge about symbolism."[1]

Sometimes symbols or elements appear in a dream that seem to have no connection to the dreamer. These may be memories of ideas or traits that the human race once experienced commonly. Freud called them "archaic remnants;" Jung named them "primordial images" or "archetypes," believing, unlike Freud, that these images are a vital part of the collective subconscious and linked to the individual by emotional factors. These universal images are a valuable bridge between our expression in the logical, linear world and the pictorial, instinctual world. They are the means of communication between the right brain's intuitive approach to the inner world and the left brain's intellectual approach to the external world.

Primitive peoples participated in life mystically by personifying nature around them. Animals, trees, the wind all took on qualities of good and evil. The spirits in nature spoke to humans through their dreams so, in their minds, fears were at least identifiable. These early women and men had their own methods of dealing with that fear.

Today you cannot blame your fears on the frog spirit in the bog in your backyard, don a chartreuse costume and leap out to meet your adversary, thus relieving some of your anxiety by actively participating in combating your terror, as your early ancestor might have done. Instead, your fear expresses itself in the form of uneasiness, vague discomforts, depression and neuroses.

Those of us who live in a modern, rational world that looks askance at frog impostors have freed ourselves from such "superstitious nonsense" while losing emotional contact with nature. We are emotionally isolated in a logical, linear world. And, as Jung suggested, even religions seem more interested in preserving the institution rather than the meaning of the symbols that those institutions represent.

The dream, full of symbols that the conscious logical mind has no control over and cannot suppress, is one of the last places where we can connect with our intuitive, instinctual world. Jung said, "dream symbols are the essential message carriers from the instinctive to the rational parts of the human mind, and their interpretation enriches the poverty of consciousness so that it learns to understand again the forgotten language of the instincts."[2]

As humanity developed, certain symbols became universal in that they were fundamental and permeated the lifestyles of many people regardless of culture, language or nationality. A mother smiling down at the new babe in her arms is a symbol of love in any culture. It stirs the roots of our primal memory of the Great Mother, when Goddess worship predominated. This image reminds us of the womb of security where we are nurtured, loved and protected unconditionally.

For example, the United States has its Sun in the astrological sign Cancer (the country's birthday is July 4). Cancer is the sign of the Great Mother. Thus, the United States proudly displays a symbol that offers this country as a womb of nurturing protection to the "poor, the tired, the huddled masses," and that symbol is a woman — the Statue of Liberty. The people of the world have lost contact with their feminine roots, even in their religions, so the need is expressed in another way. The Lady stands at the entrance to New York harbor, a symbol to people all over the world that the Great Mother still lives. Her picture needs no explanation to most because she is a symbol of a deeper need that has been denied external expression.

Symbols cannot be suppressed. They are an instinctive part of our psyches, arising from the collective subconscious, that universal pool of reference wherein resides humankind's ability to recognize things through number patterns. Universal symbols often have religious overtones, therefore, many people believe they come from a divine source and have been with us from the "beginning."

As discussed in chapter 1, religion was the outgrowth of a sacred mathematical understanding of the Universe and our place in it, a Universe created by a Great Geometrician. This Universe was constructed on the principles of proportion, order and harmony. Symbols arising from the knowledge of geometry, such as the circle, the triangle and the cube, have been used in many religions as representatives of sacred and often indescribable concepts. Religion is the clothing of the mathematical body of truth expressed through the symbolism of numbers. It is another way of examining truth.

As stated in chapter 1, our first perceptions "begin from an innate capacity in the brain/mind to recognize (count) periodic patterns of energy frequency . . ." In other words, our primary awareness begins from our ability to count. Recognition of differing patterns of energy told us that the cat was not the same as the dog, and the chair was not the table. As representatives of this counting process, numbers stand out as the original set of symbols, from which all else stems.

We have been discussing the universal process of counting patterns of energy frequency as the basis of our awareness of our environment, the numbers that represent that primal pattern, and the common symbols that stem from this capacity to count and recognize. But we must not overlook the fact that our dreams contain personal symbols that are uniquely our own. As human beings, we are alike yet unique. All of us are born in the same manner, our bodies function alike, we need air and water to survive, and eventually we die. Yet each of us has a unique personality, individual goals, drives and desires which can never be duplicated exactly by another human being.

This carries over into our dreams. Although we all dream each night that we sleep, our dreams reflect our uniqueness: your dreams are unlike anyone else's. Dreams are personal, even though they often contain universal symbols which reflect our "sameness." We are like snowflakes which all come from the same source, form under the same general conditions and fall to earth in the same manner. Yet no two snowflakes — or persons — are alike! Each snowflake has its own distinct pattern which is never duplicated. However, we can learn much about all snowflakes by observing just one. So, let us look at some common dream symbols from the personal as well as the expanded viewpoint.

Number Symbolism in Dreams

Below we will be examining the Zero and the digits One through Nine along with their geometric counterparts, and how these numbers might express in your dreams. Remember, no symbol is good or bad in itself; it just is. You should always examine any symbol within the context of your dream. The emotional content of your dream, along with other symbols in it, will reveal how you feel about any particular symbol.

If, in a dream, you are aware of a number, or its geometrical counterpart in the form of a triangular church steeple or an octagonal shaped room, or you are aware that there are three people, two lamps, eight trees in the dream, then think about what that number means to you. The symbol may have a personal meaning that comes from some experience in your past. Also, examine the meaning of that number in the following definitions. Numbers are a universal language, one that we relate to subconsciously, so that some of the basic truth of the number will most likely be part of the interpretation of your dream symbol.

The Zero: The Circle

Technically, Zero is not a number. In number philosophy it represents Spirit, the Source, the "I am that I am." It has no reference within the realm of three-dimensional experience. Form exists within it, but it can exist without form. In the material world, Zero operates beside one of the nine digits as a symbol of recycling from one set of numbers (or awarenesses) to the next, e.g., 10, 20, 30, etc.

Its geometrical counterpart is the circle, which has no beginning and no end, representing infinity and Divinity.

In *Timaeus,* Plato wrote: "Copying the round shape of the universe, they confined the two divine revolutions in a spherical body — the head, as we now call it — which is the divinest part of us and lord over all the rest."[3]

Plato was one of the philosophers who believed that mathematics was the purist and primary method of thought, and that the sphere was the perfect geometrical form. He noted that the spherical Earth, along with the other globes of the heavens, hung suspended within a Universe created by an Awareness which obviously thought round. Because of this, he argued that "the divinest part of us" resides in our heads, that spherical portion of the body which is the summit of the human frame.

As stated earlier, we need to remember who is doing the philosophizing. Plato was a man with an extremely patriarchal view of life, expressed in his belief that, during the transmigration of souls, if a "man lived a good life and overcame his baser emotions, he would be reborn in a star." If he did not do well, he would come back as a lowly woman. However, if the woman did poorly during her life, this unfortunate soul would come back in the body of an animal.[4]

Plato, who lacked a womb and certainly did not place any great value on possessing one, conveniently overlooked the fact that life begins in the womb, and "the divinest part of us" is our ability to produce life. We become co-creators with Divinity. The womb is also spherical, the perfect geometrical shape, the Cosmic Egg in which the Universe was conceived and in which it was born.

In the circle we have all of creation, the womb and the head, the emotions and the intellect, the left and the right hemispheres of the brain. Divinity does not discriminate against one sex, but includes both in the Cosmic Womb. Divinity loves all her children. And, because only females produce eggs, early peoples personified the Source as the Great Mother whose Cosmic Egg gave birth to all life.

All symbols reside in the Zero, Divinity, the Superconscious. When Zeros accompany any number, they serve to amplify the power of that number and to clarify its meaning.

When you dream of contained places such as caves, or spherical arrangements such as a group of people sitting in a circle, or rings and bracelets, you could look upon these symbols as loving and nurturing expressions because this shape symbolizes the protection of the womb. The womb is a magical place where new life stirs and comes into being. The analogy of Merlin entering his crystal cave is symbolic of the union of male and female energies to produce life.

Sample dream: I am flying over the ocean feeling wonderful when suddenly I dive into the waves and move effortlessly to the bottom of the sea. I enter a translucent cave. In its center is a golden book on a stand. I move to the book and begin to read the pages. I am elated.

The woman who had this dream had been through a traumatic divorce and had spent two years working her way through her pain. She found that the study of metaphysics offered her answers where no other philosophy could. This dream came at a time in her life when she felt she had achieved a plateau in her development. She said that when she awoke from this dream, she suddenly felt new and whole once again.

On one level, the cave and the water are certainly obvious symbols of the womb and the fluids that surround the newborn fetus. She felt reborn, and knew that much wisdom (symbolized by the golden book) lay ahead of her as she proceeded in her studies. This dream has stayed with her for years and she believes it will always be a milestone memory in her life.

It is interesting to note that in group counseling sessions, chairs almost always are arranged in a circle. This is a comforting arrangement because it stirs primal memories of the symbolism of the circle as the Cosmic Womb. Each person can see all the other people in the circle. No one is hidden; everyone is out in the open for a free exchange of feelings and ideas. Each person can feel relaxed and part of the whole. Also, this circular arrangement places no one individual in a superior or dominant position in the group. Everyone is equal.

If you have ever gone camping, you know the warm feelings evoked as you sit around the campfire at night, staring into the flames, under the black cover of the heavens. In this setting; you speak of things you might not talk about at other times. You might join hands and sing a song, say a prayer or meditation as the energy travels from one person to another around the circle. Something magical seems to happen. It is the magic of the circle.

Dreams of the "number" Zero, of circles, mandalas, caves and other symbols that convey the meaning of wholeness and fulfilled containment can be examined in this manner.

One: The Point

●   The point is the geometric equivalent of the number One. The point is the starting place of all lines. The nine digits and the Zero, the letters of the alphabet, each stroke of an artist's brush, the chair upon which you sit, the house in which you live and the beginning of a relationship, all start with the point. A thousand-mile journey begins with the first step. So does every creative endeavor, as my husband reminded me when I began this book. Everything we experience in the physical world begins somewhere with a point of focus, a desire, which then can be translated into action and ultimately a result/form. The point is the beginning of the journey, but it requires no motion. This is where the idea is born; it is the primordial impulse awakening to its self and its desire to express that self as an individual apart from others.

The point demands your intense concentration; it requires you to focus your awareness, center yourself and shut out all disturbing stimuli. When someone says to you, "The point is . . ." s/he is asking you to focus on the specific idea or thought s/he is presenting. To do this, you must disassociate yourself from any distractions in your environment so that you can give your all to the point at hand. The "point" demands separation.

Therefore, dream symbols that suggest isolation and aloneness with no one to depend on except yourself, or that separate you from the crowd in some manner, could indicate a need to center.

The point is a stirring that demands a decision. In which direction should you "point" your energies? You cannot move until you decide where you are going and/or what you are going to do. And you may need some kind of transportation to get there. So a dream of selecting an automobile or buying a house, for instance, can indicate that you have reached a "point" at which a decision must be made.

Sample dream: Symbols are highly personal, as mentioned before, so your "decision symbol" may be something that is uniquely yours. For example, one of my clients dreamt that someone threw a Milky Way candy bar to a woman who caught it with her right hand. In her left hand, she held a Gainsburger (a dog food). At the woman's feet were two pairs of shoes: a new, pink pair and a dark brown pair that was run down at the heels.

It is common to attach your own qualities and attitudes to someone else in your dreams, as my client did. The other person in your dream displays something that is actually part of you. In this case, my client was overweight and had been talking about dieting for some years. The dog food, Gainsburger, was a pun on the word "gain." The woman was gaining weight because of her poor diet, especially her craving for chocolate. And, perhaps beyond the pun, was the message that this food was "fit for a dog," (an unfortunate expression since animals should be nurtured and nourished, too, however, the point was made).

Dreams about the feet often represent our foundations. The woman in this dream was at a point of decision. Should she step into the run-down-at-the-heels shoes (a foundation upon which she had been supporting herself for years) which were suspiciously close to the color of chocolate, or step into the new pink ones (pink is the color of health) and begin a new journey?

Symbols in a dream can represent an attitude the dreamer should adopt or something the dreamer should do. This dreamer's pink shoes were such a symbol, suggesting that she should build a new foundation for health.

In your dreams, a single object upon which you could meditate or concentrate may appear as a representation of the number One. A crystal ball, a daisy or a single eye are some possibilities, but remember, dream symbols are highly personal and unique to each individual.

Two: The Line

——— The geometric symbol for two is the line. The line takes you from here to there. You were there and now you are here; you begin to compare there to here, and duality is born. The polarity is set.

In the Two, things begin to move, although often behind the scenes. You begin to understand the interrelationships you have with other things in your world.

The line, connecting one point to another, implies there is contact and some measure of cooperation between the two ends. So, the Two or the line implies polarity and cooperation between two specific things. Part of this cooperation is revealed in the expression, "You need to be straightened out," meaning you need to be more cooperative and must make adjustments in your behavior. Or, you might be told to walk the "straight and narrow" or to "tow the line."

Two, or the line, suggests that the fragile equilibrium between two opposing points needs balancing. The right brain intuition (the Yin) and the left brain intellect (the Yang) are seeking harmony of expression. You could visualize this as a seesaw, a straight line supported in the exact center. Too much Yin, and the board tips one way; too much Yang, and the board tips the opposite way.

One of the most meaningful books I have read is *Flatland,* by Edwin Abbott, a mathematician who lived in the 1800s. It presents a humorous look at the social mores of his time through a two-dimensional world called Flatland. The inhabitants of this world are squares, triangles and, that most dangerous of all creatures, the line, who is female. When she can be seen from her side — long, smooth and slender, with no sharp edges — things are in hand. But when she approaches head on she is a point, practically invisible, and also fatal because she can spear an unsuspecting soul who is not aware of her dimensions.

The message in the number Two, the line, is awareness through opposites. When we "draw the line" we are saying, "This is as far as I go. I have examined the situation, I have made myself aware of the dimensions of the problem, and I have made a decision that I am on this side and you are on that side." A boundary has been set up between two things.

Sample dream: You dream that you are standing at the beginning of a long, straight road that leads through a forest. At the other end of the road you see a dim object and you know that in order to find out what it is, you must travel down the road, through the forest.

In a number Two dream, you are at one end and something else is at the other end. You must move through the forest before you can discover the identity of the dim object, but many unknowns may lurk in the foliage so you must travel with awareness. As you prepare to travel this road you tune in to your senses and intuitions. A dream of a woman and a man also could set up an awareness through opposites, as would any two opposing symbols.

Three: The Triangle

The triangle is considered the first perfect form because it is the first that can be constructed with straight lines. It has long been a religious symbol of the trinity, the three parts of Divinity that is the moving creative force behind manifestation. The triangle also represents the three parts of the self — body, mind and soul. In ancient societies and in some contemporary ones, it is recognized as the trinity of the Goddess, signifying the Goddess in her three forms — Virgin, Mother, Crone. The triangle was the Egyptian hieroglyphic symbol for woman. In the Greek alphabet, the symbol for delta is the triangle, signifying "the Holy Door, vulva of the All-Mother-Demeter ("Mother Delta") . . . The triangle represented the Virgin Moon Goddess called Men-Nefer, archaic deity of the first Mother-city of Memphis."[5] As mentioned earlier, the downward-pointing triangle represents the female genital area.

The triangle symbolizes a gathering of universal creative energy, which is obvious in the most awesome triangular structure we have on this planet. The Great Pyramid, with its four triangular sides, is the embodiment of the triangle. This structure is considered to be a giant electrical conductor, an accumulator of creative energy awaiting release.

In 1859, Werner von Siemens, founder of the German electrical company by the same name, climbed to the top of the Great Pyramid and stuck his finger into the air over his head in a triumphant gesture. To his great surprise, he received a prickling sensation through his finger and also heard a sharp noise. Curious by nature, he wrapped a wet paper around the metal neck of a wine bottle to create a crude Leyden jar, a device for storing an electric charge. As he held the device above his head, sparks began shooting out of the Leyden jar. It appeared to von Siemens that the Great Pyramid was an electrical conductor of some sort, a focus of creative energy.[6]

Some esoteric historians believe the Great Pyramid was not the tomb of a pharaoh but was used as an initiation temple. Here the candidate for initiation was laid in the granite sarcophagus for three and one-half days while the Ka, the soul of the initiate, travelled the Universe gathering the information and experience necessary for qualification as an adept.

Also, a pyramid built with the same base angles as the Great Pyramid — 51 degrees and 51 minutes — and aligned true north, seems to focus the Earth's creative energy, which runs from the north to the south poles. Under any pyramid constructed with this specific angle, you can place a razor blade with its edge running north to south and it will remain sharp through repeated use. I know because I have done it. The number of books out today on pyramid energy attest to many more of the fascinating capacities of this pyramid.

The cone-shaped hats of witches and wizards are a solidified triangle. Was this their way of drawing in the universal energy to enhance their feats of magic, of working with the natural forces of the Earth to bring about physical change? Remember the stereotypical picture of a child who has not learned her/his lessons or is considered "stupid" sitting on a stool in the corner and wearing a dunce's cap? The dunce's hat is cone- shaped. The corner of the room is also a focus of energy because any point at which two lines intersect is a point of consciousness.

Church steeples are exaggerated triangles, reaching high into the heavens as if to draw upon cosmic consciousness. They attempt to touch a higher being, to penetrate the Awareness of Divinity.

In handwriting analysis, triangular or wedge-shaped strokes indicate people who are energetic and daring. The creative energy of their personalities shows in the triangular strokes in their handwriting.

Observe your own doodles. You may find that when you are concentrating on a problem, you tend to doodle triangular shapes. This suggests that you are attempting to find a creative solution to your problem. The triangle is the geometric symbol of the focusing of creative energy. You can analyze other doodles such as the circle and the square by understanding the energies behind the geometric forms.

Some dream symbols that suggest the Three or the triangle are a church steeple, a pyramid, a witch or dunce hat, a cone — all represent the gathering of creative energies prior to their release into manifestation.

Four: The Square

The second perfect form that can be constructed with straight lines is a square. When we talked about the elements in chapter 2, we discussed the ways Four expresses.

The square with its four sides is symbolic of the ancient sacred formula for Divinity. It also stands for the four elements of fire, water, air and earth which the Cabala said were the four stages of creation as represented by the four parts of the name Joh-Heh-Vau-Heh, a form of the verb "to be." (See Figure 5.1.) Spirit (fire/Jod) acts upon creative substance (water/Heh) which is given mental form through thought (air/Vau) and finalized in matter (earth/Heh). (Spirit in this sense is similar to "the spirit of the law," or the idea behind the law, rather than its rigid interpretation. In spirit reside the ideas, the animating yet formless forces behind creation.)

The magic square has been known from the earliest days of civilization. It was thought to have supernatural powers and was used as an amulet and talisman to ward off evil spirits, illnesses and misfortune.

This square is constructed by joining groups of squares, each of which contains positive numbers arranged in specific ways so that the sums of the horizontal, vertical or diagonal rows are always equal. One of its interesting mathematical properties is its indestructibility for, when some of its columns are transposed, it retains its original purpose. Perhaps it was this indestructibility, and its relationship to all things material, that suggested its use as protection in the material world.

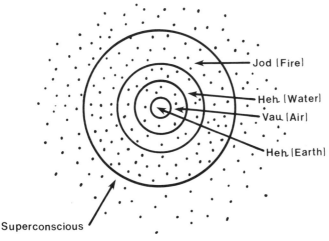

Figure 5.1   The Four Worlds of Manifestation

The square is the pattern for the building blocks of the material world. There are many common expressions using the symbology of the number Four to express earthly connections, such as the four corners of the Earth and the four winds. When we use the term "a square deal" we mean a fair and equitable agreement; to "square an account" is to settle it; a "square meal" is one that is solid and substantial. A "square" is a person who is rigidly conventional; a "four square wo/man" is unwavering, firm and forthright, one who does not go beyond the boundaries set by society; a "square shooter" is an honest person who follows the rules. The Fourth World is made up of the poorest countries of the Third World, and this designation refers to the state of their material development.

Common expressions rise from innate knowledge of truth and, in the above you find that "four" relates to earthy things: finances, food, solidity, substance, the planet itself. Therefore, a dream of a Four, a square or another symbolic image that relates to the square suggests that you are examining some aspect of the boundaries of your material world. The dream could relate to money, job security, relationships, home and family, or any facet of your life that lends a sense of solidity to your existence.

Sample dream: A man dreamt there were four ants crawling on his face. They broke into pairs and began to circle his eyes. He knew they would help clear up an eye problem he had, so he did not disturb them. In reality, this man has perfect eyesight, so he believed the message of the dream was related to seeing some situation in his life more clearly. He considers ants to be hard workers, able to carry weights far exceeding their own body weight. He, too, is a good worker, dedicated to his job and extremely reliable. This dream encouraged him to realize how valuable he was to the company he worked for and to ask for a raise — which he received.

Five: The Pentagram or Pentacle

Also called the pentangle, pentalpha, Devil's Sign, Witches' Cross, Wizard's Star, Goblin's Cross, Witch's Foot, Star of Knowledge and Pentacle of the Virgin, this symbolic figure has five points. For thousands of years, it has been used by the Pythagoreans and other philosophers, magicians and witches. It is called a pentalpha because an A (alpha), the birth letter, can been seen interlaced at five (penta) points.

Five is the value of the hypotenuse (slanted side) of the Pythagorean right triangle. The vertical line, value 3, is Spirit, or the idea, expanding to meet the horizontal line, value 4, symbol of Matter, to create the hypotenuse, value 5, nature or life. This triangle is what the ancient Egyptians called the All Seeing Eye.

As long as the Three remained Three, and the Four remained Four, there was no life — until the Five was introduced. Five symbolizes humanity; it often is depicted as a man standing with legs astride and arms outstretched, forming a five-pointed star or pentagram with his body. Here the five senses take precedence.

Five is the quickening. In early Occidental and Eastern cultures, it was generally accepted that the soul did not enter the body of the fetus until the fifth month of pregnancy, therefore abortion prior to the fifth month was not a crime. After this period, it was considered murder.

The Catholic Church expressed this belief in the Doctrine of Passive Conception, which stated that the fetus was without a soul until the fifth month and could be destroyed without punishment. It was not until 1869, when Pope Pius X announced that either God had "misinformed his church" or that He had changed His mind, that the Church's attitude toward abortion was reversed.

The Biblical story of the apple in the garden of Eden fits in here nicely, too. If you cut an apple in half horizontally, you will find five seeds inside in the shape of a pentagram, representing the five senses. It wasn't until Adam ate the apple Eve picked that they took on consciousness and awareness through their five senses. In other words, if the apple had not been eaten, Eve and Adam would not have taken on the knowledge that they had the capacity to be divine-like and make choices in their lives. They would have remained, like animals, in the Garden of Eden, and life on this planet as we know it would not exist. So, you see, Eve knew what she was doing all along. And she gets such bad press!

The pentacle in the center of the apple was the symbol of the Goddess Kore, one of the earliest names of the World Shakti or female spirit of the Universe, the inner soul of Mother Earth. Egyptians spoke of Mother Ker and Kara. The Romans knew of Carna or Carmenta, who invented the Roman alphabet. Another variation of her name was Ceres from which the word cereal is derived. "Reflection in the pupil of the eye was known as the Kore or 'Maiden' in the eye. To the Arabs, it was the 'baby' in the eye. The Bible calls either a daughter or a soul 'the apple of thine eye' (Proverbs 7:2); and of course, every apple had a Kore."[7]

The apple is a symbol of knowledge in many myths and religious beliefs. One of the seven sacred trees of the Druids was the apple tree. In Greek mythology, the four Hesperides, daughters of the Night, guarded the golden apples which grew in a wondrous garden at the western edge of the world. Today we give an apple—still a symbol of knowledge—instead of a plum or a pomegranate to the teacher.

This is a good example of a symbol persisting through the ages, in many diverse cultures, in the hands of different people, yet maintaining the integrity of its original meaning. The apple, with its five-seeded, pentagram-shaped center, represents the awakening of the senses, the ensuing experiences that are encountered and the decisions that result from those encounters.

Philosophers, magicians and alchemists often used the pentagram to signify the human being as a tiny replica of the Universe — a microcosm of the greater macrocosm. This has always been an important tenet of magic and understanding the mysteries of life. Often the pentagram is associated with witchcraft and, to those who don't know any better, it is considered an evil symbol. Throughout history, however, witches were wise women known to have magical powers, women who worked with the forces of nature to heal and create harmony. They belonged to the "old religion," Mother Goddess worship. They used the pentagram in invocations and ritual for protection because it could be formed by a single unbroken line. Evil spirits could only enter when there was a break, or a doorway, in the line.

When Father God took over, attitudes toward witches began to change, and because the pentagram was their symbol, it became associated with evil because it was part of the old religion.

The inverted pentagram, as a symbol of evil, actually signifies the senses turned upside down, or gone astray, through negative passions that drive the individual to commit evil deeds. One could say that the patriarchal Christian Church, with the deaths of two million "witches" (innocent women) on their hands, has earned the right to wear the inverted pentagram! It was man's obsession with the woman and her physical power over them — i.e., man's desire for the female body — that drove early church fathers to impose celibacy on their clergy. Their fear also led them to remove her from the trinity and they would have eliminated her entirely from religious ritual if the people had not objected to letting go of the mother goddess.

The point here is that we must look deep into the meaning of symbols rather than merely reacting to what we have been taught, especially when that teaching blankets an entire culture as evil. My question is always, "Who says?" I want to know things like who wrote that book, who is teaching that idea, where did it come from, why did they believe that, what was their ultimate purpose? Unless you understand these questions, the information you receive is less than whole. In order to have the whole picture, you must know where the information comes from and who is interpreting it.

Five, the number of the pentagram, is the number of change because it is life (the hypotenuse on the Pythagorean triangle) that is in a constant state of flux. One of the laws of physics is that the only constant is change. That is the law of Five: the law of life. Five signifies the change that had to occur when Eve and Adam ate the apple of knowledge.

As humans, we are often impatient with slow change, especially in the United States, whose birth number is 5 ($7 + 4 + 1776 = 5$). The Five requires action, therefore speed is one of the key words of this number. A good example of this is in the naming of the auto race the Indy 500. And, until recently, the United States had a highway driving speed limit of 55 miles per hour. This is probably the worst possible speed we could have selected because the double Five implies double the speed. We were psychologically motivated to break the speed limit! Even speed limits ending in 5, such as 65, still convey the impulse to move. It would have been safer if we had selected 60 or 70 as a speed limit.

When you see stars in your dreams, it does not mean that you are two tomatoes short of thick paste, but rather that your senses are involved. And, you are most likely going through changes in your life. Since the five-pointed star also represents the stars in the heavens, it can indicate that your senses are being elevated, raised to a higher level of awareness. The star can be a sign that things are changing for the better and you are heading in the right direction. The Magi didn't fare too badly.

Six: The Hexagram

Also known as the Great Yantra, the Philosopher's Stone, Magen David (Shield of David), Solomon's Seal, the six-pointed star — or two interlaced triangles, one pointing up and the other down — was adopted by the Jews in the seventeenth century as an official symbol.

However, this ancient symbol predates Judaism. The original source was the Great Yantra, which represents the union of the sexes. The triangle that points downward symbolizes the Female Primordial Image or Yoni Yantra, which was before the Universe was. In infinite time, the Goddess conceived within her triangle, the bindu, and brought forth the upward pointing triangle, the male, the lingam or "the fire." The symbol represents the eternal union of Goddess and God.[8]

The lower triangle has long been recognized as the element water, the upper triangle as fire. The hexagram was eventually de-sexed because of puritannical influences. Its message is verbally transmitted in the third sentence of the Bible describing the beginning of creation. "And the Spirit of God moved upon the face of the waters." Fire, or spirit — the male — moved "within" the face of the waters — the female — the cosmic womb, to bring about physical manifestation.

All snowflakes are hexagrams. As they fall from the sky, they are formed as the result of static electricity (fire) acting upon congealing water (water), or spirit (fire) moving upon the face of the waters (water). So, the Biblical story of creation is reflected in the creation of the snowflake.

Moses, purported author of the first few books of the Bible, was trained in Egypt by Egyptian priests, supposedly learned in esoteric lore. He is said to have written those words: "Spirit moved upon the face of the waters." Early people, who predated Moses, saw the hexagram as the symbol of the union of the sexes. What the modern world has thought to be mere imaginings of the ancient mystics is in actuality scientific truth clothed in symbolism. In the hexagram, we have a geometrical message for esoteric investigators, and a nurturing verbal story for the general public. In each individual's life, there are times when s/he needs to be comforted alternately by each of these expressions of Divinity.

Six and sex are very similar in sound and spelling. It was on the sixth "day" that woman and man were created. And Key 6 in the Tarot is called The Lovers. Older versions of this key show a naked young woman and man facing a crowned woman (Great Mother Goddess), representing the union of opposite but complementary expressions of existence. Of course, sex was part of this expression.

Therefore, in magic, which is the art of controlling and directing the forces of nature to bring about physical change, both the pentagram and the hexagram were used. The pentagram is the five-pointed star indicating the senses, discussed above, and the hexagram is the six-pointed star, representing the union of opposites. To control nature one must have control of the senses and the creative combining of opposites.

With the advent of Christianity, these symbols came to indicate, in many instances, evil forces primarily because they were associated with sexuality and the Great Mother, the adversary of the Christian church who honored the Great Father. Earlier pictures depicted the Devil as decidedly female, with bare breasts, the head of a horned creature and the pentagram or the hexagram worn on the forehead between the eyes. To the patriarchal church fathers, evil was embodied unquestionably in the female. They even named Hell after the Goddess Hel.

Key 15 in the Tarot is the Devil ($1 + 5 = 6$). In some decks it is pictured as half female and half male — certainly a better approach to the problem of evil — however, the body is decidedly masculine. Today we think of the Devil as he. I find it curious that the early fathers chose a male to personify the evils of the Mother, but of course, they couldn't accept God's adversary as being female. That would place too much power in the hands of woman. Actually, evil is the misunderstanding of the right principles of living, or Divinity inverted.

The fifteenth degree of the fixed signs in the zodiac (Taurus, Leo, Scorpio and Aquarius) are supposed to be power points in the astrological chart. Perhaps this power relates to Key 15, the Devil (embodied in the female) who has dominion over earthly things. And, as I once read somewhere, evil was never so evil before Christianity.

Sample dream: A woman dreamt that her foot lay detached on the floor. She was not alarmed or in pain, but examined the sole which was battered, calloused and rough-skinned all over. She lifted a loose flap of skin on the bottom of her foot and looked up into her leg at the leg bone. Then she covered her foot with six sheets of newspaper.

The sole of her foot was a pun on the word "soul." She felt her soul had been battered and that she was developing a calloused attitude toward the relationships in her life. Looking inside her leg at the bone indicated her need to examine the structures upon which she had built her previous relationships. Newspapers convey information, and the six sheets suggested that she needed to look at her sexual relationships in a different light, with new respect and with expectations of equality and harmony, rather than settling for a "warm body" in her bed.

Six represents the power of love, and control of the magical creative forces in nature that evolve from the equal union of the female and male energies.

Dreams of the number Six, hexagrams, snowflakes, and the Devil indicate a union of opposite but complementary forces, an urge to come together in harmonious relationships. These symbols also signify a desire to channel creatively the forces in your life. When the hexagram represents snowflakes as well as the Devil, can the Devil be all that bad? We are known by the company we keep.

Seven: The Triangle and the Square

Seven, the most mystical of all numbers, is a combination of the first two perfect forms that can be constructed with straight lines: the triangle and the square, the Three and the Four, "the trinity of spirit and the quaternary of form." The triangle symbolizes the spirit while the square represents the physical or humanity. "The union of the trine and the square signifies the interpenetration of the human and the divine. To realize such a union is the purpose of physical evolution. The process is embraced within the work of the seven creative days."[9] In the Seven, experiences are gathered and synthesized in preparation for use in the three-dimensional world of the Eight. "When the 3 and the 4 kiss each other, then the cube unfolds and becomes the number of Life — the Father-Mother Seven."[10]

Perhaps the Seven was considered the most mystical of all numbers because it is the only one that cannot be divided evenly into a circle. (360 divided by 1 = 360; 360/2=180; 360/3=120; 360/4=90; 360/5=72; 360/6=60; 360/7=51.428571 . . .; 360/8=45; 360/9=40.) The division of the circle by 7 is intriguingly close to the outer angle of the Great Pyramid: 51 degrees and 51 minutes.

We can examine the mysticism of the Seven in another manner, too. The number 22 was once considered symbolic of a complete cycle, the circle, because it reflected the twenty-two letters in the Hebrew alphabet and the twenty-two Keys in the Major Arcana of the Tarot (Keys 1-21 plus the Fool) and thus indicated one full cycle of experience. The fraction 22/7, one cycle of human experience divided by the spiritual Seven or Divinity within, was used to express our connection to Divinity. This fraction is the value of pi! or as near to it as this value can be expressed in whole digits. The discovery of pi was a breakthrough in mathematics because its value is the relationship between the circumference of a circle and its radius and diameter; pi supplied a formula by which these things could be easily measured.

Until the advent of the computer, some mathematicians spent an entire lifetime advancing the value of pi one decimal point. The computer finally solved the problem and it was discovered that, at some point, pi begins to repeat itself. Pi is unending, infinite. Pi, as the relationship between the diameter or radius of a circle and the circumference of a circle, holds a profound message. Metaphysically, the diameter or horizontal line symbolizes the earth and material existence; the circle represents Divinity. Pi, or 22/7, then, signifies the relationship between humanity and Divinity, a relationship that is eternal!

As mentioned in chapter 1, Six is the completion of the process of creating the individual patterns for the material world; Seven represents the cycle in which Divinity rests and the pieces of the first six patterns are assembled and synthesized. This is the preparation stage where outer activity ceases, and the power of thought is set into action. Seven is the gathering.

By placing the triangle above the square we create a stylized house. The Seven is the "house" pattern in which the soul will reside when it enters the "eighth" day. It is called Divinity's perfect number, and the numerous references to it in the Bible refer to the perfection of divine law. The numerical value of "the law" in Greek is 700. The Zeros amplify the power of the Seven.

We find the number Seven reflected in key places that are the underlying cycles of nature. "The formative and creative processes of nature operate in the rhythm of 7 . . ."[11] Salt first solidifies into triangular shapes, then finally transforms into the cube $(3+4 = 7)$. There are seven "original" planets — the spirits that guide our solar system also correspond to the seven major chakras in the body. There are seven notes in the musical scale and seven colors in the rainbow, Divinity's covenant with humankind. Human development occurs in seven year cycles. Every cell in the human body is replaced in seven years so that our bodies are entirely renewed in every seven-year period. Mental progress is measured in seven-year increments. This is in keeping with the planet Saturn's passage through the astrological chart: it takes seven years for Saturn to transit a quarter of the chart.

The cycles of the Moon, the basis of our early calendars, are measured in seven days, corresponding with the seven days of the week. The Celtic Runes, the tree alphabet, included seven major trees or chieftans or letters: apple, yew, holly, oak, pine, hazel and ash.

The law has a seven-year statute of limitations for most crimes, which states that a person cannot be prosecuted for a violation after a seven-year period. Seven is the final stage of planning before physical results occur.

We refer to the "seven year itch," a time when one becomes uneasy with current circumstances and sometimes makes major life changes. The uneasiness stems from an underlying urge to accumulate and analyze the experiences of the past six years. Then the whole picture can be seen, and the power of that vision gives one the impetus to move out into the material world and make decisions that will lead to the completion of the original goal.

You have seven holes naturally occurring in the head. The derisive comment that you have an extra hole in your head suggests that you are contemplating, thinking about, doing something, even though that something is considered strange by the observer. The point is that you are gathering experience and making a plan that you may carry through.

So, if you dream of Sevens or find yourself in a cabin in the woods, on an uninhabited island, in a desert or an empty room, this is a signal that it's time for a readjustment in your usual busy schedule. Analyze your situation, for you are in a formative period that requires quiet time so you can assemble the pieces you have prepared up to this point in anticipation of using that power in the outside world.

Eight: The Cube

 As stated under number Four, the square is the pattern for the building blocks of the material world. This pattern solidifies in the cube as the square moves from a two-dimensional figure into a three-dimensional world. The square (4) is the pattern for the formation of the material world, the cube (8) signifies the solidification of that pattern: the material world itself.

We express our connection to the material world in many ways, thus reflecting our innate awareness of the cube as representative of the physical plane.

The cornerstone of the temple is the cube, and the temple is that construction not made by human hands, or the physical body in which we reside.

In some Tarot decks, The Devil (card 15) is shown sitting atop a half cube to which a woman and a man are loosely chained. Since the cube represents the reality of the material world, the half cube indicates that the woman and man can only see half the truth, and they are chained to that perception which can lead to wrong choices. They could easily slip loose from their bondage, but because they are not aware, because they see only half the truth, they are chained to incorrect beliefs which imprison them.

The Devil represents the material world because it represented man's earthly desires for the sensual pleasures of the Earth. And since woman was one of those pleasures, "she" became the Devil. (You've heard the expression "she-devil," but have you ever heard "he-devil?")

The Christian church fathers wanted to frighten people away from the Great Mother who ruled the heavens and the earth. Her temples were very rich. Therefore, the Father God worshippers began to claim that the Earth and its treasures were evil and should be forsaken. That the sensual delight experienced by the followers of the Great Mother should be forsaken. The ensuing battle between God and Mammon was the battle between the Father and the Mother. (The word "mammon" comes from mammary.) So the Christian Devil represented the riches of Mother Earth, and his evil reputation was devised to lure the people away from the Mother and her rich temples. Today the rich temples belong to the Father.

The Christian cross is actually a cube. (See Figure 5.2.) This cross is a symbol of the physical body. The teachings of the Father God religion are that the body is a heavy burden we must carry through this lifetime of trials and tribulations. Patriarchy's preoccupation with pain is in direct contrast to matriarchy's preoccupation with pleasure. Therefore, the

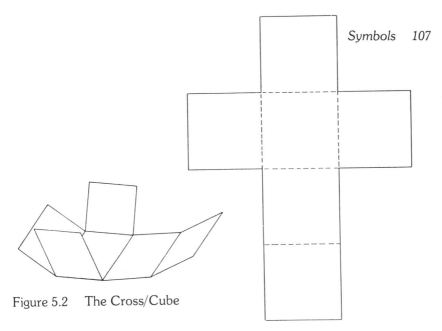

Figure 5.2   The Cross/Cube

cross, as a universal symbol, does not indicate pain — it is representative of the material world.

Also contained within this cross are the sacred Three and Four — the three horizontal and four vertical squares — which are the values of the first two sides of the Pythagorean triangle. This right triangle of 3-4-5 represents Spirit descending into Matter to create Nature.

The cube is associated with the number 26 (which adds to an 8) for several reasons. The four stages (elements) of creation which produce the material world, the cube, are found in the sacred trapezoid and its name, Jod-Heh-Vau-Heh, with its values of 10-5-6-5. These four numbers add to 26. The cube is constructed of 6 planes, 12 lines and 8 points, for a total of 26.

Wherever we find the number 26, we see an indication of the extent to which we can express in this material world, the limit within which our bodies can operate. The 26 is the fullest expression of Divinity in the material world.

In the Egyptian story of Isis and Osiris, the body of Osiris is dismembered into 26 parts and scattered about the Earth. The 26 parts symbolized the extent to which Osiris could function in the physical. Some stories say that the body was cut into 14 parts, of which only 13 were found. Thirteen is a multiple of 26, and the missing part, of course, would be Divinity which cannot be found in physical form.

Another deep metaphysical truth is found in the expression that "we are the salt of the Earth." Salt crystallizes into cubes, the symbol of the body. Solid deposits of salt exist all over the Earth; some deposits are many thousands of feet thick. The oceans, which cover the major portion of the

Earth's surface, contain salt. Salt is an essential part of the human diet. Wherever salt is scarce, its value is very high. The word "salary" comes from the Latin salarium or salt money. Roman soldiers were often paid in salt, a necessary commodity in a hot climate. Salt is definitely a solid and dense part of the material structure of this planet.

The *Encyclopedia Americana* states that "salt can be grown by very slow cooling into large and perfectly transparent cubes . . ."[12] The hidden implications in this sentence are breathtaking. We are the salt of the Earth; it is an essential part of our diets and it crystallizes into cubes, while we crystallize into the human body. Yet, by a very slow cooling (years and perhaps lifetimes of work and understanding, and a tempering of the fire, the life flame or Spirit within us) we can be transformed into perfectly *transparent* cubes (symbol of ultimate purified consciousness while in the body). A transparent cube is the purified human being. This is our fullest expression in the material world: the 26, the purified cube.

We have 26 letters in our alphabet, an alphabet that is the most widely used in the world — in English, French, Spanish, Portuguese, Italian, Dutch, German and Polish. English, with its 26 letters, is becoming the universal language — even the Turks and the Chinese are beginning to use it. These 26 letters form words then sentences that create books, speeches, poetry and communication of all types. The 26-letter alphabet is the total expression of which our minds are capable. It represents our ability to think, to comprehend, to express, to create and to communicate in the physical world.

The Hebrew alphabet has 22 letters, on which the Major Arcana of the Tarot deck is based (the twenty-one keys plus The Fool). The Hebrews considered their vowels sacred and unutterable because they were of divine origin, so we could assume that the four parts of Jehovah's name, Jod-Heh-Vau-Heh, contained those sacred hidden vowels, the remainder of their alphabet. The four vowels plus the twenty-two letters equal 26.

"The" Marathon (the Boston Marathon) is approximately 26 miles long. Who chose this length and did s/he know the implications behind the number 26? We innately know truths that we express in a myriad of ways. And, as every runner knows, at about eighteen to twenty miles into a marathon, the runner hits a wall beyond which physical endurance no longer matters. Those last miles are run on sheer will. The 26-mile marathon is a test of the will within the human body, and may represent the body's maximum physical capability.

In the Great Pyramid, called a mathematical measurement of time and space in stone, there is an Ascending Passage called the Hall of Truth which has a slope of 26 degrees. According to Peter Lesmerurier, in *The*

Great Pyramid Decoded, this upward slope represents "evolutionary progress," and the 26 degree angle of ascent indicates "human evolution."
This 26 degree slope represents human evolution, or our ability to reach
our fullest potential while in the physical plane.[13]

Note that the Precession of the Equinoxes or the Great Year is about
26,000 years (25,920 to be exact). There are 26 weeks between the sol-
stices and the equinoxes. Both are expressions of the physical cycles of
the Earth.

The four fixed physical laws of the Universe which we discussed earlier (under the section on the elements) reside in the four fixed signs of the
zodiac — Taurus, Leo, Scorpio and Aquarius. These astrological signs
rule houses 2, 5, 8 and 11 in the natural horoscope. These houses add
to 26, signifying the physical laws of the Universe.

Only the numeral 8 can be drawn over and over without lifting pen
from paper. (The 0, which is not a number, is also drawn this way; it is
reflected in the drawing of the 8 as two equal circles.) The Eight is ever
repeating, infinite, and as such, symbolizes the theme of reincarnation in
the physical world, the idea that matter is recycled forever. On its side,
the Eight is the cosmic lemniscate, the mathematical symbol for infinity.

However, some might view infinity differently. My daughter, after
a particularly harrowing day with her three little boys, described the "lying
down" Eight as a "tired Eight." While in the physical body, truth is ultimately personalized.

Will you ever look at a cube the same way again?

Dreams of cubes, the cross, running the marathon, eight people or
items, and so forth may be messages to look at how you are "running"
your life. What goals have you set for yourself and how are you progressing
toward achieving them? Eight is part of the material world with the human
body, the environment money, possessions, status and achievement as
a primary focus. Look behind the face value of the symbol to discover
deep and inspiring truths. Here you will find the reality you have built,
and a promise of what you can become. Eight is the pattern put into form.

Nine: *The Point within the Circle*

If the Zero or the circle is the cosmic womb in which all
is born and in which all exists, and the point represents
the beginning of focus where the primordial impulse
awakens to itself as separate within the whole, then the point within the
circle is the final phase of the individualized entity while in the physical
body, the person who has reached completion through recognition of her/

his individuality within the whole. This symbol represents knowledge of the self as an individual in the physical world, but also awareness that the self belongs to and is part of a greater whole. Here we have expanded awareness while in the body. We recognize that the appearance of self as alone and separated from all other things in the world is merely an illusion, that the self (the point) is connected to, or rather is in, the whole (the circle). The individual is centered in Divinity, in the "I am." The ninth letter in the alphabet is "I."

There is a natural breathing out and in which is reflected in the natural numbers One through Eight. The so-called masculine numbers, 1-3-5-7, breathe out while the feminine numbers, 2-4-6-8, breathe in, symbolizing the ebb and flow of life, opposite poles of the magnetic field. The Nine, however, is androgynous, having both female and male characteristics, or containing all.

The circle, which contains 360 degrees, adds to Nine $(3+6+0 = 9)$. When we want it all, we say we want "the whole nine yards." Someone who is "dressed to the nines" is dressed to the ultimate. Nine represents one step beyond the ordinary, beyond normal physical expression.

Nine is the number of wisdom. It has collected the events from the preceding eight cycles of living, and has centered itself in the wisdom accrued from these experiences. Nine completes one full cycle of experience.

Key 9 in the Tarot is the Hermit. He holds aloft the lamp of illumination to light the way for others who climb the mountain of attainment, choosing to rise above the physical and view it from a different perspective, appreciating its value while understanding its true function.

After reading this, you may look upon dreams of leopards and polka dots in an entirely different light.

Astrological Symbolism in Dreams

As discussed in chapter 2, the four elements indicate four basic ways of thinking, behaving and reacting to circumstances in life. Therefore, these elements represent the four basic categories into which people fall, and their fundamental approaches to understanding their worlds. Their special awarenesses are embodied in their dream symbols. If you know the dominant element in your astrological chart, you may find you can easily identify the following symbols that come under that element.

Please keep in mind that a symbol can fall into more than one category depending upon what it represents to you, the dreamer. For instance,

Vincent Price, the actor, is also a connoisseur of art. His appearance in your dream might be categorized as the element water because of the creative nature of the water element. However, if you paid far too much for something you just bought, Vincent Price could be a pun. In this case, this symbol could fall into the earth category, because the earth element is connected to values and possessions.

You must examine your own feelings as well as your current activities and concerns at the time the dream occurs. You choose most all your dream symbols for personal reasons. You are the writer and director of your dream plays. This cannot be emphasized enough.

Earth

The structures and forms we find in our dreams represent our basic beliefs and principles. Symbols that are indicative of the earth element are those that are static in the sense that we observe them as they are. We do not need to observe the motion or activity taking place in or around the form, but rather the form itself as a stationary structure without motion. By observing in this manner, we see the form that has been built up because of past activity.

In a dream, the activity around the object is often the result of the thoughts that created the condition of the object. For instance, if you dream of a house that is so rundown that you are desperately trying to repair it before it caves in, then the condition of that house is a result of your attitude toward caring for it in the past. So, the first step in analyzing this dream is to determine the condition of the house, knowing that the condition is the result of an attitude.

Form is definite. We are known by the clothes we wear, the houses we live in, the cars we drive, the creative products we produce, and the religious and philosophical tenets we profess. Much of what we know about each other comes from the possessions we have, including talents and ideas. So, when you reflect upon an object in your dream, first look at its construction and condition, things like size, shape, surface features, basic strengths.

The house: One of our most obvious possessions or structures is a house. Because we live in our houses, as we live in our bodies, houses often represent the physical body.

In the second century, Artemidorus of Daldis told of a man who dreamt that his father died in a house fire. Shortly afterward, the dreamer died with a high fever. It would seem that the house indicated the body; the fire was the fever.[14]

An eighteenth century Hebrew encyclopedia pictures a house and a human body side by side, comparing the windows to eyes, the furnace to the stomach, and so forth. In a James Thurber cartoon, a hen-pecked individual stands on the street before his home which is half-house and half-wife. Thurber depicts the building and the person as interchangeable symbols.

Metaphysical literature speaks of building and purifying the temple, an analogy to the human body. The body is the house of the soul.

The human body is the house in which the soul resides just as the structure of stone or wood we call our home is the house in which our physical bodies reside. Therefore we can see how easy it is to transfer personality traits from the human to the home, to use the rooms in the house to represent facets of that personality and the different levels of the home for areas of focus or stages of development that our consciousness has reached.

Another fascinating point that has come to my attention in working with people and their dreams is that when you physically work on your house, you are working on that corresponding facet of your own psyche. For instance, whenever my daughter Melanie moves into an apartment, she first attacks the bathroom. She has never quite finished one to her satisfaction but it is always her first choice for redecorating.

The bathroom is a place where we eliminate poisonous toxins from our bodies; we cleanse ourselves. Melanie's eating habits leave much to be desired, and her subconscious is directing her to work on the bathroom first in an attempt to send the message that she needs to cleanse her body. Because the kitchen is not involved, it would seem that she needs to cleanse herself of toxins before she begins a new eating pattern. The day she finishes decorating her bathroom is the day I know she will begin eating properly.

Before taking note of the activity in your "dream" house, examine its exterior condition — if that was part of your dream. Clean, well-kept, strong and functional houses; elaborate, intricately designed, exquisitely manicured homes; and disorderly, unstable and run-down structures — certainly the conditions of these houses reflect the attitudes the tenants have toward life and themselves.

When you drive by different types of homes, you receive impressions about the kinds of people who live in those houses. You can almost sense what they look like, how they act and dress, what activities they prefer. You know whether you would like them or not, whether they are the kind of people who fit into your social circle. Some homes are inviting, warm, charming, while others seem aloof and distant, cold and unapproachable.

Still others show undisciplined, chaotic and disorganized faces. It is the same with your "dream" houses. The type of house in which the dream activity takes place represents the attitudes behind the activity, the basic belief that brought on the action and supports it.

Sample dream: Some time ago, I met a man who told me about a "strange" dream he'd had the night before. In the dream he owned a house that was structurally weak and the furnace was so clogged he was afraid the building would catch fire. In addition, the house was so overrun by rats that he was driven out. He knew in his dream that he had to do something drastic to get rid of the rats and clean up the house so he could move back in.

My first thought was that the dream indicated illness, because rats traditionally are viewed as carriers of disease. The unstable condition of the house was another clue. Of course, it was not my place to say that before asking him what the symbols in the dream meant to him. Before I had a chance to say anything, however, he told me that he was entering the hospital the next day for major surgery. I left it at that because he obviously connected the dream with his surgery or he wouldn't have mentioned the two together.

The structurally weak condition of his dream house represented the lifestyle he had kept for years and his attitude about his health and diet. The furnace further corroborated the clogged stomach syndrome. The rats symbolized the disease that ran rampant through his body as a result of an improper health practices. His basic belief system, his lifestyle, his ideas about how to live, were represented by that house. After years of poor habits and attitudes, his health had degenerated so far that his house (body) was not fit to live in. The rats (disease) now needed to be eliminated by a radical cleansing (surgery).

I am sure this man had this or similar dreams many times over a long period of time. The subconscious does not spring surprises on you. It patiently sends messages over and over, hoping that you will listen. Certainly when something as important as your health is concerned, the warning dreams would come long before hospitalization became necessary. Your subconscious gives you plenty of opportunities to correct problems — if you listen to the messages in your dreams.

If you dream of rats, it does not necessarily mean that you need surgery, but it can indicate a need for cleansing at some level — physically, mentally, emotionally or spiritually — if rats have no other particular meaning for you. If you breed rats and love the little creatures, or if you see them as laboratory animals used for experiments, or if you just read an article or saw a film featuring rats (such as "Willard"), then the rat becomes a symbol with different connotations for you.

It is always important to remember that you are the author of your dreams, therefore your interpretation of any symbol is more important than what any expert has to say. Use your own instincts and feelings when examining symbols in your dreams, and use books like this only as a guide.

The most common interpretation of a house is the body itself; therefore, unless you have an overriding impulse to view it differently, this is the most logical approach to the meaning of the house as a symbol in a dream.

Look at the façade of your dream house. Notice the roof line, the chimney, the windows and doors, the landscaping. If you remember these details, then they are important in the interpretation of the dream.

Sample dream: A young woman dreamt she would be moving into a small cape-style house in the spring. The house was newly built and had three windows facing the street. When she awoke, she thought it strange that there were three windows on the front of the house, rather than an even number as is usually the case with cape houses.

The new house and the season of spring both indicated a new beginning. Windows often represent vision or perception because it is through them that we look out of the house, just as we look out of the body through the eyes. There were three windows in this woman's house; the number Three is the most creative and talented of all the numbers. Therefore, this dream suggested that she was about to experience a rebirth, a new outlook on life that would be extremely creative. Her talents and abilities would come to the front and be recognized (these windows were on the front of the house facing the street). As you can see from this dream, it is important to recognize numbers in your dream as important symbols as well as objects, people, events and moods.

The different levels of the house have special meanings as well. Dreams of the basement or lower levels often reflect the subconscious. Unless you have a playroom or workshop there, this is a part of the house to which you seldom go. The basement is often dark, musty and dusty. Symbolically, it contains those deeper aspects of yourself that you seldom look at. It is your subliminal world, the underworld of mythology, a place where certain archetypes are often found.

Sample dream: As a child, I had a recurring dream in which the cellar of the home we lived in played a part. The cellar was dirt with a narrow passageway that ran under another section of the house. This passageway was more like a tunnel because of the narrowness, dirt walls and lack of light.

It was my job to shovel coal into the furnace at the foot of the stairs several times a day. I was terrified of that dark place, especially in the evening. Sure some terrible monster would leap out at me from the inky black passageway, I would grab the shovel and frantically heave the coal into the furnace as quickly as I could before racing back up the stairs to the first floor, the light and safety.

In my dream, however, the drama was enacted differently. I would creep down the cellar stairs, begin shoveling with dispatch, and just as I feared, the worst happened. A shrieking witch, dressed in black, leapt out toward me from the passageway. I turned in mute terror, raced up the bulkhead steps into the backyard, and ran as if my life depended upon it because, in the dream, it did. My escape was very labored, as if I were running neck-deep in water. Finally I raced into the center of town and through the front door of my house — safe at last. Our house was actually in a wooded section on the outskirts of town, but in my dreams I always found my front door in the center of the town.

Words cannot describe the terror this repetitive dream inspired in me when I was a child. Now I realize that this dream portrayed my youthful inability to cope with certain aspects of my life, so I repressed them. I was chased by the repressed feminine side — my mother, my self — until I arrived in the middle of town (a place of visibility) and entered my front door. The front door is a direct, visible route to the house. This was a promise that these elements would be resolved and integrated into myself when I was able to consciously and visibly view them as an adult.

In this case, the witch was a model of a mother whose rejection of the maternal role threatened to devour my search for feminine identity. She was a dangerous role model — not a figure to emulate — and until I faced that undesirable feminine aspect of myself, I would never be able to express my own femininity positively.

We are chased in our dreams by those things we need to face and examine. We cannot reject them. Rather, we must assimilate them into ourselves in a loving and understanding manner. I do not remember when I stopped having that dream but, the fact that I did and it was not replaced by another similarly frightening one was an encouraging sign.

Finding treasures beneath the first floor level in a house is a good indication of subliminal talents, abilities and parts of the self that need to be brought up, exposed to the light of understanding, then used in beneficial ways. A dream of this sort may indicate that you have talents — a treasure cache — you are not aware of but from which you can draw.

Look at these lower levels in your dream houses as you would in your normal waking hours. For instance, most furnaces — the central heating system for the entire house — are in the basement. Your dream furnace could be your stomach into which fuel is pumped to produce energy to maintain your body temperature and life-support systems. Remember the man's dream above, in which the house had a clogged furnace.

Symbolically, we could say that our present attitudes are the results of conditionings that are stored below conscious awareness, in the cellar. These are traits and actions that occur spontaneously without our conscious knowledge. Some people have root cellars where garden foods such as squash and potatoes are stored for the winter, foods that nourish when the winds blow cold and the snows are deep. This analogy suggests that a cellar can symbolize a subconscious in which lies a storehouse of nourishment for times of stress and hardship. It is also a place from which to draw spiritual nourishment.

Some cellars are empty; the space is wasted and unused. An empty but clean cellar could indicate someone who is organized and efficient but does not necessarily do much in-depth thinking about his or her own life. An empty and dirty cellar, on the other hand, could suggest that it is time for a thorough cleansing and for taking a serious look at what has been accomplished up to that time in the dreamer's life.

Dream basements that are untidy, cluttered and unkept could indicate a subconscious that is full of potential, but is not organized. The dreamer has many resources available, if s/he would take the time to sort out and file the contents of the subconscious into compartments.

Laundry rooms, workshops and playrooms in the basement are certainly active places. Washing and scrubbing laundry in a dream basement could be a positive sign that the person is in the process of "cleaning up his/her act." Activity in a dream basement workshop suggests a searching mind, one that is trying to understand why things are said and done, why life is the way it is and what can be done to improve it. This is an examination of the "construction" of life. And a basement playroom in a dream may suggest a more playful and relaxed attitude upon the dreamers's part when approaching the contents of the subconscious.

If the lower levels of a dream house represent the subconscious, it stands to reason that ground levels or first floors can symbolize the conscious, waking mind. Architecture varies around the country and the world, but in some respects we all look at these levels in the same ways. The first floor is the center of activity during the daylight, conscious, waking hours. (Even in one-story houses, this still applies since usually the bedrooms and bathrooms are set away from the main entrances.)

It seems logical, then, that upper floors can indicate the higher levels of awareness, the higher consciousness. Note that we instinctively look up when calling upon higher forces. Bedrooms and bathrooms often are located on second floors. In the former we spend time dreaming, reading, changing clothes and engaging in sexual activity. In the latter, we cleanse our bodies outside through washing and inside through elimination. All these activities can have uplifting and spiritual connotations so, when we have dreams about the upper levels of the home, we should consider this possible meaning.

Attics contain items that we do not use frequently or articles that are old-fashioned and out-of-style, yet we still don't want to throw those things away. We also store our keepsakes and treasures in the attic. One rainy day we might end up sitting on the attic floor, among boxes and papers and ribbons, pouring through an old album or running a loving hand over grandmother's wedding dress. In your dreams, the attic is a good place through which to rummage, looking for treasure. It is also the highest place in your home therefore, it can represent your highest thoughts and aspirations.

The next step is to consider what kind of activity occurs in the different rooms. Each room has its unique expression and you do not find yourself there in your dream by chance. Think about what that room means to you in your waking hours.

The kitchen: For some people, the kitchen is a place of joy, companionship and camaraderie, much of which stems from the fact that we eat there, and eating gives us a sense of security, taking us back to those early moments at our mothers' breasts. We feel warm, loved and safe. This is why frustrated or lonely people tend to overeat — it gives them a subliminal feeling of security and belonging.

Some years ago, I was racing about the kitchen getting everyone ready for school and work. When I finally got around to fixing my daughter Sarah's hair, she said, "Mom, you're really lucky, you know. You can stay home in the kitchen and cook all day." Ah, happiness is surely in the eye of the beholder.

The point is, to Sarah the kitchen is a place to cook and eat; to me, it is a place to write; for someone else it may be the center for Brownie and Cub Scout meetings or to visit with friends. You need to consider the room in relation to the activities you associate with it.

Sample dream: A rather hefty man dreamt that his kitchen floor was sagging in one corner. This is a rather obvious notice that he should change his eating habits because his foundation (the floor) is weakening.

Sample dream: A young woman, unsure of her upcoming marriage, dreamt she was kneading bread in the kitchen. Bread is the staff of life; the kitchen a place of nourishment, love and security; and kneading bread is a pun on the word "need." She needed this young man. He would give her the nourishing love and security that she needed, the "bread" of life.

The living room: My daughter, April, her husband, Dixon, and little boy, Joshua, stayed with us one winter. April walked through the kitchen while I was researching this section of the dream book. Since I was looking for additional ideas on activities that take place in the living room, I asked her, "What goes on in the living room?" With a sly grin, April replied, "Do you mean when you're here or when you're not here?"

Just the word living gives us a clue to associations with this room. Frequently, dreams that take place in the living room relate to activities that we perform during our waking or living hours. We also entertain in a living room, so for some people it may be a more formal part of the home. In one sense, this room can represent the more formal but entertaining part of ourselves — the persona, personality or mask — the part we present to the general public, the part that wants to please and be accepted, to fit in, the part that is used to getting what it wants. (The outside of the house also can represent this part of the self.)

If you tend to be a more private person and do not entertain much, your living room can still indicate your general approach to life through your daily routine, even though it is not as obvious to others.

Each of us has a persona or mask of sorts, even though we may not be conscious of it. This mask features the ingrained traits stemming from early childhood conditioning and perhaps from the many lives lived before this one. This mask is not necessarily intentional, or necessarily good or bad, it just is — it is part of us.

When examining the living room in your dream, you might also consider the decor. The way you decorate each room is an indication of your approach to that part of yourself. I know a woman whose living room is thickly carpeted in rust brown. The couches are a matching print velour, soft to the touch. Drapes cover the windows and one wall is lined with books. The room is soft and inviting but also very private — notice that the windows are covered so that one cannot see in from the street too easily. Her persona or mask is reflected here. She is a private person who likes to keep relationships running smoothly. She selects her friends carefully, but those who are her friends feel warm and welcome. She is well-grounded (shown by her choice of earth colors) and likes mental stimulation (the books). You can analyze your dream rooms in the same manner.

The bedroom: A variety of activities occur here. We sleep, refreshing and repairing our bodies physically and mentally. We dream, touching part of ourselves that we cannot reach at any other time. We enjoy intimate sexual relationships with those we love. We dress and undress. Some people like to read in bed. Others find the bedroom a refuge in times of stress. This room takes us furthest from the outer world. The bedroom is also the most personal room in many respects, not only because we engage in intimate activity there, but also because we keep intimate possessions in our closets and bureaus. The dream bedroom, therefore, symbolizes a place of refuge, pleasure/sex, hidden activities and truth.

A friend told me that in the beginning of her difficult divorce, she spent most of the day in bed, under the covers, with the bedroom door shut. It was the only place she felt safe, where she could escape her overwhelming outer-world problems. She realized that this action related to her childhood experience of crawling into bed with her parents during a storm or after a frightening dream.

I often wonder if the illnesses that take us to bed are not connected with this subjective need to escape what we feel are unsolvable or overwhelming problems in the objective world. In conjunction with escape, there is a need to be nurtured and cared for, to leave all responsibilities behind. And perhaps the length of the illness is in direct proportion to the length of time we need in order to be regenerated mentally, until we feel we have received enough love and attention. This does not negate or lessen the illness. It is real, as real as the need for attention behind it.

I once read of laboratory tests conducted on monkeys. Baby monkeys were given a choice — they could go to the mother who would feed them but not love them, or to the mother who would give them all the nurturing they needed but was not able to feed them. They chose the loving mother and died of starvation. My personal feelings aside about these kinds of experiments, the evidence showed conclusively that to the monkeys love and attention are more important than life itself.

Humans react in a similar fashion, according to cancer radiologists Dr. Carl Simonton and his wife. I heard Mrs. Simonton lecture in Boston some years ago. She claimed that the reason women between thirty-five and forty-five have the highest percentage of breast cancer is because they feel they are no longer needed by their families. Their children are grown or almost grown, their husbands often are involved in their careers, and suddenly the women no longer feel necessary. (The breast, of course, is the part of the body that does the nurturing, a significant factor. In ancient and primitive cultures, the Great Mother was portrayed with large, full breasts.) A diagnosis of cancer may bring attention and assurances from family members, which is what these women wanted all along, but felt they could not ask for legitimately because it was "selfish."

So, the bedroom can be symbolic of the need to repair the body, either physically or mentally. The message to the dreamer is "rest."

The room where we dress and undress, the bedroom is a place of truth — the naked truth. Moments of truth are also indicated by the fact that we sleep and dream in our beds. Dreams can point out our strengths and weaknesses in the most graphic and sometimes comical ways. Consider the dream of the man embracing a bull in his bed. Perhaps he was too preoccupied with sex or was treating his partner in a rough and animal-like manner. This is no one's judgment but his own. It was his dream and, at some level within himself, he was reacting to his current sexual attitudes and performances.

The intimate items in our bedrooms reflect intimate feelings and emotions we often hide from one another. Hidden elements here differ from those obscure items found in the basement. Bedroom items often refer to personal relationships because of the nature of the room. The basement or lower level's hidden aspects can encompass more of the self, representing your entire foundation rather than just one aspect.

If you make reading in bed a nightly habit, certain kinds of bedroom dreams can indicate a period of learning and experience in your life.

The bathroom: Obviously, cleansing is the main activity carried on in the bathroom. We take showers or baths, shave, shampoo our hair, clean and trim our finger- and toenails, brush our teeth and eliminate wastes from out bodies. I sometimes visualize the bathroom as a rather portly hovering mother with an eagle's eye and a hen's temperament, conducting a head-to-foot inspection, inside and out. All the day's dirt must be washed away before going off to bed. And, in a sense, dreams of bathrooms do indicate the need to remove the day's dirt, a need to purify our bodies, to eliminate the toxins that can clog and poison our bodies and minds.

Sample dream: One of my clients had a repetitive dream for ten years. In it, she was supposed to move into a smaller house but she did not want to. In this new house she found an extra bedroom and bathroom on the second floor that she did not originally know were there.

If the house represents the body, then she was being urged repeatedly to move into a smaller body, to diet and lose weight. Her refusal to do so made it necessary for the dream to repeat for ten years. The extra bedroom indicated the need to give her body a rest, to allow it to rejuvenate and rebuild by reducing her food intake. She was overworking her digestive system. The bathroom symbolized the removal of toxins that was so necessary if she was to regain and then maintain her health. She admitted she had been going to a doctor for ten years — the length of time she had this dream — and she was having a difficult time staying on the diet the doctor had prescribed for her.

Bathroom dreams may suggest that the mind needs a thorough cleansing as well. You have heard the expression, "His mind is in the gutter." If you dreamt that your head was in the toilet, the message should be clear. Thoughts come from the head, and if your head is in the toilet bowl, then your thoughts are not pure. Soiled thoughts can be sexual in nature, but too often we judge others to be immoral only if their sexual attitudes and actions are different from ours. In my mind, morality has nothing to do with sexual attitudes per se, but rather represents the principles upon which we should build our lives — honesty, tolerance, compassion and love. Therefore, besides sexual acts that the dreamer perceives as negative, soiled thoughts can also relate to underhanded business dealings, hurtful talk about friends and neighbors, turning your back on someone in need, and so on. Again, these principles are very personal and may be entirely different for you than for another.

Closets: Phrases and clichés like "the closets of your mind," "skeletons in the closet" and "closet-queen" refer to places, things and people involved in dark, hidden activities. Often there is no light in a closet, which makes the hidden things that occur in this spot different from those that happen in the bedroom and basement. We reach into the closet, grab a garment and close the door. Not much time is spent there. These dark cubicles can be mysterious to a child.

I can remember, long ago, looking into a dark closet where clothes hung side-by-side like soldiers, pairs of shoes lined the floor and various hats sat on the top shelf. My impression was one of faceless, disembodied beings, suspended lifelessly, waiting for a hand to reach in and give them life. Perhaps this is where the expression "skeletons in the closet" comes from.

In the closet, we put away bits and pieces of our personalities (clothes) to be drawn out at a later time when we need them for some planned purpose. If this sounds shrouded and devious, it is only because we somehow associate negativity with closets when we talk about skeletons hanging out in there. The clothes we store in our closets are the bits and pieces we use to portray ourselves to others. At times we fool ourselves into thinking that the clothes are the real us, and that is when the skeletons rattle. We hide what we think are the real parts of ourselves in our "dream" closet, the clothes we would really like to wear, but don't because others would not like or approve of us. We know that "if they only knew," they really wouldn't approve of us.

Hidden rooms: People frequently dream of finding rooms that they did not know existed in a house. More often than not, the discovery is elating and exciting. One man occasionally finds himself in the same situation, in an unfamiliar house with many rooms. With extreme delight, he opens door after door leading through a labyrinth of rooms, each more beautiful than the last. He is an inquisitive individual, with a good mind and a desire to increase his knowledge. These dreams occur when he is the most creative, almost as if his inner self were encouraging him to go on, to explore his present concepts and line of thinking further, to "open new doors." His consciousness is growing; he is seeking inner beauty and strength of character.

I remember a few such dreams of being in a magnificent house with large elegant rooms, spiral staircases, rich furnishings. In them, I run from room to room feeling as if it is "all a dream" because it is so beautiful. After such an experience, I do not want to wake up, but wish I could remain in that fairytale place. These dreams stay with me for a long time. I can understand why the Bible says, "In my Father's house there are many mansions." These dream mansions are the compartments of our minds that we usually have no contact with during our waking hours, but at night, during sleep and dreaming, the conscious mind is "off duty," and the subconscious, creative, intuitive side takes over, leading us on a guided tour of the many mansions within us, where we can view the beauty that is the true self. And no matter how low we sink, those mansions await us.

Air

The air element represents all forms of communication. Before speaking, we open our mouths to take in air. Singers must develop large lung capacities for holding air. Air is the medium for transmitting radio and television signals. Some say that telepathic transmissions occur on the air waves. In mythological lore, birds were the bringers of messages. Mercury, messenger of the goddesses and gods, has winged feet. And spiritual tradition speaks of the "breath" of Divinity and of Divinity speaking messages of truth to mortals.

Human beings are symbols of communication in our dreams. The people we meet in dreamland are often fragments of our own psyches that take the form of other individuals. It is not the person in the dream that is important, but rather your relationship with that person that the subconscious is trying to emphasize.

Friends and relatives: A dream of Aunt Harriet may have nothing to do with her; more likely, it concerns how you feel about her. If you see a loving and nurturing aunt, then those qualities should be part of the dream's interpretation. If, on the other hand, you think of her as mean, aloof or stingy, then you must apply these traits to the dream's meaning. In such a case, you might want to examine your own actions and thoughts of the previous day or days, your present state of mind, the things that have been pressing on you recently, to determine if you acted in the same manner as the dream person. Was that dream person really you in disguise? Could it be that your conscious mind does not want to accept your own faults, therefore the subconscious cleverly projects them onto others in the dream so that you will not repress the information but accept it upon waking?

It is human nature to see and accept the faults of others more quickly than our own. Conversely, in a dream, the subconscious may present an individual we view as possessing positive traits in an attempt to encourage us to act in the same manner.

Sample dream: I had a dream that graphically supports this theory. Some preliminary information: One of my daughters is caring, helpful and considerate, but also excitable, moody and often quick to retort. She had said a few things that made me angry, but I held my tongue because I knew if I said anything in anger I would be sorry later. During the next few hours, I carried on a silent, rather heated mental conversation with her about my feelings. That evening my husband and I went to the movies to see "Private Benjamin," starring Goldie Hawn. In the movie, Goldie is dominated by her orthodox, loving but insensitive parents who do not try to understand their daughter's feelings and needs. Goldie falls in love with a Frenchman who is carefree and relaxed about love and life — an attitude Goldie has trouble comprehending.

I went to bed with these things on my mind and had the following dream. I held my youngest daughter, Sarah, by the hand. In the dream she was a toddler instead of her present age. Because her legs were unsteady, I had to help her down a stairway into a children's clothing store located in a basement. At the foot of the stairs was a narrow hallway with small cubicles on each side. The place was teeming with people, and almost all the clothes had been sold. All that remained on the racks were French-designed clothes that seemed too sophisticated for a child. There were three saleswomen: Judy and Frances — women I know — and a third unknown woman. Judy was standing in the hall telling Frances how ridiculous the owner's taste was in clothes and how obvious it was from the clothes left on the racks that no one wanted those styles. Frances gazed off as if she were only half listening. It seemed clear that she was not interested in taking part in the criticism. Sarah, who then appeared to be her present age, found a tan jumper and matching coat she liked. The tag read: $11.50. I realized the price was good but was not sure if I would buy it.

The first correspondence to the scenario of events from the previous day are the dream names Judy and Frances, puns relating to the movie: Judy was the name of the character Goldie Hawn played in the movie, and France-es related to her French boyfriend. In the dream, I played the role of an objective part of mind that had my ego (little Sarah) by the hand because it was acting immature, childish, toddling around on an unstable foundation (little legs). My mind led my immature side (Sarah) down into the subconscious (basement) where much activity was taking place (people milling around). Clothes, as mentioned earlier, can represent the persona, mask or personality. Most of the clothes were sold, gone — the mask had been nearly stripped away.

Judy, the saleswoman who was criticizing, represented my criticism of my daughter the day before. Judy, like the Jewish parents who would not listen to their daughter's needs, represented my inability at that moment to hear or see beyond my daughter's actions to the needs that motivated those actions.

I saw Frances as that part of myself that takes all things with a grain of salt — life is too short so relax, enjoy and be more loving — attitudes we attribute to the French (a relaxed nation of lovers).

The strange thing is, Judy's critical attitude and Frances' relaxed manner are part of the way I see these two women in actuality. They played themselves as well as portraying the sound of their names which, in this dream, also happened to fit into the previous evening's movie plot.

The third unknown woman may be the observer in each of us, who looks on unemotionally, observing the actions, knowing in her omniscience that everything is alright. Also, you often come across three people in a dream because .Three represents the trinity of body, mind and soul, the three parts of the self trying to reach some kind of balance and harmony through interaction with each other.

In my dream, my immature side (Sarah) becomes a little older as she is about to make a choice. This showed my willingness to think about taking on the responsibility for my actions (I was beginning to grow up).

The price tag of $11.50 also was significant. The number 11 indicated looking inward in order to bring about cooperation and harmony, standing back rather than rushing into a situation. The number 50 (5) showed a need to make decisions and then changes in my behavior. Five also is the number of communication. The final hesitancy to "buy it" (the outfit) was my final resistance to accepting responsibility for my behavior. Tan, an earth color, indicated a need to "put on" a down-to-earth, sensible attitude about this situation.

The dovetailing ability of dreams is beautifully illustrated here. Not only did the saleswomen reflect women I actually know, but their names also were a play on the nationalities in the movie I had just seen. The numbers — the three women and the price tag of $11.50 — also provided valuable information to help me interpret the dream.

Babies and the elderly: Babies, as well as very old people, are symbolic of new beginnings and final transitions. In effect, they are interchangeable since they happen at the same "time." In other words, a thing cannot die and leave a void. When something dies, something else is born at the same moment. When we close one door, another opens. When we die from this life, we are born into another level of existence, and when we are born into this life, we die from another plane of awareness. When we marry, we die as single individuals and are born anew as couples.

Sample dream: A friend of mine dreamt she was trying to dismember a chicken in her kitchen sink. Suddenly it turned into a baby. Horrified, she recoiled at her actions. Her interpretation of this dream related to her habit of analyzing everything in her life. At the time of this dream, she had the flickerings of a new idea but, rather than look at it as an idea complete in itself, she was dissecting it into its parts.

She realized from the dream her new concept was not something that could be broken up, rather it had to be used as a whole; the baby represented a whole new being, complete in itself. A baby is taken as it is, its dirty diapers as well as its spontaneous smiles. We do not isolate any one of these qualities, but realize that all these things make up a child. Therefore, infants may be a reflection of your need to be more accepting and trusting, or to be less critical and analytical, and willing to look at the whole.

It is perhaps obvious that babies represent new beginnings. The condition of the "dream baby" and the feelings you have about it indicate whether or not you are comfortable with the changes that are about to happen. Change is the keyword here, for certainly a new baby changes your life in many ways.

Very old people can symbolize wisdom or senility and, of course, much of the interpretation depends upon your association with the dream symbol. When my son was about thirteen years old, he made an observation about older people that was very wise for his years. "You know, Mom," he said to me, "kids make fun of older people, but if they stopped to think about it, they'd realize that old people have been around a long time and they've had lots of exciting things happen to them and they can tell you a lot." A parent's heart warms at such profundity.

The previous summer Matthew had been gardening with a neighbor who has lived quite a life. He's managed a farm, played professional baseball and flown airplanes. Matthew not only learned much from this elderly man, he genuinely liked and respected him, too, so Matthew views older people from a different perspective than most of his classmates.

If an elderly relative appears in your dream, first examine your relationship to that person. How would you describe that person? Use the description in analyzing the contents of your dream. If it does not seem to apply, then perhaps the dream does relate to that individual and you are picking up something that is going on in the life of your relative. You may or may not be involved with the person in actuality.

Often you pick up what the people you are close to are thinking or dreaming. For example, a woman and her father may dream similar things one night. I remember an instance of a woman who dreamt about a car that was in flames. The same night, her father also dreamt of a vehicle on fire. When you are closely connected to another individual, it is as if you are on the same wavelength, the same frequency, and you often pick up each others' thoughts.

In a dream, elderly people can represent change because older people are close to a transition point in their lives. If you dream of your ninety-year-old grandfather standing at a crossroads pointing in a certain direction, then you would expect imminent change — change because of the crossroads and the grandfather, and a change that was soon to happen because the elderly man is facing transition soon in his own life. This dream may have nothing to do with your grandfather; he may be a symbol in your mind for impending change.

When you dream of a wise old woman or a wise old man you are most likely dealing with something entirely different. Earlier, archetypes were mentioned, those universal symbols that arise from the unconscious. A wise old woman may be part of the Great Mother archetype, the wise old man comes from the Great Father figure. They represent the principle of guiding wisdom that speaks from within, the experience of the ages. Whenever we look upon the face of an aged and alert individual we see experience and wisdom etched there. We sense a knowing and we find comfort in that knowing. Such people represent a place of safety and refuge when we have problems we cannot seem to answer. We can ask them if what is troubling us ever happened to them and what they did in that situation. Although this attitude is not as prevalent today in our society as it used to be, it is an ingrained knowing that is hard to deny. Primitive cultures still revere their elderly as fonts of wisdom and experience. Perhaps one day "civilized" society will return to this ancient knowledge.

However, if the elderly in your dream do not appear in this manner, then the most logical approach is to ask what that person represents to you and go from there.

Teenagers: If, as an adult, you dream of teenagers, they can symbolize a part of you that is struggling to gain independence, yet wants to be accepted at the same time. Although we look back upon our teenage years as being carefree and full of fun, in reality, they can be a very painful and difficult period of adjustment in our lives. Teenagers are hyper-aware of their bodies and conscious of what others think of them. Everything in their lives is a crisis. They do not have the wisdom or experience to tell them that time will solve many things. They feel things have to be done now and that every pain they experience now is forever. So, when we dream of a teenager, we may be in a very vulnerable position, sensitive to the demands and judgments of others, yet struggling to gain some measure of freedom and independence.

It is important to remember that you are the author of your dream and if you visualize the teenage years as a carefree period of life, then you should use that interpretation when analyzing your dream.

Famous people: Well-known figures who visit our dreams can be archetypes in that they symbolize someone we emulate, an idealized member of the opposite sex, or the great mother or father image. An outstanding quality, trait or deed that you associate with a famous individual usually is one that you need to recognize within yourself. While we traditionally respect George Washington as our first president and father of our country, we also revere him as a truthful person because we remember that he could not tell a lie when his father asked who chopped down the cherry tree. Thus, as a dream figure, Washington may stand for the principle of honesty.

Sample dream: I recently had a dream in which Alan Alda took my hand and smiled at me. I told the three people who were with me in the dream that Mr. Alda and I were on the same set. My daughter, upon hearing this dream, exclaimed, "I know what that means. Alan Alda is a strong and outspoken advocate of women's rights. He is also very humorous."

I had this dream just as I finished writing a small book called *Broads and Narrows* which takes a humorous look at the sexual inequities in our language. My daughter felt that this dream was meant to encourage me to have faith in my book because Alan Alda had taken my hand (my hands type the manuscript) and smiled at me (given me his approval). Three is the number of expansion, creativity and joy. The book has since been printed.

Some famous figures who appear in your dreams have names that are actually puns, plays on words. (See the example of Vincent Price above.) Their names, not they themselves or their deeds, are significant in the dream.

As you delve deeper into numerology you will find that each name has a unique vibration that is an integral part of the individual or thing to which the name belongs. Your name tells what you are. A friend of mine who is knowledgeable in Indian lore says the Native Americans knew this. At the naming of every child, the tribe's chief, medicine man and the child's parents were present; they could only name the child after they had seen it. In their culture, names conveyed essences, truths about their owners, therefore the name had to fit the child. And the child became the name. I can picture the difference between a Sitting Bull, Running Deer and Laughing Brook, can't you? So, look at the meaning of your dream characters' names as well as the qualities these individuals represent.

A dream of singer/entertainer Cher, for example, could suggest a need to share; Talulah Bankhead — a head for monetary affairs; Rock Hudson — the strength of a rock or a rock head; Helen Reddy — a state of preparedness; Gregory Peck — hen-pecking; William Holden — the act of holding on, and so forth.

The names of relatives and neighbors can also be used in the same manner. A minister named Lovemore in a dream could convey the message to love more. Other names I can think of are: Failer — failure; Banks — save money; Chase — to chase or running around; Cook — to cook, perhaps as a means of nurturing; Carpenter — to build; Treat — to treat yourself; Moody — being moody, and so on. Color names such as White, Black, Brown and Green may reflect the attitudes or qualities that the colors symbolize.

Names also can reflect professions. In fact, in earlier days, people were named after their line of work — Carpenter, Parson, Woodman, Blacksmith (from which Black and Smith are derived). Since children in those days often followed their parents' line of work, they too became Carpenters and Parsons. So, today, we find people with names that match their professions such as L. Lines, author of *Solid Geometry*, Mary Breasted, author of *Oh! Sex Education*; Dr. Shuffle, a podiatrist in Washington, D.C.; Drs. Hands and Fingerman, two gynecologists in Boston; Anton Horner, a solo horn player with the Philadelphia Orchestra; Lionel Tiger, an anthropologist; Dr. Popp, a chiropractor; and Larry Speaks, White House spokesman under President Reagan.

My name, Dusty Bunker, describes my circumstances. A bunker is a small fortress dug into the hillside to protect a country against military invasion. I think of my home as a fortress, a place of security, and I defend it zealously. I am a well-organized person and keep my "bunker" neat, but dust, well, as Erma Bombeck once noted, "Such dust you wouldn't find on the moon." I have a dusty bunker!

A dream character with a name that relates to a profession may be a message about your career direction, or it could be an indication that your present activities and circumstances are somehow connected to that profession. Examine your thoughts and actions of the past few days and see if there is some relationship between the dream name and your current circumstances.

Strangers: Who are these shadowy, often faceless people you meet in your dreams? They seem to have no features, traits or mannerisms by which you can identify them. Strangers are often fragments of your own personality that have taken form in the dream to give you a message. Even if the figure is frightening and in pursuit, it is a friend because it comes to show you a facet of your psyche that you need to look at. Always keep in mind that you authored your dream, therefore you created this figure. If you created it, you can communicate with it.

If you have a recurring dream that contains a figure you cannot recognize, you can use the following technique to find out what the individual represents. Each night before you fall asleep tell yourself that if you have this particular dream, you will confront the stranger and ask it what it is doing in your dream.

In our dreams we often are chased by our own fears. These fears can take the form of strangers or frightening figures of any kind. Running away from these fears only compounds the problem, therefore it is wise to program yourself to be prepared to meet any frightening figures in your dreams so that you can determine what is undermining your effectiveness at that particular time in your life.

You also may meet a benevolent or casual stranger in your dream. If these figures appear in your dream, they are there for a reason. Use the same technique. Ask the individual what the message is.

Dreams of death and dead people/things: In my lectures I have often said that if every person who dies in our dreams died subsequently in reality, we would be orphans. Because we do not recall all our dreams, I am certain that many dreams of the deaths of our loved ones, neighbors, etc., escape our attention. Even so, many dreams of this type are remembered by people who are consciously trying to record their dreams. Death in a dream is almost always a symbol of something else. Usually it relates to one of three things: a change in a relationship, a change of attitude, or a warning. If you have a poor relationship with someone who subsequently dies in your dream, you may find that the relationship is about to improve — the negativity has died — or that the relationship is about to end. The tone of the dream should indicate which.

A death dream could relate to the death of an attitude that the dead person represents to us. If you see your neighbor as a tightwad, and in your dream he is strung up by a lynch mob in front of the local bank, you may conclude that the ungenerous, ungiving, unhelping part of yourself has just been lynched, done away with, killed, eliminated. You have changed, gone through a death, a transition, and if you scrutinize your current actions and attitudes, you may find this is true.

Sample dream: The following dream incorporates both death and a stranger. At a seminar, a man told the following repetitive dream. He and a man he did not know were roommates. Each night, his roommate went out into the city and murdered someone, then returned to their apartment. The dreamer knew of his roommate's nightly activities but did not want to get involved by informing the police. He felt cornered and frightened, and was becoming more fearful for his own safety with each passing night.

This man was friendly, but somewhat aloof and restrained. He came across as the intellectual, scientific type who needed logical reasons and explanations for everything he did and experienced. He said that he felt emotionally bottled up because of his factual mind, and he did not think it was proper or safe to let his emotional side loose. The stranger/roommate played the emotional side of himself, a side he did not recognize. Yet, in his dreams, he let it loose many times to roam the city (his consciousness) looking for victims. He was killing parts of himself by not getting involved (bottling up his feelings). He was the victim each night.

Some death dreams come to warn us that our present course of action could lead to trouble. The aggressive driver who dreams that s/he dies in a fiery automobile crash is being admonished to slow down or end up exactly that way. Most likely, the dreamer will slow down for a week or so because of this dream, which may be all s/he needs to get beyond a potentially dangerous future situation. Whenever we have this type of dream, we tend to be more careful regarding the dream conditions when we encounter them in waking life. The purpose of the dream is then fulfilled.

Some symbols become entrenched in some people's minds as symbols of actual physical body death. Occasionally, they do presage death. Some of the more common symbols are muddy water, crossing a river, stopped clocks, broken mirrors, birds and letters edged in black. If the dreamer accepts such a symbol as a harbinger of physical death, then it will become a death symbol for him/her. Such symbols have been established in their personal dream dictionaries, but for each person the symbol is different, and some people may not have one particular symbol. If you dream of one of the above mentioned symbols it does not necessarily mean death — unless you have established it as such.

Until I began studying dreams seriously, I did not have a conscious death symbol. Some experiences within the last few years, however, have led me to think that I may have recently adopted a common death expression as my personal symbol. A few weeks before my stepmother died, I dreamt I received a letter from her sister. It was edged in black. I made note of this in my dream notebook. A telephone call two weeks later informed me of her death.

One September a few years ago, I dreamt I was reading a letter from my stepfather. I noticed a small black smudge in the bottom left-hand corner. Again, I recorded this dream. Three months later I found out, quite by accident, that he had died the previous August. Because of a strange set of circumstances, I was not notified. I had that dream a month after he died but no one in my household and no one I associated with had any knowledge of his passing. Perhaps the smudge of black indicated that the message would not be clear or timely.

A friend of mine knows that whenever she dreams of a faceless body lying in a coffin, within a few hours she will be notified of a death. Her daughter dreamt of a skull and crossbones on two occasions, both times on mornings that family members died.

Shortly before his assassination, Abraham Lincoln had a number of dreams that foretold his own death. The dreams incorporated common death symbols. In one, he dreamt that he entered the Capitol rotunda when a national funeral was in progress. The guard told him that the President had died. Lincoln was the President.

Just before he died, Lincoln dreamt three times that he was in a boat on a large rolling river and that he was falling in. (This is closely linked to the mythological ferryman Charon who transported dead souls across the River Styx to the underworld.) The day of the evening that Lincoln attended Ford's Theater, he commented to a number of associates: "Gentlemen, something extraordinary will happen, and that very soon."

If family members, friends or famous personalities that have died appear in your dream, again you must ask yourself what those persons represent to you. If an individual was a nurturing figure for you, then s/he has appeared in your dream to nurture you through some unsettling situation in your life. Whether the person appearing in your dream is symbolic or is actually that individual reaching out to you through time and space, no one can prove. The point is that you are being comforted by a figure you trust. The message has been transmitted and the effect is the same.

Other common symbols in dreams are those which involve the human body. The separate parts of the body indicate the way we think, understand and transmit our understanding.

Hair: Since hair grows out of our heads, it often represents the process of thought. The length, quality, condition and color of your dream hair suggests the thoughts that are behind or under it. Gorgeous shades of healthy hair indicate a positive use of the attitudes we associate with the color of the hair, whereas that same color hair, frizzled and unkept, indicates misuse. Long, black shiny hair suggests that you are delving into the mysteries of life with positive results. A dream of two people, one with black hair, the other with white, may symbolize an attempt to look at everything in terms of black and white, an extremist view of life. The number Two (two people) suggests a need to compromise.

Red hair may present thoughts of passion or activities that require additional spurts of energy. Blonde hair, golden as the sun, emphasizes the qualities we associate with the sun: optimism, gaiety, happiness, light, understanding. The quality of your dream hair represents the quality of your thoughts. When Samson was shorn of his curly locks, he lost his physical strength.

Actually, the story of Samson and Delilah revolves around the setting of the Sun. Samson means "sun god," and Delilah means "she who makes weak." Each evening, the Sun is pulled down under the Earth by the night; its rays are cut. This is the true story behind Samson having his hair cut. It does indicate the loss of the Sun's strength during the night when the moon takes precedence.

Eyes: Dreams of the eyes can relate to an need to look at something more carefully, to examine the fine print, to look beyond the surface. Such dreams can also be extremely spiritual and uplifting. When asked who are you, Divinity said, "I am." When we are asked who we are, we say, "I am Dusty" or "I am Carole" or "I am Matthew." What we are really saying is that our names are Divine Carole, Divine Matthew. The "I am" represents the divine within us. And because we pronounce "I" and "eye" the same way, we sometimes use them interchangeable in our dreams.

Sample dream: Starr Daily, author of *Love Can Open Prison Doors,* was a repeat offender finally confined to prison for twenty years without hope of parole. Because of his rebellious behavior, he ended up in solitary confinement. As he lay sick on the cold floor, staring up at the black ceiling, he realized that this was the end of the line. He was in prison for what amounted to a life sentence at his age — in solitary confinement, totally alone and sick. He could sink no lower. Then one night he had a dream. In it, Jesus stood in a garden before him. His lips moved as in prayer. His eyes enveloped Daily in a love he had never known. As the figure faded, the word Love appeared in misty letters where Christ had stood.

This incident changed Daily's life. Through a slow and disciplined process, he rehabilitated himself, gained an early release from prison and went on to lecture and write books that inspired many thousands of people.

A friend of mine was sitting in the audience as Starr Daily walked down the aisle to a podium to speak. She said she had never felt such a wave of love sweep over her as when he passed her aisle seat. The point of this story is that the eyes, which are often called "the windows of the soul," transmitted a deeply felt message. Starr Daily was told that he was loved. The eyes of Christ asked nothing of him, demanded nothing from him. They just said, I love you. Those eyes flooded Daily's mind and soul with insight, understanding, compassion and wisdom.

Hands: Hands are the most obvious way in which we communicate. We recognize that hands are a symbol of service when we say "lend a helping hand." An open hand, stretched out to join with another, is a sign of friendship, acceptance and warmth. Our hands stroke and fondle a child or loved one, give comfort to the sick and aid to the needy.

A closed hand is aloof or restrained, a fist defiant, indicating a "hands off" attitude. We gesticulate or pantomime our thoughts with our hands. You must know people who would have trouble talking if their hands were tied behind their backs. Motioning with our hands is a natural part of communicating. When you dream of wearing precious rings or bracelets, you can be sure that the kind of service you offer is highly prized by your inner self.

Feet: Feet are the foundation of the body, the part upon which you stand. In this respect, they represent the condition of your stability. Dreams of tiny feet under a huge body certainly suggest an imbalance in the dreamer's basic foundation. Feet that are much too large for the body could indicate that the dreamer places too much emphasis on security to the exclusion of growth in other areas of life.

If you had an important decision to make that would greatly alter your present circumstances and you asked your dreams for guidance and the answer you received was a picture of yourself standing in front of the bus station with roots growing out of your feet deep into the ground, the solution would be clear. You are not going to budge. The change is not for you.

We move from one place to another on our feet, so dreams of feet can indicate a new journey or direction in life. Or, such dreams may mean that you are treading the same path in your dream that you have been on before. This could suggest that you examine the path to determine whether to stay on it or change direction. Other symbols in the dream as well as how you feel when you awaken should tell you whether the direction is right or wrong for you.

Skin: Your skin, as the largest organ of elimination in your body, may be a symbol of your ability to let go of the toxins or the negativity in your life. Clogged pores, pimples, boils and the like suggest festering thoughts that are plugging up your physical/mental processes. A good fast, cleansing your body inside and out, letting go of all the negative thoughts and feelings about yourself and others, will help eliminate this problem and give you a "peaches and cream" complexion and attitude. The mind and the body are intimately connected so that what we do to one we do to the other. When we clean and discipline our bodies, we clean and discipline our minds. Dreams relating to condition of the skin often refer to this phenomenon.

Animals: We communicate to and through the animals we choose as our companions. In the Walt Disney film, "101 Dalmatians," one scene shows different kinds of people walking their dogs. The comical thing about this scene is that the owners look exactly like their animals. This is not as far fetched as you might think, because the things we choose to own, such as our automobiles, are an extension of our personalities. Animals fall into this category, too. Think about people you know and the types of animals they keep.

My husband favors German shepherds which are sleek, dark strong animals. He is dark, slender and very strong, and exercises daily to keep himself healthy. I tend to favor English sheepdogs who, my husband tells me, have the same hairdo I have. My mother-in-law loves collies. I remember seeing her sitting in her car with her collie, who was also in the front seat. She has beautiful smooth hair and, that day, she had on a coat with a large fur collar. From the back, they looked identical.

The point of this is that we assign human qualities to animals, using them as symbols of the way humans act and think. We might "roar like a lion" or be as "meek as a lamb." We have moments of being as "stubborn as a mule," "busy as a bee," "sly as a fox" or "eager as a beaver." These creatures indicate ways in which we choose to think or act at any particular moment as well as the way others see us. Dreams may incorporate animals as symbols to reveal our human qualities. A dream of your mate with the body of a human and the head of a bull is a perfect description of his or her being "bull-headed."

As always, you must ask yourself what the symbol means to you. If you have a particular association with a creature that is different than what the dream books say, you should use your own interpretation. It is your dream.

Sample dream: A friend of mine had a dream that she was going on vacation but, at the last minute, changed her mind because she could

not leave her cat behind. Cats can be symbols of wisdom, agility, independence and mystery. In ancient Egypt they were considered sacred. In the
Middle Ages, when Christianity had gained a foothold, the cat was associated with those witches who still worshipped the Goddess Freya whose
chariot was drawn by two large white cats. Since the Christian church was
trying to convert everyone to the Father-God, they conveniently overlooked the fact that Freya was the Goddess of love. In the witchcraft trials
of the Middle Ages, her followers were accused of every sort of diabolical
magic such as flying to their meetings on broomsticks, often accompanied
by their familiars, their cats. Cats today still retain an aura of mystery.

Before applying the universal meaning of a cat to my friend's dream,
I first asked what the cat meant to her. She replied that it was like a member of the family and required a lot of work. So, in this case, a cat meant
work and responsibility. This woman did not want to go on vacation because she did not want to leave her work. This is a good example of what
I have been saying throughout this book — when analyzing your dream,
you must ask yourself what the symbol means to you before you apply
the universal meaning.

Dogs are dependent creatures, our "best friends," faithful, loyal and
long-enduring. Research has shown that because men have the need to
dominate, they favor dogs; dogs can be controlled. Women, on the other
hand, favor cats because women generally are less concerned with domination. Have you ever tried to get a cat to heel?

Water

Water is the universal solvent. Given enough time, it can dissolve even
granite. It is the most viable and changeable element, taking three different forms: solid (ice — Scorpio), liquid (Cancer) and gas (steam, fog —
Pisces). In liquid form, it adapts to any container and flows in the direction
of least resistance. It can cleanse, destroy or, through inactivity, become
stagnant. Two-thirds of our planet is water.

Symbolically, we can apply these descriptions of the three different
states of water to the part of our psyche that water represents: the emotions. Our emotions are a universal solvent. Given enough time, a caring
attitude can dissolve the hardest heart. Our emotions take these forms:
cold, frigid and icy (solid); flowing, adaptable and giving (liquid); fiery,
eruptable and blistering (steam), or vague and uneasy (fog).

At their most positive, our emotions are adaptable and moving,
cleansing and refreshing. Flowing emotions, like flowing water, can
cleanse the body and the mind. Like water, emotions can run shallow or
deep.

Contained emotions and feelings can create stagnant conditions and ultimately disease. We must learn to release our feelings properly or they can "blow up" and scald us and others. Medical sources claim that our bodies are predominately fluid (we are basically emotional creatures) and that most of our diseases are psychosomatic, a result of unfulfilled emotional needs.

Weather: Like emotions, the weather is unpredictable in many parts of the world, therefore we tend to use weather conditions in dreams as symbols of our emotional conditions. Terms like "stormy seas," "rough sailing," and "ill winds" can be indications of mind states and, even if they symbolize the actual state of affairs in our lives, they show our emotional perception of the events. Expressions like "smooth sailing," "calm seas," and "clear skies" signify peaceful states of mind.

Whenever you encounter weather in your dreams, ask yourself what it means to you. How does it affect the mood of the dream and does it suggest your current attitude toward a particular situation in your life?

Sample dream: A woman dreamt that she sat on a beach watching large waves breaking on the shoreline. In the distance she could see small children dressed in snowsuits standing on the crest of the waves, laughing and joking as they rode them in toward the beach. The woman was both amazed and frightened for the children.

During analysis, she explained that she does not like the ocean. To her it represented a rhythmic flow to which she could not adapt her own life. She found it difficult to be emotionally adaptable, therefore she found the constant rhythm of the ocean an uncomfortable reminder of her rigidity. The children symbolized an unquestioning faith that she needed to adopt — children will believe anything. We are told that we must have the faith of small child if we are to discover what is possible for us. It was the children's faith that allowed them to ride the waves without sinking. Their snowsuits represented her view of such a believing attitude. Clothes, as you recall, signify the persona, the outer mask, the personality and how we appear to others. The children's innocent attitude seemed inappropriate to her just as it was inappropriate for the children to be wearing snowsuits while riding the waves. But the tots were happy and carefree, unconcerned about the conditions that she viewed as dangerous. This dream came to tell her to adopt a more childlike attitude toward life, to be more emotionally flexible and carefree.

Clear skies indicate a clear view of life, free from obstacles and obstructions. Fair weather clouds, those big puffy white cotton patches that often adorn the summer sky, may bring pleasant messages or creative ideas that need to be absorbed and utilized.

Sample dream: A woman asked if she were making spiritual progress, and had a dream that featured applauding hands emerging from the clouds. This was a perfect answer to her questions about her progress.

But be aware that even pleasant, puffy white dream clouds can be obstacles to growth if they represent an attitude of laziness and complacency. Then you are in danger of stagnation through egotism or the silver-spoon-in-the-mouth syndrome.

Clouds can indicate a gathering of activity that portends difficult conditions. Dark, threatening clouds suggest internal conflict. When storm clouds gather on the horizon, there is trouble ahead if the dreamer does not examine the cause of those clouds and the emotional content that formed them. Clouds also interfere with our ability to see into the distance, so whether the dream experience is pleasant or not, the dreamer should realize that it is important to understand the reason for the clouds existence.

Of course, if you love storms because they provide excitement in your life and make you feel more alive, then the storm symbols may indicate a state of mind that is necessary for you in order to accomplish your goals. We are supposedly more alive when faced with danger and death than at any other time. Perhaps for you, storms signify this stimulus.

The Sun: The Sun creates weather conditions as well. Without the Sun, life as we know it on this planet would not exist. The Sun warms the soil and our bodies, provides the impetus for new life and growth, and is a source of inspiration and faith as it rises each morning with its promise of eternalness. But, as with all things, it must be used in moderation. Anyone who has suffered from a painful sunburn knows what I mean. The Sun can create a lush tropical paradise with food in abundance or a stark parched desert where the balance of life changes minute by minute under scorching heat.

Desert landscapes have been robbed of their moisture, their water, their emotional content, and are left dry and arid. Constant dreams of deserts can indicate that you feel emotionally arid, parched and drained of all emotion.

Analysis of this kind must be approached with caution, though. Walt Disney's fine film, ''The Living Desert,'' changed many people's concept of these ''forsaken'' lands. After viewing this film, I realized how alive the desert is, how beautiful and captivating its creatures, and how awe inspiring the depth of life that lies beneath its silent, harsh surface.

When fire suggests an emotional state it falls into this *Water* category because here it represents an emotional perception of your environment.

Water is also a creative force, and the source of much of the inspiration that has produced lasting monuments to human creativity. Creative people are often immersed in their feelings (water) and are extremely sensitive. The *kundalini* is a creative fiery liquid, a blend of fire and water. Creative desire (water) is embodied in the kundalini. The Hexagram, geometrical counterpart of the number Six, also signifies this elemental blending.

The kundalini force is depicted as a serpent that coils around the spine. The caduceus, used as a symbol of the medical profession, shows a staff entwined by two coiled serpents, representing the kundalini, the creative life force, as it embraces the spine from which nerves connect to all parts of the body. The kundalini feeds the entire body.

On a recent plane trip, I looked at the earth below and saw long, snake-like rivers, flowing over the flat terrain. I wondered if the ancients had looked upon these same rivers and mused how they appeared to be serpents, lovingly embracing their blessed Mother Earth, nourishing and sustaining her in her productive work.

Early people certainly knew that without water they would die, as would their earth. Water was a life sustaining element, one that creates life (water "breaks" before a child is born) and sustains it (humans, plants and animals need water to survive).

Jealousy, anger, hate and revenge may also be signified by heat and fire. Observe how the body heats when any of these emotional states are experienced. We say he "saw red," or that she is "hot-headed," or "hot under the collar."

Broadcasters often comment that, by the time the firetrucks arrived, the fire was "fully involved." How can a fire be fully involved? The phrase has such a human connotation. But we use terms and phrases regarding fires and sexual relationships interchangeably. The phrase, "fully involved," when applied to two people means an intimate sexual relationship, one that is heated, passionate, intense, just as a fully involved fire is heated and intense. By examining our descriptive phrases about phenomena outside ourselves, we learn a great deal about how we use that phenomena in symbolic exchange in our dreams.

Food: Although food is a material substance, it often has emotional connotations. If we trace our associations with food all the way back to the beginning of our lives, we find that it is tied to our sense of security. Usually, the first person who feed you is your mother. In most countries around the world, an infant is breast-fed. And whether the mother breast feeds or bottle feeds, the child is usually held by her, fondled, talked to and loved — emotionally and physically nourished.

During childhood sicknesses, you may have been given "special" foods to eat. When I was little, I had strep throat several times, and I still associate ginger ale with those illnesses because then I was allowed that "treat." Adults often find that during times of insecurity and depressions, we tend to overeat. This subconscious gesture gives us a sense of security, a link to that past when "mother" loved us. Someone cared, we were important and the center of attention in someone's life. Many of our psychological connections with food are tied into this association, therefore, food can symbolize security and nourishment on the emotional level. And, of course, nourishment and "mother" are associated with the astrological sign Cancer, a water (emotional) sign.

Nutritionally-conscious parents know that candy and sweets in general are not good foods, yet we carry on a strange relationship with them. We tell our children that candy is not good for them — they should eat their vegetables. We force spinach down their throats. Popeye eats it and look how strong he is. They must eat their greens, and oranges and proteins.

But when we want to reward them for something special, we allow them a candy bar. What a strange concept! As adults, it becomes almost a conspiracy with ourselves. We feel we have worked hard and stayed on that diet, or have just run a mile, or spent the day cleaning the desk, so we reward ourselves with a sweet. Then we feel guilty about it. We know it is not right but we feel we deserve it.

Knowing this, we can understand why food represents many emotional states, some of them quite confusing. Our relationship with food — like that we often have with our parents — may be a love-hate one.

We may see food as a temptation. And although Eve was not tempted by a chocolate bar in the Garden of Eden, she was beguiled by a serpent offering an apple. Maybe the message is that even an apple, symbol of knowledge, can take on negative connotations in your dream. No symbol has an absolute meaning.

Sample dreams: Two opposing messages came through the following food dreams. A man dreamt that he paid eighty cents for a candy bar that was worth only forty. His dream expressed the fact that the price he was paying for his sweet tooth was too high, and that his body would have to pay a greater price. (Both the Four and the Eight relate to the physical body and the temptations of the material world.)

A woman dreamt that her kitchen table was covered with the most beautiful, brightly colored vegetables she had ever seen. A dark blue ribbon, the prize for first place, hung from the table's edge. Here, she was being applauded for her current activities that were providing nourishment for others. She was "feeding" the "hungry" in spiritual ways.

Colors: Colors are an important factor in dream interpretation. In common expressions, we associate colors with emotions, and whether or not we all dream in color all the time is not the issue here. The point is if we remember any part of our dream in color, we should look at that portion of the dream through the meaning of the color itself and what it is attached to in the dream.

In reality, color affects us both psychologically and physiologically. A network of nerve fibers leads directly from the retina in the eye to the midbrain and the pituitary gland. The pituitary is one of the major glands in the body's endocrine system, a system that secretes powerful hormones into the bloodstream and affects personality and character. Because the pituitary stimulates or inhibits the other glands' secretions, it is called the master gland. Color vibrations seen by the eyes are sent along the connecting nerve fibers to the pituitary or master gland, which in turn controls the secretions of all the major glands in the body, and they in turn affect behavior. In this context, it is easy to understand why and how colors influence us physically, mentally and emotionally.

Common expressions that include references to color reflect our unconscious knowledge of the impact colors have upon our psyches. We say that someone is "in the pink" meaning in good health. Having "the blues" means that you are depressed. We can be "green with envy" or have "a yellow streak" or "see red."

We innately know that each color contains specific emotional content and we incorporate those colors correctly into our language and our dreams. We tend to attach certain emotions to specific colors, but it is important to remember that the color itself is neither good nor bad. It is how *you* view that color that matters in the interpretation of the dream. If, at this time in your life, you feel that blue is a depressing color, then the expression "blue Monday," which signifies a state of mind, may apply to your dream symbol. However, if you love blue, it can mean progress, that things are looking up just as we look up to see the blue of the heavens. Blue, symbolic of the experiencing mind, is the collegiate color of the department of education and signifies the advancement of the mind. Colors are emotional factors in our lives, producing states of mind that can be depressing or uplifting and inspiring.

Fire

In dreams, the element fire indicates the will, the motivation and the force that drives you. History reveals a common tendency to associate fire with the concept of immortality. The Greek philosophers believed that fire was the constituent part of all form, indeed, the divine force or primordial ener-gy in all matter including humans.

In his book, *She,* H. Rider Haggard tells the tale of a beautiful woman who bathes in a column of fire to stay young forever. This shows the con-cept of fire as immortality.

In the last section, I mentioned the kundalini, the fiery liquid of the life force which twines around the spine. The serpentine force is also repre-sented by the cosmic lemniscate, a horizontal figure eight, which is the mathematical sign for infinity (immortality). In past times, the serpent was a symbol for supreme wisdom. Ancient adepts were called Serpents and were taught to remain silent concerning their craft. The four elements are symbolized by the four "serpent signs" in astrology: Taurus, Leo, Scorpio and Aquarius.

Many life patterns travel this serpentine line: electrical currents, brainwave patterns as registered on an electroencephalograph, bio-rhythms, numerological cycles, the life current that flows through our bod-ies. When we say the Lord's Prayer, we are supposed to be activating the spiritual centers in the body in this figure eight fashion.

Knowledge, symbolized by the serpent, can be corrupting as well as enlightening. The serpent in the Garden of Eden, wound about the apple tree in a pose similar to the serpents on the caduceus, is the life force which, in this case, represents the temptation to become divine-like crea-tures, taking on knowledge or self-awareness and decision-making capaci-ties. Eating the apple was not a sin but an act that gave humankind the ability to become divine-like through decision-making that influenced the outcome of events.

Because we have the ability to make decisions, we have the ability to break universal law. This is where sin enters. Many of the symbols that fall into the category of fire have a theme of recreating the battle between good and evil, between the prompting of the will, the divine spark within, and the urgings of the self that break universal law seeking to satisfy ap-parent needs. Will is a force that motivates us on either a personal level, through the little ego, or on a more evolved level, through the principles by which we live. In spiritual teachings, we often hear, "Thy will not mine." Fire, as the divine energy or higher will, is the motivating force behind our actions. It is the vehicle we use to arrive at our destination and to achieve our highest goals.

On the personal level, the will is expressed through personality, the vehicle we use to get what we want and to get where we want to go. Your personality is a vehicle of the will.

Vehicles: One of the most common personality symbols in a dream is the vehicle we use to transport us from where we are to our desired destination. Vehicles of transportation come in all shapes and sizes in our dreams. These dream vehicles are similar to the house as a symbol; both can represent the human body. Vehicles, however, relate to the way we use and direct our energy, and to the condition of that energy, rather than to the way we view certain areas of our lives. We get into a vehicle in order to go someplace, to reach a destination for any number of reasons. Therefore, a dream vehicle indicates action on the part of the dreamer, a facet of the psyche that is in motion heading toward a goal. The ease or difficulty with which one reaches that goal should be apparent by the accompanying symbols in the dream as well as the feeling and mood one experiences upon awakening.

The vehicles we use to transport us from one place to another allow us mobility and movement. Think how closely we identify with our cars and trucks. Men traditionally call them "she," washing and caressing and generally pampering them, taking better care of their vehicles than they do themselves. The care with which we handle our dream cars reflects the care we take of our bodies.

Automobiles: Have you ever noticed how people defend their choice of automobiles as if they were a part of themselves which, of course, they are in some respects. The choice of a car reflects one's personality. Think of the different types of people you'd expect to drive a shiny red Trans-Am and a Ford Country Squire station wagon with a roof rack. The first driver is motivated by a need for freedom, power, fun and perhaps a swinging social life whereas the second is concerned with practicality, convenience and responsibility for others. The car expresses the personality and motivating force behind the driver.

The operation of the dream car often relates to the way you operate your own life, how you "drive" yourself. Are you on a mad dash to success and money, or just taking a leisurely Sunday drive through life? Of course, this driving attitude changes as you go through attitude changes in your daily life.

In an article in the *New Hampshire Sunday News,* John Martellaro mentions people who experience personality changes behind the wheel: "the easygoing or even timid soul who becomes Indiana Jones once inside his own personal temple of glass and steel." Donald Rey, commander of the traffic division of the Kansas City Police Department, says, "I don't believe personalities can change that quickly. It's more that their real self comes out."[15]

Brakes: Different parts of the car represent corresponding parts of the human body. A common dream is one in which the dreamer is driving a car, comes upon a situation that requires the use of the brakes, and finds that no matter how hard s/he presses the pedal the car won't stop. It is still heading for an intersection, a tree or a cliff —and sure disaster.

In this case, the brakes can indicate the condition of the dreamer's willpower. Obviously it is not working. The dreamer cannot slow down the vehicle, cannot apply the brakes or the will. If the dream car runs into a Sara Lee delivery truck, the message is that you need to exercise will power over your eating habits. It if smashes through the office walls, then someone at work may be testing your good nature and you need to draw upon all you willpower to resist a conflict. Accompanying symbols should tell you where you need to exert more control.

Headlights: The headlights on your dream car can be symbolic of your eyes, your ability to see, your insight and perception. If, in a dream, you are driving in a dense fog and reach out to switch on your headlights, there may be a situation in your life that is not clear, things seem foggy and uncertain. It is here that you need to exercise clear perception, to see things as they really are and not as you (or someone else) would like you to see them. Reaching out to switch on the headlights may be a promise that you will soon be able to clearly see the situation as it really is.

Tires: The tires on a vehicle suggest the strength, endurance, elasticity or mobility of your personality. The entire car rests upon the tires, therefore, they can symbolize responsibility. We have expressions that refer to tires when describing certain personality types. A "flat tire" is someone who does not want to join in and be part of the fun, or who does not seem to have much to offer in the way of company. People who "spin their wheels" make a lot of noise, perhaps for attention, but do not necessarily accomplish much or go anywhere.

Steering wheel: The steering mechanism indicates the direction in which you are headed and, perhaps, the ease with which you set and accomplish your goals. Do you have an automatic transmission or do you chose to shift the gears yourself? Do things come to you automatically, with ease, or do you shift for yourself, working hard for the things you want? Will the recent decisions you have made be carried out easily or will you have to struggle with or guide them (keep your hands on the wheel)?

The driver: Who is in the driver's seat? This is an important question in any dream that involves vehicles. When you are a passenger and someone else is driving, you should ask why you are not in the "driver's seat," why you are not in control of your vehicle, your destiny. On the other hand, given the appropriate symbols, perhaps you should not try to be in control of certain things in your life at this time. You need to look at the dream as a whole and relate its meaning to the current circumstances in your life.

If another person, someone who is a positive figure in your mind, one that you associate with good qualities and high principles is driving then the dream may suggest that you should adopt those same principles, using them to aid you in steering your course. If a negative figure holds the wheel, then a less than desirable situation has you in its control and may be "driving" you in directions that you should avoid. If you relinquish control of your vehicle, be sure it is to someone you respect, but always keep in mind that you must eventually move into the driver's seat yourself because this is your life. You are here to accomplish certain goals and you should do it under your own volition. No one can do it for you.

A heavy car could suggest an overweight condition. A luxurious vehicle intimates ornamentation of the body and the need for luxuries in life, or it could be a promise of things to come. A low-powered car, one that lacks horsepower, may symbolize a lack of stamina and energy, a weakened condition. Running out of gas is an obvious association with running out of energy.

Before the invention of the automobile, a common form of land travel involved the horse. Even today, we associate travel with horses when we assign "horsepower" to our vehicles. And, in one sense, horses and automobiles have much in common in dream symbology - both represent the rider or driver's personality.

Trucks, buses, trains and planes are also transporting vehicles and, as such, fall into this category. Since these modes of travel are high-powered, performing extra-duty service, carrying a large load or number of people, they can symbolize individuals who try to carry too much, who overwork or take on too much responsibility. Do not overlook the possibility that vehicles of this kind can also relate to an overweight condition or an over-powering personality.

Trucks also are used in work situations so their appearance in a dream may relate to your work condition. Buses, trains and planes may also fall into this category as they also are used in business.

Trains and planes, which require tremendous amounts of energy to operate, suggest personalities that are highly motivated to accomplish as much as they can, as quickly as they can. These individuals want to get there yesterday. They may have bottled energy which needs to be released in constructive ways, but once they have set a worthwhile goal, watch their dust. Planes, because they rise above the earth, can indicate the need to rise above your problems. They also may have spiritual connections.

Sample dream: An unemployed school teacher had the following dream. He was being chased down a railroad track by an old-fashioned locomotive with a cow-catcher attached to the front. He stumbled into a train station and safety. The train rumbled up to the platform and stopped before him. He stood there wondering if he should get on.

The man was in the midst of a career change. Although he appeared quiet and unassuming in many ways, underneath he had a flamboyant personality that sought expression. In his new career as a metaphysical lecturer, he was toying with the idea of using stage theatrics to dispel certain taboos surrounding his subject matter. His dream revealed his reticence about adopting this new plan. The locomotive was the high-powered personality he wanted to adopt, chasing him because he was still uncertain about this new role. The cow-catcher was sweeping away negative ideas concerning his subject so the track would be clear for others to follow. The station may have been a play on words, regarding his "station" in life, his professional standing. And the old-fashioned train symbolized his lecture material that deals with the past.

Walking is a mode of travel that should not be overlooked. Two friends who have been working on inner development were sharing their experiences. During meditation one had a vision of walking up steps to the edge of a cliff; the other was on a Budliner traveling toward the edge of this cliff. In this context, the cliff was a stepping-off place for flight, mental elevation and higher awareness. But the curious thing about these similar visions is that one chose to walk and the other to ride a fast train. The different choices related to the personalities of the individuals.

Madame Blavatsky, a turn-of-the-century metaphysician, spoke of three paces of development: the turtle, the fish and the hare. The turtle obviously takes its time, moving one step at a time, sure and slow; the fish swims forward, then back and forward again, more flexible and flowing than the turtle; and the hare dashes with all dispatch toward its goal, like the white rabbit in *Alice in Wonderland,* muttering all the while, "I'm late, I'm late, for a very important date."

One of my friends likens her development to the turtle: she walks toward her goal. Another associates his pace with the hare: he takes the quickest route. No one path is right or wrong; each person finds his/her own pace.

Clothing: Clothing is another vehicle we "get into" or "put on" to express our personalities. Too often we make judgments about people according to their dress. Although there is subconscious truth behind this assessment, the clothes are not the true value of the wo/man. We have all heard stories of rich people, like Howard Hughes, who travel in ragged clothes without a cent in their pockets, as well as tales of poor persons who drive sleek sport cars and wear designer clothing yet their homes are shacks.

However, we can in part determine personality and feeling by our clothing because the clothes we choose to wear express our feelings on that day. Sometimes these decisions are made consciously as we stand before the closet door thinking, "I have a prospective client or a job interview or a club meeting today and I want to make a good impression." We have specific goals to achieve and our clothes will help us do that. On other days, we may decide to stay at home and relax, and our clothing reflects this intent, too. Even the person who claims no attachment to clothes, who wears whatever is near at hand, projects an image that tells a story. This individual may be less concerned about etiquette and more motivated by a nonconformist lifestyle.

So, when you see yourself in a dream, notice your clothes. Just as the old-fashioned locomotive in the unemployed school teacher's dream suggested old-fashioned methods and materials, so might the style of your dream clothing suggest something that will advance you toward your goal.

Sample dream: A man told the following dream: "I am at the office but instead of wearing my usual business suit, I am dressed in tennis shorts and huge, clown-like sneakers that are bright red. I am talking with a client who does not seem to notice my peculiar dress. The biggest surprise of all is that my boss, who is standing nearby, does not object to the way I look. This would not be his reaction outside the dream."

The dreamer was a workaholic who neglected his family and his health. His dream was a message that he needed to change his motivations, to take a more relaxed attitude toward his work. The large sneakers represented the strong foundation he needed to build in his life with reference to recreational activities. Red indicated extra energy that he should apply to this phase of his life in a carefree, "clown-like" manner. As players in the dream, he, his boss and the client could be the three parts of himself that needed to be brought into alignment. His boss, or Higher Self, approved of the motivational change. This dream indicated a need to take more time from work to enjoy life, exercise, get out in the sun and spend time with his family.

Activity: In a dream, what you are "doing" or the occupation or role you are playing signifies a motivational force in your life at that time. Keep common expressions in mind when you look at your dream activity. Skating on thin ice is a perfect analogy for a dangerous situation that may be present in your waking life. Standing up could suggest the need to stand up and be counted, to take a stand on some issue about which you are presently concerned. Walking forward on a path may represent your journey on the path of life. Coming to a fork in the road symbolizes a choice and decision. Walking backward could mean losing ground, whereas retracing your steps might suggest a review of something you may have disregarded or overlooked.

Sample dream: Some months before I wrote *Dream Cycles,* in 1981, I dreamt that I was walking down a path through a sparsely-wooded area. I was hugging a book against my chest. As darkness descended, I decided it was time to return home. On the way back, the heavens suddenly came ablaze with colors, fireworks and moving scenarios. It was such a spectacular sight that I could not take my eyes away, and I was keenly aware that I needed to keep my feet on the path and watch where I was walking. Then a voice called me from behind and above. I somehow knew it was "Peter."

I analyzed this dream in *Dream Cycles.* I felt that the book in my arms was the dream book I had not yet written and that I needed to go back and take it off the shelf where I had put the idea some years ago. The maze of heavenly colors encouraged me in the sense that this display could be seen by many people.

Keeping my feet on the path has many associations for me, one of which is my compelling need to present my work in a logical, concise and useful manner to the reader. In other words, I feel it is essential that ideas be expressed so clearly and simply that the information can be understood by everyone. I like to read books I can understand and, although I admire a good vocabulary, I find it extremely irritating to have to look up every other word in the dictionary.

I had this dream in 1981, before the publication of *Dream Cycles* by Para Research. At the time of this dream, I thought that Peter was St. Peter, whose stance at the pearly gate indicated a new gate opening for me. As it turned out, however, this dream was not complete; I had not yet met the right "Peter." Six years later, Para Research's book division was sold to Schiffer Publishing, Ltd. The president of the company is Peter Schiffer.

In my dream, the voice I heard behind me on the path while I was carrying the dream book, was the voice of Peter. I had to retrace my steps, go home. I look upon this now as the need to rework the original dream book. In *Numerology, Astrology and Dreams* I have incorporated astrology — the blaze in the heavens — as well as the knowledge of numerology and dreams that I have acquired since then, and taken it "home" to Peter, my new publisher.

This is a wonderful example of how a dream can carry meaning for years, if we only record it, and occasionally review it in keeping with our progress.

If you seem to be unprepared in your dreams, you may need to examine your work load. Perhaps you take on more than you can handle or you have a hard time saying no to requests for help. Or, you could look at the way you manage your time. Careful preparation and efficient use of your time could eliminate these problems.

It has been said that being unable to cry out or to escape in a dream suggests an improper diet — which may be true in some cases — but more often, it seems, this condition has deeper implications. The dreamer may have a feeling of impotence, of being unable to control certain behaviors and situations in waking life. Or, the dreamer may have the sense of such overwhelming opposition that s/he gives up entirely and becomes totally passive.

Inaction is as decisive as taking action — they both require a decision. In one, the dreamer has decided not to act; in the other, the dreamer has chosen to act. Both stances are motivated by deep inner convictions about how to handle a situation and achieve some sort of result.

Falling dreams are fairly common and suggest what the word itself means — a fall from the esteem in which you hold yourself or in which the higher self sees you. When you fall, you are "taken down a peg or two," and forced to look at your failings. You are humbled. In this context, the falling dream indicates that you should look at your actions, thoughts and plans of the previous few days to see why you have "fallen." Are you doing or thinking about something that is not up to your standards? Of course, if you have a fear of falling, this type of dream may have a very different meaning.

Flying dreams can suggest a need to escape from or rise above daily problems. They can also indicate sexual feelings, the release that comes from orgasm. You should look at the accompanying symbols and examine your mood upon awakening.

Then there are flying dreams in which you are exhilarated, in complete control and feel you could travel anywhere in the Universe. I remember one such dream in which I was flying through our solar system out to the planet Jupiter. I felt absolute freedom and mystical awe at the sights around me. Upon arriving at my destination I circled Jupiter, examining its rings which were luminous and breathtaking. When I returned to Earth, I found myself flying just above the treetops over a small fishing village moments before the break of day. It was autumn, my favorite season, and the leaves were brown and dry. I reached out, took one of the leaves and crumpled it in my hand. I could hear the brittle sound as it disintegrated. The feeling of wonder was still with me.

Experts could give me many rational explanations about what this dream means, but I know it was something out of the ordinary, unlike most of my dreams. I was really *there*. And who knows. Perhaps we do leave our bodies when we fall asleep, perhaps we experience out-of-body-experiences as the astral body leaves the physical and moves through uncharted space to be shown the wonders of creation. Perhaps we can be taught more than our A-B-C's and arithmetic, in other schools in other dimensions.

The professional roles you play in your dreams may represent approaches you should implement in order to achieve your goals. A carpenter builds with careful, deliberate and well-ordered plans. This could indicate the approach you need to use in your current circumstances. A police officer represents the authoritative, controlled, disciplined side of self; a fire fighter suggest controlling your sexual appetites or aggressive tendencies; a doctor signifies the healer within the self; a banker symbolizes the material side of life; a judge indicates a need for judgment or decision-making, and so on. Whatever role you play in the dream may show a means to an end. Walter Mitty aside, you may need to adopt those very qualities to solve a difficult problem or to accomplish the goals you have in mind at the time of the dream.

If it were not for a dream, *Man and His Symbols,* the only book in which Carl Jung explained his concepts to the general public, would never have been written. Jung's ideas and theories were known to his colleagues and a select group of intellectuals through discussions and papers printed in specialized literary publications. In his dream, however, he took a very different role. He stood in a public place addressing many people who listened to him "with rapt attention" and understanding. In this dream, he took on the role of a public lecturer and teacher.

Inspired by this dream, Jung allowed himself to be persuaded to write *Man and His Symbols* with contributions from a few carefully chosen colleagues. Deep within, Jung understood the public's need to become associated with his ideas, and perhaps he had an inner need to share his ideas with the multitudes. Whatever the motivations, the dream had the desired effect. The book was written and Jung's ideas became known to thousands of people.

Finding money, gold, jewels and other treasure in a dream can prophesy a real situation, of course, but more often it symbolizes spiritual progress on the part of the dreamer. A crown on the head suggests elevated thoughts and ideas; precious jeweled rings and bracelets indicate spiritual service; richly embroidered robes represent an aura of perfection; gold or jeweled sandals show valuable foundations.

Rainbows are special symbols of wholeness. The rainbow body (a balanced aura) and the pot of gold at the end of the rainbow (the head and heart) containing immeasurable treasure were aptly depicted in "The Wizard of Oz." When Dorothy went over the rainbow and traveled the yellow brick road to arrive at Emerald City, she was in search of truth. In this green city, the color of balance and healing, lay the treasure she sought. The message of the rainbow and Emerald City was balance, proportion and a respect for polarities — night and day, summer and winter, female and male — as separate and independent, yet dependent opposites. The rainbow is a promise that by respecting opposites and their value, by understanding the feelings and opinions of others, by allowing space for differences, we find our own balance, create a wholeness and discover our true inner gold.

Lamps and lights represents mental or spiritual illumination or the lack of it, depending upon how the symbol is incorporated into the dream. Light dispels darkness, allow us to "see," therefore we associate light and its accompanying accouterments with understanding, awareness and insight. Phrases such as "it dawned on me" and "I see the light" characterize our understanding of the esoteric affiliation with light.

When I was a teenager, I lived in a Massachusetts town near Marblehead. We used to say "Light dawns on Marble-head" when we finally caught on to something we had been slow to understand. In cartoons, a light bulb often conceptualizes an idea, new insight and understanding. In the Tarot, Key 9, the Hermit, holds a light from atop the mountain of attainment, symbolizing enlightenment and truth for those who will follow it. The eternal flame represents the truth of the spiritual self that is never extinguished, the flame that flickers through eternity. So, in a dream with obvious higher consciousness intonations, whether you dream of a faulty fluorescent in Macy's or the burning bush on Mt. Sinai, you are experiencing the true self.

One last thought before we close this chapter. A friend told me about a dream in which he was caring for a well-cultivated garden and taking great pleasure in it. I told him this was a good sign, showing that his efforts toward raising his consciousness were beginning to come to fruition.

He said that a woman friend had told him to beware because flowers meant death. She then asked, "Where do you always find flowers" and answered her own question with, "At a funeral." He replied that his flowers were in a garden. Her comment was, "That doesn't matter."

This kind of thinking is not only wrong, it is dangerous. To this woman, obviously flowers were a death symbol. That was her personal association with that symbol. But, this does not mean that flowers are a death symbol for everyone else. The dreamer's instincts about the meaning of any symbol come first! Never allow anyone to convince you that a symbol means other that what you instinctively know it to be. You can listen to other definitions, but ultimately you must decide if it is right for you. Even coffins covered with mounds of posies may be indicative of a positive transformation. There is no such thing as an absolute meaning for a symbol. The interpretation varies with the dreamer.

Above all, remember that there are no absolutes. Believing that a symbol always has a certain meaning is a dangerous trap to fall into. Respect the dreamer's association with any and all symbols in her/his dream. S/he is the author of that dream.

Notes

1. Jung, Carl G. *Man and His Symbols,* (Garden City, NY: Doubleday & Co., Inc., 1964), p. 55.
2. Ibid., p. 52.
3. Blakemore, Colin *Mechanics of the Mind,* (Cambridge, England: Cambridge University Press, 1977), p. 1.
4. Ibid., p. 13.
5. Walker, Barbara *Woman's Encyclopedia of Myths and Secrets,* (San Francisco: Harper & Row, Publishers, 1983), p. 1016.
6. *Encyclopedia Americana,* Vol. 29, (NY: Americana Corporation, 1966), p. 84.
7. Walker, pp. 514, 782.
8. Ibid., p. 565.
9. Helene, Corinne *Sacred Science of Numbers,* (La Canada, CA: New Age Press, Inc., 1971), p. 57.
10. Ibid., p. 58.
11. Ibid., p. 60.
12. *Encyclopedia Americana,* Vol. 24, p. 198.
13. Lesmerurier, Peter *The Great Pyramid Decoded,* (NY: St. Martin's Press, 1977), p. 56.
14. Jung, p. 78.
15. Martellaro, John, "Driving: That's When 'Real You' Surfaces," *New Hampshire Sunday News,* March 15, 1987, p. 4H.

6

Personal Year Cycle Dreams

It would appear that this Universe was created by Spiritual Love, fire and water, a force which understood and respected structure and order, and incorporated these principles into its creation. Thus, all events must occur within this structured Universe in predictable ways, in ordered and dependable cycles.

As creatures living on Earth, within this solar system, we are a part of this structured and cyclical existence and are influenced by it. Cycles are an integral part of the order of the Universe, our planet and our personal lives. As above, so below.

Therefore, to understand the dream process and the contents of your dreams more thoroughly, it is necessary to be aware of your own personal rhythms. *Your dreams are influenced by the energies of the cycle you are presently experiencing.* One of the easiest and most accurate methods of determining which cycle you are in now is by using the numerology method we discussed in chapter 1.

Astrological Influences on Dream Cycles

In addition to examining your dreams within the context of your personal year cycle, you also will want to consider your astrological makeup. Your attitude toward your annual cycles — your yearly "assignment sheets" — will be influenced by your astrological characteristics.

Element Influence

Determine if you are a fire, water, air or earth-type person, which means, do you have a preponderance of planets and sensitive points in any one of these elements? (See chapter 2.) If you find that you do, keep this in mind as we discuss the following nine personal year cycles. Your astrological element, which shows how you think and react, does affect the way you approach each of the years in your nine cycles. Therefore, your dreams will contain specific symbols that are expressive of your attitude toward each year's assignment. Your dominant element influences your approach to your dreams — perhaps so much so that you avoid the other elements.

For instance, if you are an earth-type person, you like the security of knowing your perimeters and want to be in control of your material world. Thus, you might have some difficulty with cycles One, Five and Nine because they require new beginnings, making changes and ultimately letting go. You would rather dream of the house you lived in as a child and, if you astral project, you might choose never to leave your neighborhood.

The other possibility, as Adler suggested in his compensation theory, is that you might compensate for what you feel you lack and emphasize your weakest element. For example, I have only one air planet in my birth chart (Venus in Libra in the third house) with no angular emphasis in this element. (I realize that this is an elementary look at the chart, nevertheless it has merit.) I have always been fascinated by the world of ideas and thought. My fondest desire has always been to sit at the feet of a great teacher and learn the mysteries of the Universe. I admire people with good vocabularies, who express their ideas fluently. Many of my dreams involve flying (the air element) and these dreams have increased my awareness and inspired my writing. Today, I am a writer, teacher and researcher, seeking understanding through my mental wanderings.

So, the first step in understanding your dream cycles is becoming aware of your element. Do you stay within that element's domain because it feels comfortable and natural, or do you reach out and compensate for the element that you feel you lack?

Your Birthday Number

The number of the day on which you were born is significant because it indicates how you approach your everyday life and your attitudes and behavior during your waking hours. If you were born on the 7th of the month, for instance, you will want to be more aware of the dreams that occur around the 7th of each month. (Look at the dreams you have during the three days preceding and the three days following the 7th, too.) The messages you receive on these dates are attempting to aid you in dealing with the energies of that month. The message will change on your birth day of each month, (in this case, the 7th).

This is a smaller cycle within the larger yearly cycle. These monthly cycles work toward the integration of the whole, the personal year cycle.

The Moon's Influence

The Moon rules your personal moods, as well as those of the general public. The Moon moves through all twelve signs of the zodiac every twenty-nine days or so, and spends approximately two and one-half days in each sign.

One of my students noticed that disc jockeys often play music which relates to the position of the Moon on any particular day (without being conscious of doing so, of course). The Moon's position not only reflects the disc jockeys' moods, but the mood of their public as well. A DJ who is sensitive enough to be in touch with the Moon's cycles also would be attuned to public mood swings and, therefore, probably would be successful with her/his show.

The Moon represents your nurturing side, the side that is hidden in the subconscious, the side that motivates you in instinctual ways that you do not understand consciously. The Moon is the Cosmic Mother who wants to nourish you through whatever sign it is in at the moment. Knowing the placement of the Moon on any given day tells you how you should nurture yourself during that period. Your dreams will reflect this need.

On the physical level, you need to indulge yourself in those things that are related to the sign in which the Moon is positioned. If it is in Libra, for instance, go to lunch with a friend or spend a special day with your partner. If the Moon is in Pisces, spend time alone with your feelings, sit by the sea, listen to inspirational music or offer your assistance to those who are less fortunate than yourself.

Pocket Astrologers are available for a few dollars and show the Moon's movements during an entire year. A Pocket Astrologer not only gives the Moon's position on each day of the year, it also contains the glyphs (symbols) of the planets and signs, and brief descriptions of their functions so that even if you are not an astrologer, you can read this calendar. You can purchase a pocket calendar calculated for either Eastern Time or Pacific Time; directions for making adjustments for other time zones are included with the calendar. (See the Appendix at the back of this book for the address.)

Personal Year Cycle Dreams

Now let's take a look at the types of dreams you might have in each of the nine personal year cycles. Keep in mind that the dreams listed under each cycle are typical examples, however, they may not be the only kinds of dreams you will have during that period.

Begin by determining the cycle you are currently in, then turn to that section. The kinds of dreams listed under your current cycle are those that will have the most meaning for you now. They are meant to aid you in the evolvement of this year's lesson.

To review: To find your personal year cycle, simply add together the numbers in the date of your *last* birthday. For example, this is being written in May of 1987, so if your birthday is October 13th, as of this writing your last birthday was October 13, 1986. Remember to include the "19" in 1986 or you will arrive at the wrong number. Add the number for October, which is a $10, +13+1986$, or $1+0+1+3+1+9+8+6 = 29$. Add again, $29 = 2+9 = 11$. Add again, $11 = 1+1 = 2$. With a birthday of October 11th, your personal year cycle is Two as of this writing.

Keep in mind that your *personal* year runs from your birthday to your birthday. It has nothing to do with the calendar year. That is why it is called your Personal Year.

At the end of each cycle following, you will find a brief description of how people whose birth charts are dominated by one of the astrological elements might react to that particular yearly cycle. Each element will be explained.

Personal Year Cycle One Dreams

Symbol - The point
Principle - Action
Purpose - Self-centering, motivation, independence

In this cycle you are experiencing what is called the process of individuation, or your development as an individual apart and separate from anyone else. During this time, you need to stroke your ego and to sing the praises of your self, as Walt Whitman wrote in "Song of Myself" from *Leaves of Grass*, "I celebrate myself and sing myself . . . " Your present stage of growth places you as the central character in the play of life. This is the year when you will feel the most individualistic.

Your dreams will show how your life will be most strongly affected by expressing your will and placing your personal stamp on all that you do. Independence is the impetus behind many of your dreams this personal year.

Since independence requires that you do many things for yourself, you will find that your dreams now will be full of symbols that are aggressive, thrusting and suggestive of forward motion. They are meant to recharge your batteries, to give you the drive to reach out and dare to do those things you might not ordinarily attempt. It's time to try new things.

One of the symbols you could encounter is fast-moving vehicles such as racing cars, trains, airplanes, rockets and so forth, modes of transportation that get the adrenalin going. You might also dream of pioneering vehicles such as canoes, kayaks, wagon trains and space ships. You could sail a dhow to Zanzibar or trek to Andromeda with Mr. Spock. The speed with which you travel and the period of time in history is not as important as the selection of the vehicle, for the vehicle represents your need to move beyond your present stage of existence, to reach out for different experience on your own, to travel to distant horizons and discover new lands. This is your pioneering year.

Other symbols you might encounter in your dreams now are those that signify major transformations such as the birth of babies, weddings and funerals. These all represent new beginnings. When a child is born, life changes dramatically for the parents. When a person marries, life as a single person ends and a new lifestyle as united souls, a partnership begins. When death symbols appear in your dreams, they signify the death of an old way and the birth of a new direction. This death/birth symbolism signifies changes of áttitudes, relocation, new relationships, different jobs or any experiences that change your lifestyle in a meaningful way. In many ways, birth and death are interchangeable and synonymous as symbols, for when one thing ends, another must begin.

Sample dream: A fifty-five year old man dreamt that, as he looked through the door of an old, rundown office building, he saw dead man lying on the hallway floor. The man resembled him but he, the dreamer, was standing on the busy sidewalk where the sun was shining and the leaves on the trees were rustling in the spring breeze.

This man had taken an early retirement in order to begin another career. The dead man in the dream was indicative of an old way of life that had been cast off like the skin of a snake. The office building suggested that the dream referred to his work. His new career promised to be busy (the busy sidewalk) and happy (sunny), filling him with the anticipation and vitality of springtime. So, although death was part of this dream, it was not frightening because it signified a new beginning.

In a personal year cycle One, you could also dream of figures that frighten you into action. Who's going to sit calmly reading movie magazines when an angry, saber-toothed tiger is hovering over the back of the couch? This tends to be a stimulating, activating dream, one that is designed to get you moving. Frightening creatures can pull you out of the doldrums and set you on a path toward accomplishment.

You dream of those things which you are capable of attaining in some manner. After all, you are the creator of your dream; it comes from your subconscious so, if you can conceive it, you can achieve it.

During cycle One, you may, like Walter Mitty, dream of yourself as the hero/ine, the valiant one who snatches others from the jaws of death or who faces death without flinching. And although Walter Mitty dreamt of glory to lighten his drab daily existence, he was expressing personal desires that could have materialized if he had backed them up with personal effort. This reminds me of a story about a great musician who was approached by a gushing fan. "Oh, if only I had your talent," said the fan. The musician replied, "Sir, if you had practiced eighteen hours a day for forty years, you would be just as talented as I am." Our Walter Mitty dreams of glory can come true.

Sigmund Freud suggested that many wishes are fulfilled in our dreams. Carl Jung went a bit further, intimating that our deep psychological needs expressed through dreams may manifest later in actual events, in, I believe, our wishes come true.

In cycle One, your personal desires and wishes come to the surface through your dreams. But it would be foolish to say that, because they are only wishes, they have no meaning. On the contrary, I believe the things we yearn for the most deeply are those things that have the greatest impact on our lives if they come to pass.

As a child of five, I thought writers were the greatest people in the world. I would stand before bookcases, staring up at the multi-colored bindings, wondering how anyone could possibly know enough words to fill all those pages. I marveled at the magical minds that could organize those reams of information, and dreamt of being a great writer some day. Even now, when I read an especially well-written book by an author who obviously loves the language and caresses the words, I am deeply moved.

I bring this up for a reason. To say that my childhood dreams of becoming a writer were mere wish-fulfillment and nothing else would be a terrible injustice to the use of the dream's energy. To date, I have written eight books. Six have been published, two are collecting dust; this is my ninth. After years of typing from my ironing board — about the only use I ever had for it — I bought myself a desk and chair with the royalties from my first book. I now own a personal computer. I am proud of those possessions, which I have tucked into the corner of my kitchen beside the window that looks out over a small rock garden by a lovely old maple. (Yes, my chart is dominated by the element earth.) As I sit here at my desk working on my books, I sometimes stop for a minute to gaze out that window and dream about becoming an Edwin Abbott or a Marie Corelli or a Jules Verne . . .

So, in your cycle One, dream your dreams. Let others say they are merely wish-fulfilling. Let others suggest your dreams are a waste of time. Let others live in a world devoid of dreams if they so choose. But go after yours. They are precious, they are fulfilling and they are *the real you.* While you are in your personal year cycle One, you have the energy and impetus to begin the journey to achieve the dreams that can come true for you.

Fire-type response to cycle One: I am in my element. There is nothing I would rather do than get out of that old rut. I've been there long enough and there are new worlds to explore. All I need is one minute to pack a toothbrush and a change of underwear, and I'm ready to face new adventures with spontaneity and enthusiasm. I'll lead, and I don't care if I don't have a map. I'll make my own.

Water-type response: I'll go but first, I have to make sure the family is okay, that there's enough food on the shelves and everyone's had the chicken pox, and there's enough money in the sugar bowl to tide them over until I get back. What if we get lost or we meet some unsavory characters along the way? I don't know. Maybe, on second thought, I'd better contemplate this a little longer.

Air-type response: This adventure would be good for me. Think of all the people I will meet and the experiences I will have. Why, I could gather all that information and put it into a book. I'd better take along plenty of pens and pads of paper, and maybe a small tape recorder and a video camera. I don't want to miss a word or nuance.

Earth-type response: No way! I'm not leaving my possessions and the career I've worked so hard to build!

Personal Year Cycle Two Dreams

Symbol - The line
Principle - Attraction
Purpose - Nourishment, imagination, reflection

Your previous actions in personal year cycle One set up an equal and opposite reaction. The One, moving out, caused the Two, moving in. Therefore, during this period, you must pull back and let the law of attraction work for you.

All the activity that was generated during your previous personal year cycle One resulted in the accumulation of many new experiences which must now be dropped into your subconscious for processing and nourishment. The seeds you planted then, your external experiences, now need to be cared for in the secret recesses of the dark moist soil of your subconscious where they can be analyzed through your feelings, emotions and instincts. Your cycle Two is your hall of mirrors, where personal illumination comes through seeing reflections of the energies you expended last year: you made a decision and this is the potential result. In cycle Two, you begin to use your psychic awareness.

The dreams that come to you now will reflect this hidden, creative process. These dreams are especially important because they reflect the new path you have chosen for the next eight years. Many of these dreams will be precognitive in that you will be told of something before it happens.

I have come to realize that, for me, dreams of babies or pregnancies indicate precognitive dreams. If, in the dream, I or someone else is pregnant, I count the number of months until the child's delivery and mark that date on the calendar. If a small baby appears in the dream, I take note of the baby's age — it has always been months — and mark ahead that many months to the day on the calendar. This has been uncannily accurate.

Sample dream: During the early part of my career, I dreamt I was lying in bed with my husband. I looked down at my stomach and realized, with great pleasure, that I was three months pregnant. That morning I made a note on my calendar exactly six months from that day (since most dreams come in the morning, I start counting from the morning of my dream).

About a month later, a colleague invited me to travel with her to Michigan where she was to speak before a convention. I had never heard of the group and was about to say no, but finally reconsidered and accepted. At that convention, through a series of strange circumstances, I ended up lecturing three times and making contacts that have proven important to me. Those contacts led to my lecturing and conducting workshops for numerous other groups across the country, something I am still doing today. At that first convention, I also picked up valuable information which I used in my last book. And yes, that first convention opened on the day I had circled on my calendar, exactly six months from my pregnancy dream.

This is a good example of cycle One and cycle Two dreams. The energies I put forth in my One cycle were dropped into my hall of mirrors where I saw reflected, through the pregnancy dream, the possibility of things to come.

Many famous individuals have had dreams that were the result of seeds dropping into the subconscious, dreams that had profound effects upon history. Otto Loewe discovered the interaction between active chemicals and the nerves in a dream; his dream changed the world of chemistry.

Elias Howe, who invented the lock-stitch sewing machine, had struggled with his invention for ten years. One night he dreamt that he was surrounded by cannibals who threatened to boil him alive if he did not solve his problem. In terror, he looked up at the spears they were holding and noticed that each spear had an eye-shaped hole at the end. He had been placing the hole in the center of the needle. He awoke and dashed to laboratory, carved the needle he had seen in his dream, and the lock-stitch sewing machine was born.

During your personal year cycle One, you tended to separate yourself from others. When you enter the Two cycle you become aware of that isolation because it now is time to repair any bridges you may have torn down. Therefore, you may have dreams that help reorient you to others.

Sample dream: A young mother dreamt that she looked out her kitchen window and saw cobwebs on the swing set in the back yard. This woman views her kitchen as a nurturing room where the lines of communication are very busy. The family eats there, and conversations about the day take place over dinner. The children tell their parents about school and play, and she and her husband discuss their days and make plans for tomorrow.

Cobwebs indicate a place that is undisturbed for long periods of time. The swing set referred specifically to her three little boys. Prior to this dream she had been feeling guilty because she had not spent as much time with her children as she thought was necessary. She was finishing up her cycle One year and had put a great deal of time and energy in starting her education at the university. Her dream had come to tell her that her playtime with the children (the swing set) was practically non-existent (gathering cobwebs), and the lines of communication (the kitchen) needed to be opened (looking through the window of the kitchen).

She had this dream at the onset of her personal year cycle Two, near her birthday in the spring. The woman realized that she needed to work out a schedule that would allow her both to study and spend more time with the children.

You could look upon cycle Two as your processing playground where all the possibilities are tossed around, swung back and forth and spun about. Some of these dreams may involve extra sensory perception (ESP) or astral travel, sometimes called out-of-body-experience (OBE). Perhaps a few of these dreams may relate to past-life experiences, if that is part of your belief system. In the case of past life recall, it may be necessary to review some events from another lifetime in order to process the material you are working with in your current cycle.

Sample dream: The following dream of Hermann V. Hilprecht, former professor of Assyrian at the University of Pennsylvania, is a good example of the possibility of past life recall. It is also a psychic dream, specifically a retrocognitive dream (in which one picks up information about a past of which one is not aware).

The professor worked late one evening in 1893, trying to decipher the cuneiform markings on two drawings of agate fragments which he thought were finger rings from the Babylonian period. He classified one fragment but was unable to do so with the other. When he finally went to bed he had a dream.

In the dream, a pre-Christian Nippur priest appeared and led him to the treasure chamber in the temple where the agate fragments had been found. The priest then proceeded to explain in great detail exactly what the fragments were. They were not finger rings. The priest explained how the cylinder came to be broken into three parts, and that the third fragment would never be found. It was like a guided tour of the past, with the priest explaining the archaeological history of the agate fragments that Hilprecht had worked on so diligently.

As soon as he could, the professor went to the museum in Constantinople where the fragments were kept. They were in separate cases because no one knew they came from the same piece. He fit the two fragments together perfectly, thus confirming the information given him by the priest in his dream.[1]

Whether this was a retrocognitive dream or a glimpse into his past during a lifetime when he had actually worked with this dream priest, no one will ever know. But the possibilities are intriguing.

So, during your personal year cycle Two, you are drawing to you those things that you asked for during your One cycle. The law of attraction is at work. It is a calm and receptive period in which you can process and balance your energy. You are "under construction" now and need to nourish those seeds that you feel will accomplish the goals you have set for yourself.

Fire-type responses to cycle Two: Give me a break. I've got better things to do than to stand around and wait for a seed to work its way up through the soil. Booooring!

Water-type response: Does a fish love water? Here is where I can immerse myself — in the waters that permeate my being. Here, in the subterranean emotional recesses of my mind, I find ideas floating on the creative fluids of my imagination. Here, I encounter dragons and the Hobbits and the shining Emerald City over the rainbow. Here, I can mistress the possibilities.

Air-type response: If you think about it, this isn't a rational way to approach life. And actually, a rainbow is an arc of spectral colors that often appears when sunlight refracts and disperses in raindrops or mist. Let's exercise our powers of reason and philosophize about principles and ideas, but leave the fantasizing to those emotional types.

Earth-type response: If I can't eat it or use it, what good is it?

Personal Year Cycle Three Dreams

Symbol - The triangle
Principle - Expansion
Purpose - Creative unfoldment, encouragement, growth

The "under construction" sign placed upon your path during your personal year cycle Two has been removed. It's time to get into your vehicle and move out, to experiment with those things you have been nurturing, to use your talents to entertain others, to enter the social world where you can encounter the feedback that you need to gain confidence in yourself.

In this Three cycle, you need room to grow out into a world you have not encountered previously. Your dreams come to help expand your horizons, to show what you can do if your "reach exceeds your grasp."

Sample dream: Italian violinist and composer Giuseppe Tartini, at age twenty-one, had a dream in which he sold his soul to the devil, then handed his violin to the horned creature. He wrote: "But how great was my astonishment when I heard him play with consummate skill a sonata of such exquisite beauty as surpassed the boldest flight of my imagination. I felt enraptured, transported, enchanted; my breath was taken away, and I awoke. Seizing my violin I tried to retain the sounds I had heard. But it was in vain. The piece I then composed, the 'Devil's Sonata,' was the best I ever wrote, but how far below the one I had heard in my dream!"[2]

I would imagine this type of dream to occur in a Three cycle because it has the element of reaching beyond what one feels can be accomplished. Although Tartini never recaptured the essence of his dream sonata, he produced his best composition. He had reached into his creative pool and touched the music of the spheres. His skills then allowed him to composed the sonata. If he had not been prepared, the music would have been lost forever. He had put in the time, nurtured his creative imagination and allowed it the room to expand into a timeless piece. There is an order in the Universe.

Your dreams come to encourage you to grow beyond what you think is possible for you, to reach for the stars, to speak out as Carl Jung did after his dream of lecturing in a public place to large numbers of people who listened "with rapt attention" and understanding. This encouraged him to write for the general public, which he did in his book *Man and His Symbols.*

Sample dream: One of my clients dreamt he returned to his home and picked up the mail on his way in the door. There were the regular bills and fliers along with three large manilla envelopes. Two were from companies he usually received mail from, but the third was sent by a national real estate chain. This envelope had a gold band across the top.

The dreamer was toying with the idea of investing a large sum of money in a new business. He had been thinking about this for two years. A conservative person, he was quite hesitant to make the plunge but, after this dream, he felt differently. He made the investment and has been more successful than he imagined possible. His dream came to encourage him to enlarge his sphere of thinking, to reach beyond what he had previously attempted, to broaden his beliefs about what was possible. The gold band across the envelope was a symbol of the positive aspects of his contemplations. Perhaps the "real" estate chain was a play on the word "real," meaning his dreams were realistic. And a business chain implies that the business has grown and expanded. The *three* envelopes indicated the expanding energy that was about to take form. Things happen in Threes, the triangle that creates life.

Often, when you encounter three people in your dreams, you are looking at the three personal aspects of yourself: body (earth), mind (air) and soul (water), or the three in one (fire) symbolized by trinities. These three represent the complete and whole you. It is important to look at these three individuals and what roles they play in your dream. There is usually an authority figure or one who seems to be in charge while the other two seemed paired in some manner. The one who stands apart should be examined first because s/he represents a part of yourself that is not in accord with the other two. This person has been singled out so that you will examine his/her role in your dream.

Sample dream: A woman told me this dream: "I am a passenger in a car driven by a lovely Chinese woman who is pregnant. She is about to have her baby. We stop at a garage for gasoline. It seems there is snow piled everywhere so she has to plow through snow drifts to reach a tank. The Chinese woman then gets out as an attendant, who seems unsteady on his feet, almost drunk, approaches the car. The woman has to be helped back into the car because her labor pains have started. I offer to drive and she accepts. I wonder why I hadn't offered before."

Her associations with the dream symbols were as follows:

Chinese woman — oriental philosophy which is different, wise, and noticed in our society. Oriental women are very beautiful with thick shiny hair and clear skin. This seemed to indicate clear thinking. The dreamer sees these women as traditionally passive when relating to men, but the Chinese woman in the dream was not.

Gas/garage — a place where you refuel for your car or energize yourself.

Snow — clean and invigorating, but deep drifts can make moving ahead or progress difficult.

Attendant — one who watches over his/her energy supply. In this case, the attendant was drunk, unsteady and not in control.

Labor pains — something is about to happen.

Offering to drive — time for her to take control. Maybe she should have done this earlier.

At this point in her life, the woman was going through major changes (birthing) in her philosophy. She was an assertive woman, as was the Chinese woman in the dream, however, she felt that she should display that assertiveness in a more feminine, loving manner (Chinese women traditionally are receptive). This new attitude would require hard work (difficult progress through the snow drifts) but it was time for her to take control of her life (drive her car) in a more positive manner. She had been using her energy in an unsteady manner (gasoline station attendant) and needed to dole it our more efficiently.

This dream is a good example of the three parts of the self trying to come together into a creative, expanding unit. The two women were together and the third individual, the man, was the one who symbolized her unbalanced use of her efforts to achieve the goals in her life. Without the proper fuel supply, without a balanced attendant caring for her vehicle, she would not be able to blend the two remaining parts of herself: the assertive woman with Western ideas and the receptive woman with Eastern ideas. She came to realize that she could express her feminine self and still be in control of her destiny. She did not have to be a man to be in charge of her life; her feminine power was revealed to her. By wedding these two attitudes, the assertive and the receptive, she experienced the fullest expression of her feminine role.

Since personal year cycle Three is a period of expansion, travel to distant places may be theme in your dreams during this time. My dream of flying around the planet Jupiter was certainly a mentally and emotionally expanding experience. It came at a time when I needed to understand that I was not limited by my thinking and that what I could conceive, I could achieve.

When you are in personal year cycle Three, your dreams come to encourage you to test your creative wings, to expand your circle of reference, to move out beyond the normal, because now your "reach should exceed your grasp."

Fire-type response to cycle Three: I'm ready to go but, if there's going to be group, I'm the one who is the most qualified to take the lead. And let's not get caught up in details. Let's just go and see what adventures will greet us.

Water-type response: Well, spontaneity has its place, but I'm not going off half-cocked. I mean, we do have responsibilities to think about. If you're talking about expanding my horizons through something like taking private acting or art lessons, okay. But, I'm not sure I want to get too involved in groups; that fellow in the last group was a bit outspoken and I was uncomfortable through the whole class.

Air-type response: You water types are too sensitive. Why not rise above your feelings and examine the experience this year can afford? I am mentally stimulated by the possibilities. But I do think we need to be more concerned about what the other people involved in these experiences think. After all, isn't that what life is all about?

Earth-type response: Sure, I'd love to invest some money in that new adventure. It sounds like it has plenty of room to grow. But, can you guarantee that I'll get a good return on my investment? No? Well, what kind of an operation are you running anyway?

Personal Year Cycle Four Dreams

Symbol - The square
Principle - Formation
Purpose - Organization, structure, respect for the material

In a Four cycle year, you are rooted in the physical and material world. You need to become involved with your earthly ties and to examine them. It's time to realize that the Earth and its products, including your body, are spiritual containers, in and of the One Divinity that created your mind and soul. Too often, spiritual literature and teachings are misinterpreted by individuals who seek to escape their temporal bonds or by religious institutions who desire to control the masses through teachings of poverty. Such organizations teach that in order for you to be spiritual, you must relinquish all ties to the Earth. Granted, there are people whose path is one of poverty however, it is not for everyone. We should examine our feelings toward the Earth and its resources, including money, during this cycle. Perhaps your destiny is to be the steward of Mother Earth's bounty, to handle money and power, and use your physical body with respect and for the betterment of your own life and the lives of others.

Often, in my travels, I meet people who believe they should give up their ties to the physical in order to be "spiritual." They struggle with this belief because it is not in their nature to do so. In my opinion, their struggle is between religion, a codified set of rules set up by men, and spirituality, the true laws of the Universe. One does not have to be religious in order to be spiritual.

The Earth and its resources — power, sex, money, the physical body — are spiritual expressions of Divinity. It may be your destiny to work with these expressions. It is the intentional misuse of these gifts that is evil, not the gift itself. All you have to do is examine history to discover that religious institutions have committed as much evil as the secular world.

Therefore, in your personal year cycle Four, it is time to get in touch with your physical needs, your contact with the temporal world. Listen to what your dreams have to tell you about your position in these matters.

Sample dream: A young married woman dreamt she followed a police car to her local Shop and Save supermarket. In back of the building, her younger sister's car was in flames. She was frantic until she discovered that her sister was not in the car.

Her association with the symbols was as follows:

Police car — to police or watch where she was driving herself.

Shop and Save — be careful when shopping. Shop when necessary but save your money. Shop when necessary. Shop and save.

Her youngest sister — extravagance. She tries to maintain a car that is too expensive for her small income.

The woman who had this dream was in the process of giving up her job to stay at home with her small children. She knew she had to curb her spending habits, which were considerable. She has Venus (the planet that represents things that please us) in the second house (the sector associated with personal possessions) square (challenging relationships) to Pluto (obsessions) in the sixth house (the sector of work). Therefore, her obsession with owning things that please her could put her in a challenging position where she would have to overwork in order to pay for the items. She could easily get herself into considerable debt because of her burning desire (car in flames). She had to police her actions (follow the police car), save when she shopped (Shop and Save) and curb her appetites (food is found in a supermarket). Her youngest sister was an aspect of herself, the side that was too extravagant, perhaps because of immaturity and lack of experience. The dreamer's sister was not in the burning car, therefore the woman was not out of control. She had time to correct the situation. It had not surfaced to a dangerous extent (burning car in back of the supermarket, out of sight).

This dream dramatically showed the young woman's connection to her material world. In fact, she had been discussing this very situation with her husband the day before she had the dream. The graphic dream came along to support and guide her through the battle against her desire for material possessions that could have led to difficult financial situations for her family.

In your Four cycle, you desire security. You need to own things that lend substance to that need, and since personal possessions qualify, you find yourself buying land, property, and becoming involved in other substantial financial investments. The young woman's dream is a good example of this need that was surfacing during her Four cycle; the Four emphasized what had not been so obvious prior to this cycle.

Satisfying this desire to own often forces you to organize your life and budget your money. Dreams in your personal year cycle Four are meant to aid you in organizing on many levels, one of which may be financial. Look for tips on how to earn and save money. Clean out your house and garage and have a yard sale.

Since your personal year cycle Four is a physical year, the theme of healing may arise. Remember the man who had rats in his dream house and could not reenter it until he had exterminated the problem? If you have any physical problems with health or weight, this is the year to take care of your personal structure, your body. Look at your dreams in this light if it is applicable because you can glean much information about your health from your nightly scenarios. Hippocrates, the father of medicine, obtained much of his medical knowledge from his local temple where cures, obtained from the dreams of the infirm persons who had slept there, were inscribed upon the walls.

Sample dream: A woman who had decided to go on a seven-day diet plan was faltering in her efforts after the second day. She told her husband that she hated dieting because eating was so much a part of enjoying life and she thought she might give the whole idea up.

That night she dreamt she was dressed in white tights with an overblouse belted at the waist. Her husband took pictures of her while she was performing. She was horrified at the pictures because her hips and thighs looked huge. She also dreamt that she had gone off her diet by mistakenly eating the incorrect foods on the fifth day of the seven-day plan.

This dream did not need much analysis. Upon awakening, she was so disgusted at her dream photographs that she decided to stay on the reducing plan the full seven days. Also, the fifth day — Five is a number of change — indicated that she would make a mistake if she changed her plan to continue the reducing regime.

You may dream of houses and buildings frequently during this personal year cycle because, in many cases, they relate directly to your body. Examine the condition of the structure of your buildings because you need to build a sound foundation during this period of time, to prepare for the changes that will occur in your next cycle. Your dreams will supply you with the tools and the materials you need to construct a proper home.

Fire-type response to cycle Four: I can see the value in having a yard sale so why don't I get things rolling, assign the duties and then you and I can take that trip to Machu Pichu. I hear that's a very metaphysical place and I've never been there. How about you?

Water-type response: Well, I'd rather be at the yard sale. Why don't we have it at my house? You can take charge and I'll take care of the cash box. We can pool our resources. There's strength in numbers. I also think it would be a good idea to tithe some of what we make. Think of the starving children in Africa.

Air-type response: I'll do the advertising. And I have loads of friends I can invite. I'll kind of move around through the crowd and keep the conversation going. It will help sales.

Earth-type response: You can depend on me. Besides, I probably can make some good money. But I will have to think about what I'm going to sell. You never know when you're going to need something but, if the price is right ... We'll need tables, and tags and stickers, and hangers for clothes ... I'll take care of the details. Do you suppose the neighbors will mind if there are cars lined up along the street? I am a banker and we do have an image to uphold.

Personal Year Cycle Five Dreams

Symbol - The pentagram
Principle - Change
Purpose - Freedom, communication, experience

Your five senses are heightened this year so you can focus on issues of freedom, communication, experience and change. You are extremely restless with the status quo, and seek to make new and exciting contacts. The dreams you have now are designed to assist you in making contacts that eventually will lead to awareness of the opportunities that are being presented to you. It is as if your mind is sending out invisible antennae, scanning the atmosphere, picking up subtle nuances in your environment. You are emitting messages to which others will respond. The end result will cause you to consider making changes in those areas of your life that now are unsatisfactory.

Any type of vehicle can be a prominent symbol during this cycle. Vehicles take you from one place to another, and therefore, connote freedom and change. If you feel stuck in an uncomfortable situation in your life at present, you may dream you are in a red Ferrari or boarding a plane bound for parts unknown. Examine the accompanying symbols to learn the specifics of the message as to how the change can be accomplished.

Books, libraries, schools and class situations also fall into this category. Since learning is part of your experience, it can be a key issue now. Therefore, you may dream of being back in school or sitting in a library, surrounded by the ideas of thousands of authors, present and past. A wealth of information is available to you under this cycle.

Sample dream: A woman who was searching for meaning in life dreamt: "I am a student in an old-fashioned school where the books are stored inside the desk. We were given the problem of absorbing a pile of gold money. I laid my head on the desk. In a few minutes I had absorbed all of the gold into myself."[3]

School, for most people, is an obvious symbol for learning. The books stored inside the desk suggests that the dreamer has not yet gained access to the information. When she laid her head on the desk (applied her head to the problem) she absorbed all of the gold (symbol of spiritual wealth, in this case) into herself. Since she "absorbed" the gold, she may have been using her right intuitive brain rather than a rational, traditional education.

This dream may have come to encourage her to continue the process, the learning, through which she was going in order to reach her goal of finding her purpose in life. A Five cycle implies that changes are occurring, and this dream suggests that the changes in her life were positive ones.

Dreams of receiving letters, telephone calls, newspapers and so forth fall into this category as well. People often dream of receiving letters when an important change is about to occur in their lives.

We subconsciously recognize that Five is the number of change. We have five fingers on one hand; our hands reach out to greet new people or to acknowledge acquaintances we don't see every day. These people bring a change of scene, different ideas and lifestyles into our set routines. Some of these people and their ideas will affect changes in our lives.

Contact with others can involve you in sexual experiences. Five is a sexually-active cycle because close contact with another person is one way of heightening your senses so that you can experience life to its fullest. If you are in the market for a new relationship, this cycle can bring one; or, it can enhance an existing relationship. Your dreams will mirror this activity.

Sample dream: A young man dreamt that he was with four friends from high school whom he hadn't seen since he graduated three years ago. The five of them were ogling a voluptuous woman who walked by wearing tight black shorts and high-heeled shoes. Out of the group of five, he seemed to be the only one who noticed another young woman across the street who was dressed in jeans and a T-shirt. She was not especially attractive, but she appeared to be walking in a glowing light thrown from a large, transparent stone she carried in her arms. He felt so drawn to this woman that he left his friends and crossed the street to talk with her.

After discussing this dream, the young man felt that he had gone through changes in his attitude toward women. He was no longer one of the group as he had been in high school, following the crowd, attracted to physical appearance alone. He was not going to sell himself short (woman wearing shorts) but was looking for quality (the glowing light that only he noticed) in a woman. He knew that a real relationship stemmed from more than someone's physical beauty and that is was something to be cared for (carried) and treasured (the large transparent stone).

He had made a decision about what he wanted in a mate. The element of change and choice was indicated by the number of friends who were gathered (five) and in the dreamer's noticing of the woman across the street. To cross a street, bridge or any divided section indicates a decision to change since you move from one vantage point to another.

Whenever you find the number Five arising in your dream, through the number of people as in the dream above, or objects such as five trees or five pencils lying on a table, or symbolized in a star, the pentagram, or any five-pointed figure, you should consider that the message has something to do with communication and change. Remember, the five-pointed star is a symbol of the wo/man standing astride; the points represent the head, two arms and two legs. S/he is ready and reaching out into the world to experience, through the five senses.

In your personal year cycle Five, examine your dreams with the knowledge that you are in a period of restlessness and change. You need freedom in your relationships and in the decision-making process. Your dreams will offer encouragement, suggestions and solutions to aid in this process.

Fire-type response to a Five cycle: This sounds like an exciting year. I'm always ready for a change. But let's not get bogged down in talking too much about it. That spoils the spontaneity of the moment. I'll just make the decision and do it.

Water-type response: Don't you think we ought to wait and see how we are going to feel about it, plan ahead a little? We may not want to change when the time comes. What if we like things just the way they are? I mean, I feel good about how things are going. If we change, then we have to shift emotional gears.

Air-type response: However, if you think things through, you don't have to get involved in an emotional upheaval. Besides, you can take a course in planning, talk with other people and see how they handled the same situation. We learn through understanding how others think. Communication is the key.

Earth-type response: Talk all you want. I'm not budging.

Personal Year Cycle Six Dreams

> **Symbol** - The hexagram, the philosopher's stone
> **Principle** - Balance
> **Purpose** - Love, responsibility, external perfection

Since six is the first perfect number in mathematics, its presence always implies the search for perfection. In your personal year cycle Six, you search for external perfection which translates into a need for balance and harmony in your environment, whether this is in your home or in your community. Your creative energies are accentuated and you should express them through beautifying your external world.

Sample dream: A woman had the following dream: "I planted a vegetable and flower garden very neatly in rows. It was full of healthy plants of all kinds but nothing seemed to be blooming yet. The soil was very dry and I noticed a water spigot that was spraying a small amount of water, as if the pressure were on but the water could not get through the opening. Then I realized that I could have been using that spigot all along instead of dragging a hose from another faucet further away.

Her analysis of the dream was as follows:

Healthy, but not blooming plants — her creative efforts were healthy and about to come to fruition. These efforts were both practical (vegetables nourish the physical body) and etherial (flowers beautify the environment).

Dry soil — she had grown this beautiful garden in spite of the lack of feedback, the lack of nourishment (water) from those around her.

Spraying but partially clogged spigot — her creative and emotional line was ready to burst. She needed to release her creative flow.

Using the closer spigot — depending upon herself rather than going outside herself for nourishment for the garden.

The woman was in the midst of many family changes and her dream came to assure that her efforts to nourish and support her family members would soon be rewarded.

Dreams of plays, the opera and symphony, works of art and places of beauty can fall into this category of promoting your sense of aesthetics during a personal year cycle Six. If you are creative in the physical sense that you like to paint, write music, sculpt, garden or perform any other activity that requires your creative input, use this cycle to your advantage by listening to the dreams that come to you now.

Since this is a period when you need to express your love towards others, your dreams will reflect this attitude through the symbols they contain. Your need to love can be expanded to include wider social responsibility, too, such as caring for the homeless or the hungry in your community or the world. Some of your dreams may urge you to participate in this form of support through financial contributions or through participating in worthwhile projects. This was the energy of the sixties: the flower children whose slogan was "make love not war."

If you dream of going to bed with Cher, the implication may be a play on words. You need to make "sharing" an instinctual part of your life. Look around you. What are the needs in your area? You might want to volunteer your time to help the elderly through visiting nursing homes, or work with the young through the Big Sister or Brother organization. Your dreams will guide you to the right path.

Solutions to long-standing problems can come to you through dreams now because, in a Six cycle, you need to finish things that you have been concerned about or involved in for some time. Examine the trend in your life for the past five years to discover what the paramount concern has been. You began a new nine-year cycle five years ago, and now, in this Six cycle, you can arrive at creative solutions to any problems that have arisen as the result of past decisions and actions or to problems that have arisen without your apparent input. The answers lie here in your dreams during this Six year, so examine your nightly scenarios with problem-solving in mind.

Your Six cycle is similar to that mystical moment just before the Moon gives way to the Sun in the early morning. This period of time has fascinated and intrigued wo/man from the beginning of awareness. The ancient Egyptians knew that sunrise was a precarious transitional point, a moment of perfect equilibrium between Matter and Spirit, a mingling of darkness and light in perfect harmony and balance. They thought of dawn as a door between two different worlds, a portal that allows us to move in either direction. The Hermetic doctrine states that in those few minutes around dawn, Psychopompos, Herder of Souls, shuffled souls between the land of the dead and the land of the living, or between sleeping and waking. The ancients believed that this point of perfect harmony lasted about three minutes.

At this moment in time, at Moon set/Sun rise, there is perfection, as if opposing forces recognized and bowed to each other's spirituality and importance in the cosmic plan. In this philosophy, we can see the Six, the hexagram, the two triangles of the Sun and the Moon in an equal and opposite embrace at Moon set/Sun rise. In this suspension of time, we, as souls, are free from domination by external affairs or internal promptings. We are in complete accord, able to see our wholeness and truth, our Sun and Moon in harmony.

Your personal year cycle Six embodies some of these concepts because you are seeking perfect harmony in your life during this period. This balance is necessary to prepare you for the coming cycles. Your dreams are suggesting ways in which you can find the balance and harmony necessary in your life during this period.

Fire-type response to cycle Six: I would love to be a Big Sister. Every child needs a role model, someone s/he can look up to. And I can think of a thousand places we could go together and tons of things we can do. I just don't want to get bogged down in red tape. After all, it's the activity that counts, not the paperwork.

Water-type response: The poor kids. They need someone to nurture and comfort them. They've had so many difficulties, so many emotional traumas. I can remember how my aunt helped me when I was growing up and how much it meant to me, so I will be glad to be a Big Sister. Every child needs a safe haven.

Air-type response: These kids need to get out into the world and find out how the other half thinks. Different cultures, different customs and ways of communicating. I think it will be important to introduce the child to other people who can broaden her/his intellectual and social horizons.

Earth-type response: This is a long-term commitment and shouldn't be taken lightly. A child needs continuing support, not only emotionally but physically. My role as a Big Brother will be to give the child a sense of self worth and dignity, teach him some skills so that he can make his way in the world on his own.

Personal Year Cycle Seven Dreams

> **Symbol** - The triangle and the square
> **Principle** - Rest
> **Purpose** - Rest, analysis, internal perfection

Your body needs rest now but your mind is highly activated; your energy has turned inward. You are piecing together the pattern from the past six years into a cohesive whole in preparation for your debut next year. There is a simplicity in the number Seven that reflects the simplicity of the origin of the Universe. Scientists say that the Universe began in a state of perfect simplicity, a state that is reflected in the atom. Einstein searched for that simplicity in a unified field theory, that one single equation that would account for every fundamental process in nature. This may be found in the nucleus of the atom which embodies the "elegant simplicity underlying the wild diversity of the universe." Every atom in your body was once inside a star. Therefore, to know the atom is to know the Universe and to know the Universe is to know the atom and yourself. Such thoughts may occupy your mind during this cycle because you are seeking to unify your past six years into a simple formula that can be used in the material world in your next cycle Eight.

Now that you have expended the necessary energy in your outer world, you must withdraw into the inner recesses of your mind to discover what externals need to be processed before you send them out once again in your next cycle Eight. Thought precedes reality and Seven is "a bridge for the Superconscious to perceive the material world." Before sending your energies out into the material world, they need to be perfected. Six is the cycle of external perfection, Seven is the cycle of internal perfection. For the past six years you have been building. Now you have reached the point where you must select those experiences that will serve you best and analyze them carefully. This requires that you spend more time alone so that you can look at the skills and experience you have acquired without interruption. Therefore, the higher forces decree that you will feel more tired, less inclined to socialize, so that you will want to spend time alone with your thoughts. Your thought processes must be perfected before they are externalized. Your dreams will reflect this state of mind.

You may dream you are alone on a tropical island, on a solitary trek across the Sahara on a camel or hurtling through space in your own Starship Enterprise. Wherever you find yourself in your dreamscape, look at your place in the environment in terms of how you can draw upon your past experience to deal with the situation at hand. Your dreams will rely only upon your specific talents, abilities and awareness, so analyze them with this in mind.

Time seems to have no sway over your dreams, especially in cycle Seven. You can travel light years through space in seconds, breaking time barriers and entering other worlds, perhaps worlds that you once lived in. You understand that you are not bound by time and space; you know that the Big Dipper in the heavens is seventy-five light years away and when you are seventy-five years old, you will be viewing that starry arrangement as it was on the day you were born. Your dreams can seem magical and mystical.

Sample dream: Some years ago, I laid down on the bed one afternoon to rest before the children came home from school. It was a warm spring day, the windows were open and the curtains were blowing gently as I shut my eyes. I could see myself and seven long-robed figures standing before an Egyptian sarcophagus. I knew they were about to reveal to me the secret of their embalming methods, a sacred ritual known only to the initiated.

Just as suddenly as the vision came, it disappeared. But the effects of those few moments have stayed with me ever since. I knew I was in the presence of something mystical and meaningful. I felt honored. This dream/vision came in a personal year cycle Seven, a time when my mind was searching for answers to some of the questions in my life, questions that invariably arise when you are in such a cycle. This is where the expression, the "seven year itch" comes from. Under a Seven, we become mentally restless, examining our past and present. We are want to know where our future will lead and what it is all about. Your dreams will explore these avenues of thought. This is a learning cycle that takes place on an inner level, and at this time your spiritual self is closer to your consciousness than usual. Listen to its dictates.

Also, watch your dreams for indications of your state of health because, if you do not slow down, if you persist in trying to actively cope with the outside world instead of letting it go as much as possible, your body may suffer the consequences. If your dreams are suggesting that you take care of your health, you had better listen. Under cycle Seven your body does need to rest. It is an essential part of this cycle. The body slows down; the mind speeds up.

Sample dream: A woman who had a recurring dream for many years was suddenly motivated to tell me about it when she was in a personal year cycle Seven. In her dream, she was encouraged to buy a smaller house that she didn't want. The large house that she owned in the dream had an extra bedroom and bathroom on the second floor that she didn't need. There was more to the dream, but this segment was most telling in terms of her personal cycle. The house was her body and to move into a smaller house suggested she move into a smaller body or lose weight. She was quite overweight, to the point where it was beginning to affect her health. The large house that she didn't want to give up was her present condition, her large body. She was not consciously aware of the severity of the situation, as suggested by the extra bedroom (where activity occurs that is not obvious — in this case, the activity was not obvious to the dreamer herself). The extra bathroom indicated the need to cleanse her body of poisonous toxins, a double-duty job because of her excess weight. Because she was in a cycle Seven and thinking about her "place" in life, she recognized the message and set about to correct her problem.

When you are in a cycle Seven, if it is necessary to cleanse your body, your dreams will suggest that you do so in order to fulfill one phase of internal perfection. However, the primary purpose is to think, to analyze your past, present and future direction, and to gain some understanding of your importance and place in the Universe.

Fire-type response to cycle Seven: Don't fence me in. I don't see any need to lie around and do nothing all day. What good is that going to do? I need space to move and get things accomplished. I won't get anything done just sitting here chanting ooooms.

Water-type response: I think ooming would be very soothing to the nerves. We can do it as a family, get in touch with our feelings and discover how our emotions regulate our moods. After all, it is feelings that count.

Air-type response: What a great intellectual exercise. I can imagine the beneficial aspects of ooming. I'm not sure I want to do it as a life's occupation, but it would be interesting to analyze the results and see if they have a measurable effect upon my metabolism.

Earth-type response: I've always wondered about you pointy-headed intellectual types with your pie-in-the-sky ooming. If you can't eat it or use it in some practical manner, what's the sense of it? Things should have a useful purpose.

Personal Year Cycle Eight Dreams

Symbol - The cube
Principle - Manifestation
Purpose - Power, sex and money

Did I get your attention? Those three words always seem to do the trick. Actually, they are accurate descriptions of your personal year cycle Eight. Now you are responsible for the energies you generate in the material world, a world which is caught up in power, sex and money. The word "responsibility" is a prime mover for you because you will be involved in these issues, and may well be the steward of vast resources and power which you should learn to use wisely. You will be tested during the Eight on how well you formulated your plans in your past cycles. Now it is execution time. Your cycle Eight gathers all the energies from the previous seven cycles and gives birth to them in your material world. Karma, or the total effect of your conduct over the past seven cycles, determines your present destiny. The law of cause and effect is in progress. Your dreams will offer guidance in the enactment of your karmic blueprint.

Since this is your power year, the dreams that come to you are likely to encourage you to reach for the stars, to go to the very top of the heap and show others and yourself what you are capable of accomplishing. You need to experience feelings of personal accomplishment and prestige.

A young woman was very nervous about presenting her ideas to the board at her place of business because her promotion rested upon the quality of her work. Shortly before the meeting, she had the following dream.

Sample dream: I was at the Academy Awards celebration. The place was only half-filled, but I knew it would soon be jammed with people. The ceremonies were about to start. Everyone was wearing black sequin suits which were very beautiful and expensive. It seemed that I was going to get an award. People in the audience were complimenting me on my black sequin jacket and the soft arrangement of my hair. Walter Mathau arrived. I knew that I would be sleeping with him that night because we were going to California together the next day. I was excited but fearful that I would be homesick. Mathau looked at me and smiled and I was no longer afraid. I looked forward to loving him that evening.

This woman was in her personal year cycle Eight and her dream suggested that she was about to receive a reward, quite fitting for this period in her cycle. The expensive clothes pertained to the elegant layouts she had prepared for her presentation to the board members. Her hair represented her personal ideas and thoughts because it grows from her head.

She views Walter Mathau as a very talented, relaxed and humorous actor who is flexible and adaptable. These were qualities she should embrace (loving him) during her presentation. Maintain a flexible attitude and a good sense of humor. California, to her, stands for a place where the wealthy and recognized people live. That was her destination in the dream. As a result of her work, she was on her way toward her goal of recognition and wealth. Her fear of being homesick disappeared when she received a smile from Walter Mathau and she thought about loving him that evening (exchanging sexual energies). She was a bit fearful of leaving the relative security of her present position with the firm (being homesick) because she was comfortable with it; she knew her job well. But, she needed the challenge of a new place within the company so she looked forward to being with Mathau in her dream because she would take on some of his flexibility and adaptability. She would welcome a new adventure.

The dream was effective in giving her the confidence to present her material in a relaxed yet professional manner, with a little humor thrown in. This dream has all the essential elements of a personal year cycle Eight — power, sex and money — presented in such a way that the woman could use it as a guide to achieving her goals. She handled these energies properly and today is successful in her field.

Dreams of receiving rewards or recognition for something that you haven't achieved in reality is the dream's way of encouraging you to reach for something that you think is beyond your grasp, to try something you think you can do but you are not sure about. It requires that you rely on skills you have built, but perhaps have not yet tested.

We humans have a strange quirk. Many of us think that the other person is smarter or more talented than we are, and that the things we can do, anyone can do, because they are easy for us. We tend not to value those things that come easily to us, failing to realize that someone else might find difficult those very things we can do so easily. So we give away our power. We let someone else do it, receive the recognition and glory, and then sit back and say, "I could have done that. That's not so difficult. In fact, I probably could have done it better." We need to learn to value our ideas and abilities. This is what the personal year cycle Eight desires to point out to you.

Intense sexual relationships are often part of this cycle as well because an exchange of sexual energy is one method of releasing your inner power. Therefore, dreams involving imagery that represents sexual energy is part of this cycle. Symbols such as a high-powered vehicle or a mountain that waits to be conquered could be part of your dreams now. Or, you may dream of a relationship with someone you know, perhaps someone famous, such as in the dream above. In cases similar to the one above, take the qualities you associate with that person and apply them to yourself. See if that works for you.

Any symbols that represent a reward, a point of attainment, an accomplished goal may be part of your nightly scenarios. The rainbow would certainly qualify. As a mystical symbol in numerology, I see it as the aura that you build around yourself during the first seven cycles of your nine-year cycle period. In the Eight cycle, you weave a "coat of many colors," your aura, a result of all the energy you have expended during the past seven years. To some people, it is the visible result of their efforts.

Dreams that come to you during your personal year cycle Eight are meant to encourage you to go to the very top, to attempt those things that you might not have dared before this time, those things that you are truly qualified to do, but still lack the confidence to take on — perhaps because you feel that your abilities are not up to the standards of others. In this cycle, you should try your wings, test your abilities. You may be surprised at what you can do and how others will respond to your capabilities.

Fire-type response to cycle Eight: It's about time. I know I can do it. I never had any doubt about it because I belong at the top.

Water-type response: Oh dear. Well, I'll give it a try. But I don't want my name in the paper. I don't mind working behind the scenes, but let's leave the glory to the ones that like the spotlight. I prefer to work quietly, without a lot of fanfare.

Air-type response: Have I got some ideas about how to improve this business! We should start with the advertising — the image the company presents to the public. And also, relationships within the office are extremely important to any thriving enterprise. I'll be in charge of that.

Earth-type response: I've worked long and hard for this top position. I think I can handle it if perseverance and longevity count for any-thing. I've had plenty of practical experience. And you can count on me when the going gets tough. I don't let go easily.

Personal Year Cycle Nine Dreams

Symbol - The point within the circle
Principle - Dispersement
Purpose - Fulfillment, release, wisdom

In this cycle, you are coming to the end of your nine-year period. It is time to let go of those things that are no longer a necessary part of your life. Part of the lesson during this period is realizing that you can let go and still have. Nature abhors a vacuum so that when one thing leaves, another thing enters to fill the void. Symbols of major transition such as birth, death, marriage, divorce are likely elements to appear in your dreams now. As I mentioned in chapter 5 on symbols, death does not necessarily mean a physical death, but rather the death of a current situation or atti-tude that brings about a major shift in your lifestyle.

Doorways in your dreams are another symbol for this transitional year in your life. Janus, the Roman solar deity, was the god of all door-ways. His insignia was the key which opened and closed the doors along with the stick which drove away those who had no right to cross over the threshold. His two faces allowed him to observe both directions, inside and outside. Your personal year cycle Nine allows you to observe both directions as well. You look over your past eight years — the doorway to the past — and incorporate those experiences into your soul growth. Then you observe what you have gained from the Universe, what suste-nance nature has provided for you, and in payment, you give back some measure of your bounty in thanks. You have come to the point within the circle, where you begin to understand your individualized energy within the cosmic womb, or Divinity, your place in the scheme of things.

Dreams of moving into a new house indicate the changes that are occurring in your life now. In order to change your residence, you must let go of the past and those things that are familiar to you. You have to readjust your lifestyle. The new house represents the new attitude you are adopting.

Sample dream: During a Nine cycle, I dreamt that my husband and I were shown a few rooms in an old house. They needed a lot of work — the walls were plaster with wooden slats beneath and no insulation and the wind was blowing through the loose windows. I loved the house and we decided to put a $50. deposit on it without seeing the rest of the building. I was amazed at the low deposit because the house was so big and I knew it was worth a great deal.

Later, I began exploring more of the house and to my amazement, it was palatial. It seems two large old houses had been joined by a huge, open room three floors high. This interior room was elaborately adorned with wall paintings. I ascended to the second floor and there was a library filled with books. Beyond that, the entire second floor, which was the size of a warehouse, was filled with books and people sitting at tables reading. I was amazed at the size of this house that I had purchased for such a small price.

When I asked someone if this was a library, she said no. It was a re-search business where people read all day and supplied information and ideas. I was overwhelmed that I owned this place.

I look upon this dream as my reward for the years of study I had put into this field that I love so much. I am a researcher, and here was a vast library at my disposal, in the upper recesses of my house, my mind, hidden away from the casual observer. Here was a glimpse of the wisdom possible when I pursued my studies.

You may dream of precious gems and metals, pots brimming with gold or caves full of untold treasure. This is your pot of gold at the end of the rainbow, your reward for the years of struggle you have invested in your future. You may also find that your dreams suggest that you share your good fortune with others because you have to make room for the next cycle. You can't go dragging your pot full of gold into the next cycle One or there will be no room in it for new gems of experience. It is time to empty it, to let go. In this cycle, it is in the giving that you gain. As Gibran said in *The Prophet,* all that you have will someday be given, so why not give now, and let the joy of giving be yours. This is the wisdom of the Nine.

Your personal year cycle Nine dreams will focus on these issues of transition, tithing, release and wisdom. Examine the symbols with these ideas in mind as a starting point. You may find that your dreams will be much clearer when you have the information about your current cycle at hand.

Fire-type response to cycle Nine: Sounds good to me. I'm always ready for a change, new scenery and adventure. It's not good to remain too tied to the past. It just drags you down and often prevents you from going when you want to. I like my freedom.

Water-type response: Wait a minute. What about the kids? And my husband and parents? And the dog and cat? And the elderly woman I visit next door? I mean, you can't just take off and leave them without some kind of support system. Who's going to watch out for them?

Air-type response: Oh, they'll be alright. Besides, you can make new friends wherever you go. There are groups and clubs and you can always look through the newspapers to find out what's going on in a new place. And, you know, you shouldn't get so attached to things. It's not healthy.

Earth-type response: What? Give up the possessions I've worked so hard for, and the security I've built up over the years and my reputation in the community? Are you crazy?

Well, there you have it. The nine personal year cycles, the type of symbols you might find emerging through your dreams during these cycles and the possible reactions of the four basic personality types as they experience each of the nine cycles. Obviously, it would be impossible to cover every conceivable symbol that you might weave into your dreams during each of these cycles, but I hope that you now have a feeling for the basic energy of the cycles One through Nine as a starting point for interpreting your dreams.

Notes

1. Garfield, Patricia *Creative Dreaming,* (NY: Ballantine Books, 1974), pp. 42-44.
2. Ibid., pp. 41-42.
3. Sechrist, Elsie *Dreams, Your Magic Mirror,* (NY: Cowles Education Corp., 1968), p. 141.

7

Recording Your Dreams

In this chapter, I will go over the steps I find the most effective in organizing and setting up dreams for analysis on a daily basis. Then, as an example, I will examine a dream I had just this morning to illustrate the procedure and to show how effective this process is.

1. First, you will need two notebooks and a box of tabs. The first notebook is for recording your dreams. I find a spiral bound notebook is best because it lies flat when the pages are folded under, making it easier to write in. Use the 8½ X 11 size or a smaller version, depending upon your taste. Make sure the paper has a large left margin, usually about an inch, so you'll have plenty of room for making notes.

The second notebook is for your dream dictionary. It is better to use a loose leaf notebook for your dictionary because you may want to insert pages or move them around. Again, use whatever size you prefer. In this notebook, attach twenty-six tabs, one to the outer edge of each of the twenty-six pages. The tabs should be labeled "A" through "Z." By placing the tabs one below the other, you'll be able to find the letter you are looking for easily. Include several sheets of paper in each lettered section.

Keep a few reliable pens and your two notebooks on a bedside stand or somewhere within arm's reach of your bed. Now you are ready to begin your journey.

2. Develop an interest in your dreams. You need to care about what your dreams are trying to tell you. Give them the respect they are due

and realize that they come from a creative source that can be a pool of nourishment for you. They are your pipeline to inspiration, encouragement, problem-solving, creativity and guidance.

Watch television shows, and read books, newspaper and magazine articles on dreams. Familiarize yourself with the process and the potential inherent in this other part of your life.

Let your subconscious know that you are interested. Talk to it, even name it if you like. I call mine Charlie. Whenever I have a problem or am looking for something, I talk to him. And I thank him when he helps me. You can do the same. Or, you may choose to talk to your teddy bear, a doll or a real or fictional person, whatever you find most comfortable. Many people prefer talking to the opposite sex part of themselves because this seems to help balance the Yin and Yang energies. But that is a personal preference. If you like this idea, choose whoever or whatever feels right.

3. As you approach bedtime, slow down. Too often in this hectic world, we rush pell mell through the day, brush our teeth and drop into bed exhausted. Sometimes we watch a television program with a violent theme — a police, detective, thriller show — or an emotionally moving piece. By the time our heads hit our pillows, we are practically vibrating off the bed. Needless to say, this isn't the way to approach bedtime and it certainly isn't beneficial when you're trying to record and recapture your dreams.

Make an effort the slow your pace before retiring. Take a warm bath or listen to soothing music. Drink a glass of warm milk. (Science has proven that this old remedy works because warm milk soothes the central nervous system.) Bend over and brush your hair slowly from the back toward the front of your head. Any one of these techniques will help calm you down.

During the day you might also want to take a few minutes to mentally stop the activity that usually engages you, to relax your mind and listen to what is going on inside you. Even in a busy office you can stop, take a deep breath, close your eyes, clear your mind of all that is crowding in on you, and visualize a pastoral scene or hear your favorite melody. These few moments in the midst of a busy routine give your inner self the opportunity to speak to you.

4. You've brushed your hair, had your warm milk and listened to the Moonlight Sonata, and now you're tucked into bed. The next step is to take your dream notebook and make a few notations. First, record the day's date. I write this in the margin and underline it for easier reference while keeping the text to the right of the margin.

Next, write down the number of your personal year cycle. I use the abbreviation "PYC 4," for example. Mentally review what this cycle means for you and what you are supposed to be accomplishing during it.

Then, note your personal month cycle and whether today is close to the beginning of this cycle. For instance, if your birthday is April 14th, your personal month cycle begins on the 14th of each month. If the date you are entering into your dream notebook is the 13th, 14th or 15th, (one of the three days surrounding the beginning of your personal month cycle), indicate that. Your dreams may give you new messages for the coming month. I write "PMC" if the date I am entering is close to the beginning of my personal month cycle.

5. Enter the position of the Moon if you are know what it is. Remember, you can obtain a Pocket Astrologer from the address in the appendix; this calendar gives the Moon's sign position for each day of the year. If you are not familiar with the meaning of the position, look in the front of the Pocket Astrologer where each position is briefly delineated.

The Moon sets the mood for that period of time, affecting everyday affairs and our interactions with others. The Moon also has a great deal of influence over the subconscious. Therefore, it also influences the content of dreams.

On the next line in your notebook, to the right of the margin, write the word Observations. I find circling this word sets it apart from the text as well as from the date (which is underlined).

In this section you can make note of events that happened during the day that are meaningful to you, and any thoughts that are on your mind, whether they relate specifically to today or not. Use your instincts and write whatever comes to mind. This is an important part of the process because as time goes on you will consciously forget these details. When you go back over your dreams at a later date, you will have a "hook" to hang your dream associations on if you have noted your state of mind at the time of the dream. These are good reference points for the dreams of that day as well as dreams that may follow.

6. In the margin, following the section titled "Observations" denote another section as "Dream," and circle the word. This is where you will record your dream(s) of that night.

Although it takes pages to explain these procedures, it take just a few minutes to do it, so don't be discouraged by my lengthy explanations. I am a detailed person (Mars conjunct Jupiter in Capricorn in the sixth house) so it's my nature to be exacting.

7. Now that you have made the above notations, lie back and relax. As you fall asleep, make this suggestion to your subconscious: "I will remember one dream." Start with just one; that's all you need now. Clear

you mind and say over and over, "I will remember one dream." Hold on to this thought as you drift off to sleep.

Some dream books suggest setting your alarm clock at intervals during the night to help you catch a dream. I am convinced the authors of these books are sadistic. I believe if you follow the instructions I am outlining here you will not have to subject yourself to such masochistic techniques. Trust your subconscious to aid you in remembering.

8. When you wake, lie very still. Relax. Wait. Soon . . . a word . . . a thought . . . an image . . . will come to you. Once you catch a thread of your dream, the entire skein will begin to unravel and voilà! You have a dream. Once your dream recollection begins, you may have more than one. They often flood in upon your consciousness so fast it is hard to keep up with them in writing. Record what you remember of your dream under the "Dream" section in your notebook.

If you do not catch a dream the first night, do not be discouraged; it may take a few days. Your subconscious has to be convinced that you are serious, and you both have to be trained to follow these steps.

9. Record every detail of your dream. No matter how insignificant the information may seem, if you remember it, it is important and should be included along with other pertinent observations. Sometimes seemingly unimportant details turn out to be most enlightening.

10. After recording your dream in your notebook, you'll want to write your analysis of it. The first part of the interpretation should be your mood upon awakening. How do you feel? Your waking mood is the result of the dream scenarios you have just enacted. You may recall days in the past when you woke feeling happy or grouchy or tired. These attitudes are often carried over into the day. Getting at the root of these feelings will place you in a position of control and understanding, and will provide you with one key to interpreting the meaning of your dream.

11. The theme of your dream is also important. Look upon your dream as a story written by an author — you. What is the author trying to say? What is the plot, the theme of the story? What is the essential action? Who is doing what to whom? What is happening to whom? Focus on the action in the dream while looking at it impersonally. Take away the identity of the players and objects. For instance, if you dream that you bought an old car from Al Capone, you would extract the theme by saying, someone is buying something from someone. This is the theme of the dream. Since symbols vary so widely, even with the same dreamer, try not to interpret them prematurely.

12. Now look at the symbols in your dream. If no immediate meaning comes to mind that feels right to you, there are three effective techniques you can use to stimulate your associations.

a. The first is *amplification,* used by Carl Jung. In this technique, you take a symbol as the central focus, searching for associations while returning to the main symbol each time. For instance, if there is a ladder in your dream, use it as the focus in the amplification technique. Ladder — height. Ladder — caution. Ladder — access to otherwise inaccessible places.

b. A second technique is Freud's word association. Rather than return to the central symbol each time you arrive at an interpretation, you continue from the association itself on to another and another, like a chain. For example, ladder reminds you of height. Height leads to a position above the crowd. Above the crowd means a better view. And so forth. One of these associations may suddenly pop up at you causing an "Of course!" reaction. Then you will have a clue to your dream's meaning.

c. Third, you can take the part of that symbol in a process called role-playing, a technique used extensively by those who practice Gestalt therapy. This technique requires you to *become* the symbol and act out a role. The more involved you get in the character of the person, animal or thing in your dream, the more insight you achieve in the final analysis. For instance, you might begin by saying, "I am a ladder. I am here to help people reach higher than they might have thought possible. Without me they could not discover things that are hidden in high places." By becoming the ladder, interesting attitudes may emerge from subconscious levels that you did not know were there. This technique is extremely effective. You may want another person to help you by asking questions such as "Why were you left leaning against that wall rather than being put away?" and "Who owns you?" If you would rather work alone, you can do so by closing your eyes, relaxing, clearing your mind and beginning by simply saying, "I am the ladder." Then continue to expound on how you feel as the ladder.

13. When you experience symbols that appear to be important in your dreams, you may want to record them in a dream dictionary. This is your second notebook with the tabs arranged alphabetically. In our example of the ladder, you would enter this word under "L." Make reference to the date you had the dream of the ladder and leave a few blank lines. Then, write a brief description of the dream along with what you think it means. Keep this short because you can refer back to the dream in your dream journal if necessary. These notes are merely to jog your memory.

Once you have collected enough information under "ladder," you may find that it becomes a symbol you will use frequently in your dreams with the same general meaning each time. This makes it easier for you to analyze future dreams that contain this symbol. After your dream dictionary gains substance, you'll be able to refer to it when analyzing symbols in the future.

14. Finally, each night before you go to sleep, look over your dream book, reread the dreams of the past week, let your instincts guide you in turning the pages. On occasion, you will come across a dream that has obvious significance to something that is currently happening in your life. The dream may provide answers to a problem you are working on, answers you didn't notice at the time your recorded the dream because, perhaps, the solution was being presented in segments for some reason. Or, you may notice a dream you had about something that was about to occur — a precognitive dream. When this happens, make a note in the margin next to that dream and date your observation. (This is the reason for the wide left-hand margin. It makes it easier for you to pick out such observations and to note which dreams seem to be special in that they know no time or space. They are your personal pipeline to a pool of universal wisdom that contains all answers.)

Dreams supply you with information about a past of which you know nothing, a present with which you may have no current contact and a future that is yet to be in conscious terms. The world of dreams is a landscape of wonders.

Sample Dream

Some background information to set the stage. Today's date is June 5. On March 6, I missed one step on a stairway and sustained a third degree sprain, which required me to wear a cast on my leg for two months. I spent the first six weeks mostly on the couch with my leg elevated on pillows. The few times that I was mobile, I had to use crutches. During this period of inactivity, I gained twenty pounds.

I had been on an exercise schedule for three weeks and a strict diet for a week, but on June 4th (yesterday) I decided to treat myself to pizza. When I gave my address to the young man at the pizza house, he repeated it incorrectly as "Hoggs Street." I laughed and corrected him.

That night, I entered the date in my dream book as June 4th, 1987. Next to it, I wrote PYC 4 (personal year cycle Four), then I noted PMC (personal month cycle, because my birthday is November 5, and this date of June 4 is close to the beginning of my personal month). Then I entered the Moon's position in my notebook (Moon in Virgo).

Under "Observations," I made some notations about the events of the day such as going off my diet, the conversation with the young man at the pizza house and my feelings about giving in to eating something I shouldn't have until I get down to the weight I want to be.

When I awoke early the next morning, I recorded the following dream. I was packing and cleaning up a motel-like room, trying to organize a group of kids who were running around, and wondering where my husband was (he was supposed to be helping me get ready to leave). We were going home, a long trip across country. I realized we needed maps, something I had almost forgotten. I walked across the floor, which rippled like a trampoline as I moved over it, and reached up onto a high shelf to retrieve one of the maps that lay there. I could not reach the others as they seemed to be four floors up. A man offered to get them for me. He proceeded to climb a tall ladder and obtained the others maps for me. As I walked over to the ladder, the floor began to move again, and he and the ladder fell, but he was not hurt.

Under "Analysis" in my journal, I noted my mood upon awakening, which was one of some frustration and also an underlying humor which I couldn't quite account for until later.

The theme of this dream was "someone helping someone get something," so the dream had to do with assistance in obtaining a goal.

Looking at the symbols in this dream, I arrived at the following conclusions.

Ladder — reaching for a goal that seemed very high above me and needing help to get there.

Maps — a tried method that should be followed, the diet plan.

The motel — a temporary place of residence or the temporary condition of my body (the house or motel is the body where the soul lives).

The maps on a shelf four floors above me — the Four relating to my personal year cycle Four, and the need to get my "house" in order.

I was looking for my husband, my higher self, to assist me but he was not around — my going off the diet the night before.

The children were the distraction — the immature side of myself that needed instant gratification.

I was going on a long trip across country, going home — to the normal condition of my body.

It would be a long trip — it would take a while to get back into condition.

The wavy floor — my shaky foundation when I wavered and went off my plan, diverged from the map.

The man who fell from the ladder but was not hurt — my fall from my diet; it was not lethal, just one small slip.

So, the dream seemed to indicate my guilt feelings at going off the diet before I had reached my desired weight. I had fallen in the eyes of my conscience, but the damage was repairable once I got the children under control and paired up with my husband, the Yin and the Yang working together in harmony. It was also interesting that the maps were four floors up, indicating both my personal year and the need to get organized.

The next morning, while I was telling this dream to one of my daughters, I mentioned that I had "pigged out" eating pizza the night before. Then I began to laugh because I remembered the young man on the telephone at the pizza house referring to my address as Hoggs Street. Right then I should have gotten the cosmic message.

The dream referred to my personal year cycle Four in which I was to get my house organized. In addition, I was beginning a new monthly cycle, which meant I should start anew with my determination to achieve my goal.

Also, the Moon is in Virgo, the sign that rules the house of health and diet. Virgo also rules the small intestines which discriminate by separating the foods we ingest into what the body needs and what has to be eliminated. The message of the dream was that I needed to be more discriminating in my choice of foods.

This is the method I find most effective in analyzing dreams. It incorporates three ancient systems — numerology, astrology and dreams — each of which supplies important insights into the processes of the human mind. I hope this book and the methods I have presented awaken some interest in your dreams and in astrology and numerology and that together, they will help you discover the "light being" that you are.

Appendix

There are several places from which you can obtain a copy of your natal chart. These services require your birthdate, place of birth, and exact time of day if possible (they will correct for daylight time). Midnight, 12:00 AM, begins the day. Noon is 12:00 PM. They use what is known as the Tropical/Placidus system, the most commonly used in this country, unless you request otherwise. The charge for calculating your birth chart is usually about $2.00. It is worth your while to find out your correct birthtime. You can obtain a copy of your birth certificate from your town/city hall. Do not rely on your mother's memory. It has been my experience that mother's memory can be quite a few hours off. After all, she was pretty busy at the time.

If your birthtime is not on your birth certificate, try the office of the Department of Health in your state. As a last resort, you could write for the pamphlet, *Where to Write for Birth and Death Records,* Superintendent of Documents, U. S. Government Printing Office, Washington, D.C. 20402.

Two organizations that will calculate birthcharts for you are: Astrolabe, Box 28, Orleans, MA 02653, (617) 255-0510; and Astro Computing Services, Box 16430, San Diego, CA 92116-0430, (619) 297-9203.

For a copy of the Pocket Astrologer or an astrological calendar, write to Quicksilver Productions, P.O. Box 340, Ashland, Oregon 97520. Indicate whether you want Eastern Time or Pacific Time. You can easily make corrections for the time zones in between.

The Pocket Astrologer is a handy size that will fit in your pocketbook. Complete with the astrological glyphs, it gives a brief description of the signs of the zodiac, followed by the Moon through the signs. It then describes each of the planets and their functions. A section on aspects and time corrections also is included. For each day of the month, the sign in which the Moon is positioned is noted as well as what time the Moon moves into the next sign, (which happens approximately every 2½ days).

This information is handy when noting the position of the Moon in your dream notebook, as the Moon sets the mood for the day.

For a copy of my book, *Broads and Narrows,* send $6.00 plus $1.00 for postage to Dusty Bunker, P.O. Box 868, Dept. NAD, Exeter, NH 03833.

About the Author

Dusty Bunker, numerologist, astrologer and symbolist, is an internationally-known author, lecturer and teacher. Her first book, *Numerology and the Divine Triangle,* was co-authored with Faith Javane. She is also the author of *Numerology and Your Future,* and co-authored *Birthday Numerology* with Victoria Knowles. *Numerology, Astrology and Dreams* is her sixth published book, and incorporates portions of an earlier work *Dream Cycles* that is now out-of-print. Dusty lectures nationwide and appears frequently on radio and television programs.

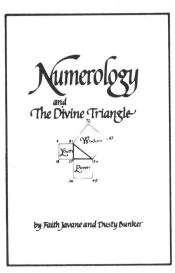

NUMEROLOGY & THE DIVINE TRIANGLE

Faith Javane & Dusty Bunker

Now in its fifth printing, this major work embodies the life's work of Faith Javane, one of America's most respected numerologists, and her student and co-author Dusty Bunker, a teacher and columnist on metaphysical topics.

Part I introduces esoteric numerology. Topics include: the digits 1 through 9; how to derive your personal numbers from your name and date of birth; how to chart your life path; the symbolism of each letter in the alphabet; the life of Edgar Cayce, and more.

Part II delineates the numbers 1 through 78 and, illustrated with the Rider-Waite Tarot deck, synthesizes numerology, astrology and the Tarot. *Numerology & The Divine Triangle* is number one in its field.

ISBN 0-914918-10-9
280 pages, 6½" x 9¼", paper $14.95

NUMEROLOGY AND YOUR FUTURE

Dusty Bunker

In her second book, Dusty Bunker stresses the predictive side of numerology. Personal cycles, including yearly, monthly and even daily numbers are explored as the author presents new techniques for revealing future developments. Knowledge of these cycles will help you make decisions and take actions in your life.

In addition to the extended discussion of personal cycles, the numerological significance of decades is analyzed with emphasis on the particular importance of the 1980s. Looking toward the future, the author presents a series of examples from the past, particularly the historical order of American presidents in relation to keys from the Tarot, to illustrate the power of numbers. Special attention is paid to the twenty-year death cycle of the presidents, as well as several predictions for the presidential elections.

ISBN 0-914918-18-4
236 pages, 6½" x 9¼", paper $13.95

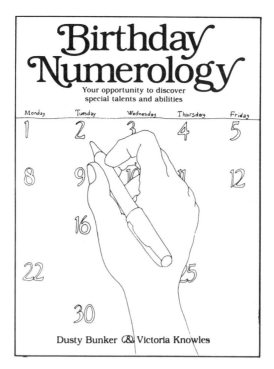

BIRTHDAY
NUMEROLOGY

by Dusty Bunker and Victoria Knowles

One of the unique things about you is the day on which you were born. In
Birthday Numerology, well-known numerologist Dusty Bunker and psychic
counselor Victoria Knowles combine their knowledge of numerology, symbolism
and psychic development to present a clear and coherent presentation of how the
day you were born affects your personality.

Unlike other methods of divination, the beauty of this book lies in its
simple and direct presentation of the meaning behind personal numbers. Rather
than having to perform complicated calculations, all you need to do is know
your birthday. The book is uncannily accurate, written in a warm and engaging
style and, above all, is easy to use.

The introductory chapters discuss the foundation and validity of
numerology and will help you discover why the date of your birth is crucial in
determining your personality. From there, *Birthday Numerology* examines the
traits and characteristics inherent in people born on each day of the month.

Dusty Bunker and Vikki Knowles have written a book that is much more
than just a delineation of various personalities, it is truly a guidebook to your
journey through the 31 days.

ISBN 0-914918-39-7
228 pages, 6½" x 9¼", paper $13.95